THE
LAW OF NATIONS

J. L. BRIERLY

THE LAW OF NATIONS

AN INTRODUCTION TO
THE INTERNATIONAL LAW
OF PEACE

———

SIXTH EDITION

EDITED BY

SIR HUMPHREY WALDOCK
C.M.G., O.B.E., Q.C., D.C.L.,
CHICHELE PROFESSOR OF
PUBLIC INTERNATIONAL LAW
IN THE UNIVERSITY OF OXFORD

OXFORD
AT THE CLARENDON PRESS

Oxford University Press, Walton Street, Oxford OX2 6DP

OXFORD   LONDON   GLASGOW
NEW YORK   TORONTO   MELBOURNE   AUCKLAND
KUALA LUMPUR   SINGAPORE   HONG KONG   TOKYO
DELHI   BOMBAY   CALCUTTA   MADRAS   KARACHI
NAIROBI   DAR ES SALAAM   CAPE TOWN

ISBN 0 19 825105 X

© *Oxford University Press 1963*

First edition 1928. Reprinted 1930
Second edition 1936. Reprinted 1938
Third edition 1941. Reprinted 1945
Fourth edition 1949. Reprinted 1950, 1953
Fifth edition 1955
Reprinted lithographically 1956, 1958, 1960
Sixth edition 1963
Reprinted lithographically 1967, 1972, 1974, 1976, 1978, 1980, 1981

Printed in Great Britain by
Billing & Sons Limited, Guildford, London and Worcester

PREFACE TO FIFTH EDITION

THE purpose of this book remains what it was when it was first published in 1928. It is not intended as a substitute for the standard textbooks on the subject, but as an introduction for students who are beginning their law courses, or, I hope, for laymen who wish to form some idea of the part that law plays, or that we may reasonably hope that it will play, in the relations of states. That question cannot be answered by *a priori* methods which lead too often either to an under-estimation of the services that international law is already rendering, or to an equally mistaken assumption that it offers us the key to all our international troubles. The truth is that it is neither a myth on the one hand, nor a panacea on the other, but just one institution among others which we can use for the building of a better international order.

J. L. B.

Oxford
December 1954

PREFACE TO THE SIXTH EDITION

THE previous edition of this book, prepared by Professor Brierly himself, appeared in 1955, a few months before his death. The purpose of the book, he wrote in his last preface, remained what it was when the book was first published in 1928, that is, 'an introduction for students who are beginning their law courses, or for laymen who wish to form some idea of the part that the law plays, or that we may reasonably hope that it will play, in the relations of states'.

The judgment, vision, and scholarship that characterized all Brierly's work, combined with the simplicity and brevity of his exposition, made *The Law of Nations* a masterpiece in its own genre and won it a wide popularity in many different countries. Even in ordinary circumstances, therefore, the preparation of this edition would have been a responsible and delicate task. It was rendered more difficult by reason of the really immense developments that have taken place in international organization and international law during the years which have intervened since the author's death.

In the first place, the world community itself has undergone a radical change through the transformation of many colonial, protected, and mandated territories into independent states. The process of transformation, it is true, was already under way in 1954, when the previous edition went to press; but its tempo quickened dramatically after that date, and the emergence of a large number of new African and Asian states has fundamentally affected the structure, politics, and work of the United Nations. In the second place, in handling crises in the Middle East and the Congo the United Nations has been led to undertake experiments in the formation and operation of international police forces which are of the greatest importance. In the third place, there has been a large expansion in the economic and technical activities of the United Nations and the Specialized Agencies. As a result of these and other developments, the United Nations and the Charter have acquired a significance in relation to the international legal order which was not yet fully apparent in Brierly's lifetime. In general international law also there have been a number of important developments, such as the Geneva Conventions on the law of the sea, the Vienna Convention on diplomatic intercourse, the growth of a legal régime for international rivers and for outer space, as well as other more detailed matters.

Much as he would have preferred to leave Brierly's own text largely intact, the present editor has not thought this to be a possible course to adopt. Although the book, as already mentioned, is essentially an introduction, and not a textbook, some two-thirds of it deal with the existing framework and principles of international law; and it would soon lose its value, even as an introduction, if this part did not reflect the present rather than the past state of international law. The editor accordingly decided that he must displace the original text with new material, wherever necessary, to prevent the book from falling behind the quickening march of international law and international institutions. The present edition in consequence contains not only additions to cover new developments but also, in some places, quite extensive substitutions of new material for Brierly's text.

The first two chapters, apart from some new material in Chapter II on the International Law Commission, have been left almost as Brierly wrote them; but in the next edition it may be desirable to expand his statement of the sources of international law to take account of the decisions and resolutions of international organizations as a source of law. Chapter III contains additional material on the Security Council, the Uniting for Peace Resolutions, the Economic and Social Council, and the Specialized Agencies, as does Chapter IV on succession to membership of international organizations. Otherwise these chapters also are much as Brierly wrote them.

In Chapter V the sections on prescription, colonies, and trust territories have been substantially revised; those on maritime territory and the continental shelf have been written *de novo* by the present editor, who felt it necessary that the law should now be presented in the terms of the Geneva Conventions of 1958; and the section on territorial air space has also been written by the editor. Chapter VI, dealing with

jurisdiction, has been rearranged so as to place all
the examples of internal waters in the same section,
while the part dealing with rivers has been revised;
new sections have been inserted on jurisdiction in
territorial air space and on the limits upon a state's
treatment of its own nationals. The sections on the
territorial sea and on the high seas have been completely rewritten by the editor, as here again it is
necessary to state the law in the terms of the Geneva
Conventions of 1958. Another section completely
rewritten is that on 'Jurisdiction with respect to
Foreign States, their Property, their Agents, and their
Armed Forces'; for it seemed desirable to include in
this section a number of important developments in
regard to state immunities, while the Vienna Convention of 1961 in any event made it necessary to re-
state the law of diplomatic immunities in terms of
that Convention.

Chapter VII on 'Treaties', with two exceptions,
has been left virtually as Brierly wrote it. The first
exception is the insertion on page 326 of a paragraph
concerning treaties having objective effects. The
second is the incorporation into the text of the passages on 'Peaceful Change' which in the previous
edition were simply appended to Chapter VII in the
form of a 'Note'. These passages have at the same
time been considerably shortened without, it is
believed, losing anything of their substance. In
another edition, this chapter may have to be revised
to take account of the work of the International Law
Commission since 1955, but the chapter is so charac-

teristic of Brierly that the editor preferred in this edition to leave it as it is.

In Chapter VIII, Section 2 contains new material on the Optional Clause and the advisory jurisdiction (pp. 355–66), while Section 6 has been considerably expanded in order to provide an up-to-date account of the working of the Charter system for the handling of international disputes. The last chapter—Chapter IX—on international law and resort to force has been written by the present editor and takes the place of Brierly's brief chapter on this subject.[1] It seemed essential to the editor that any account of the law regarding the use of force should today give a much larger place to the law of the Charter than was the case in the previous edition.

Despite every effort to keep down its size, the book has grown by just over 100 pages. The chief reason is the developments in international organization and international law which have already been mentioned. In one or two places also the legal material has been slightly expanded in order to provide a somewhat fuller framework for those readers who are 'students beginning their law courses'. Finally, the index has been enlarged in order to make it rather more serviceable, while the table of cases has in the ordinary course of events grown a little larger.

With all the changes that have been made, the present edition still reflects only partially the transition that is taking place in international law in

[1] In writing this chapter the editor has drawn upon material contained in lectures delivered by him to The Hague Academy.

consequence of the increasing organization of the international community. Another edition may have to go even farther in expounding the general principles of international law in the framework of the United Nations and other related international organizations.

C. H. M. W.

Oxford
June 1962

CONTENTS

CONTENTS

I

THE ORIGINS OF INTERNATIONAL LAW

§ 1. *The Rise of Modern States*

THE Law of Nations, or International Law, may be defined as the body of rules and principles of action which are binding upon civilized states in their relations with one another. Rules which may be described as rules of international law are to be found in the history both of the ancient and medieval worlds; for ever since men began to organize their common life in political communities they have felt the need of some system of rules, however rudimentary, to regulate their inter-community relations. But as a definite branch of jurisprudence the system which we now know as international law is modern, dating only from the sixteenth and seventeenth centuries, for its special character has been determined by that of the modern European state system, which was itself shaped in the ferment of the Renaissance and the Reformation. Some understanding of the main features of this modern state system is therefore necessary to an understanding of the nature of international law.

For the present purpose what most distinguishes the modern post-Reformation from the medieval state is the enormously greater strength and concentration of the powers of government in the former.

The national and territorial state with which we are familiar today in western Europe, and in countries which are founded on, or have adopted, western European civilization, is provided with institutions of government which normally enable it to enforce its control at all times and in all parts of its dominions. This type of state, however, is the product of a long and chequered history; and throughout the Middle Ages the growth of strong centralized governments was impeded by many obstacles, of which difficulties of communication, sparsity of population, and primitive economic conditions, are obvious illustrations. But two of these retarding influences deserve special notice because of the imprint which they have left even to this day on the modern state.

The first of these was feudalism. Modern historical research has taught us that, while it is a mistake to speak of a feudal *system*, the word 'feudalism' is a convenient way of referring to certain fundamental similarities which, in spite of large local variations, can be discerned in the social development of all the peoples of western Europe from about the ninth to the thirteenth centuries. Bishop Stubbs, speaking of feudalism in the form it had reached at the Norman Conquest, says:

'It may be described as a complete organization of society through the medium of land tenure, in which from the king down to the lowest landowner all are bound together by obligation of service and defence: the lord to protect his vassal, the vassal to do service to his lord; the defence and service being based on and regulated by the nature and extent of the land held by the one of the other. In those states which have reached the territorial stage of development, the rights of defence and service are supplemented by the right of jurisdiction. The lord judges as well as defends his vassal; the vassal does suit as well as service to his lord. In states in which feudal government has reached its utmost growth, the political, financial, judicial, every branch of public administration is regulated by the same conditions. The central authority is a mere shadow of a name.'[1]

Thus to speak of a feudal 'state' is almost a misuse of terms; in a sense the feudal organization of society was a substitute for its organization in a state, and a perfectly feudal condition of society would be not merely a weak state, but the negation of the state altogether. Such a condition was never completely realized at any time or anywhere; but it is obvious that the tendency of feudalism to disperse among different classes those powers which in modern times we regard as normally concentrated in the state, or at any rate as under the state's ultimate control, had to pass away before states in our sense could come into existence.

On the other hand, there were elements in the feudal conception of society capable of being pressed into the service of the unified national states which were steadily being consolidated in western Europe from about the twelfth to the sixteenth centuries, and influential in determining the form that those states would take. Thus when its disintegrating effects on

[1] *Constitutional History of England*, vol. i, p. 274.

government had been eliminated, the duty of personal loyalty of vassal to lord which feudalism had made so prominent was capable of being transmuted into the duty of allegiance of subject to monarch in the national state; the intimate association of this personal relation with the tenure of land made the transition to *territorial* monarchy easy and natural; and the identification with rights of property of rights which we regard as properly political led to notions of the absolute character of government, of the realm as the 'dominion' or property of the monarch, and of the people as his 'subjects' rather than as citizens. Feudalism itself had been an obstacle to the growth of the national state, but it left to its victorious rival a legacy of ideas which emphasized the absolute character of government.

The other influence which retarded the growth of states in the Middle Ages was the Church. It is not necessary here to speak of the long struggle between Pope and Emperor, although one incidental effect of this was to assist the growth of national states by breaking up the unity of Christendom. More significant in the present context is the fact that never until after the Reformation was the civil authority in any country regarded as supreme. Always governmental authority was divided; the Church claimed and received the obedience of the subjects of the state, and its claims were not always limited to the purely spiritual sphere. Even in England, always somewhat restive under papal interference, the idea of the omnicompetence of the civil power would have been unthinkable. Men might dispute exactly how far the powers of each of the rival authorities extended; but that there were limits to the powers of the state, that the Church had *some* powers over the members of the state which it neither derived from, nor held by the sufferance of, the state, was certain. States might often act as arbitrarily as any absolute state of the post-Reformation world; they might struggle against this or that claim of the Church; but neither in theory nor in fact were they absolute. But just as the state was gradually consolidating its power against the fissiparous tendencies of feudalism within, so it was more and more resisting the division of authority imposed upon it by the Church from without; and this latter process culminated in the Reformation, which in one of its most important aspects was a rebellion of the states against the Church. It declared the determination of the civil authority to be supreme in its own territory; and it resulted in the decisive defeat of the last rival to the emerging unified national state. Over about half of western Europe the rebellion was completely and evidently successful; and even in those countries which rejected Protestantism as a religion, the Church was so shaken that as a political force it could no longer compete with the state. The Peace of Westphalia, which brought to an end in 1648 the great Thirty Years War of religion, marked the acceptance of the new political order in Europe.

This new order of things gave the death-blow to the lingering notion that Christendom, in spite of all its quarrels, was in some sense still a unity, and there was a danger that the relations between states would be not only uncontrolled in fact, as they had often been before, but henceforth uninspired even by any unifying ideal. The modern state, in contrast with the medieval, seemed likely to become the final goal of unity, and Machiavelli's *Prince*, written in 1513, though it formulated no theory of politics, had already given to the world a relentless analysis of the art of government based on the conception of the state as an entity entirely self-sufficing and non-moral. Fortunately, however, at the very time when political development seemed to be leading to the complete separateness and irresponsibility of every state, other causes were at work which were to make it impossible for the world to accept the absence of bonds between state and state, and to bring them into more intimate and constant relations with one another than in the days when their theoretical unity was accepted everywhere.[1] Among these causes may be mentioned (1) the impetus to commerce and adventure caused by the discovery of America and the new route to the Indies; (2) the common intellectual background fostered by the Renaissance; (3) the sympathy felt by co-religionists in different states for one another, from which arose a loyalty transcending the boundaries of states; and (4) the common feeling of revulsion against war, caused by the savagery with which the wars of religion were waged. All these causes co-operated to make it certain that the separate state could never be accepted as the final and perfect form of human associa-

---

[1] Cf. Westlake, *Collected Papers*, p. 55.

tion, and that in the modern as in the medieval world it would be necessary to recognize the existence of a wider unity. The rise of international law was the recognition of this truth. It accepted the abandonment of the medieval ideal of a world-state and took instead as its fundamental postulate the existence of a number of states, secular, national, and territorial; but it denied their absolute separateness and irresponsibility, and proclaimed that they were bound to one another by the supremacy of law. Thus it reasserted the medieval conception of unity, but in a form which took account of the new political structure of Europe.

§ 2. *The Doctrine of Sovereignty*

Out of the new kind of state which developed from the Reformation there arose a new theory of the nature of states, the doctrine of sovereignty. This was first explicitly formulated in 1576 in the *De Republica* of Jean Bodin, and since sovereignty has become the central problem in the study both of the nature of the modern state and of the theory of international law, it is necessary to examine its origins and its later development with some care.

Like all works of political theory, even when they profess to be purely objective, Bodin's *Republic* was deeply influenced by the circumstances of its time and by its author's sentiments towards them; indeed one of Bodin's merits is that he drew his conclusions from observation of political facts, and not, as writers both before and since his day have too often done, from supposedly eternal principles concerning the nature of states as such. France in Bodin's time had been rent by faction and civil war, and he was convinced that the cause of her miseries was the lack of a government strong enough to curb the subversive influences of feudal rivalries and religious intolerance, and that the best way to combat these evils was to strengthen the French monarchy. He saw, too, that a process of this kind was actually taking place in his own day throughout western Europe; unified states were emerging out of the loosely compacted states of medieval times, and the central authority was everywhere taking the form of a strong personal monarchy supreme over all rival claimants to power, secular or ecclesiastical. Bodin concluded therefore that the essence of statehood, the quality that makes an association of human beings a state, is the unity of its government; a state without a *summa potestas*, he says, would be like a ship without a keel. He defined a state as 'a multitude of families and the possessions that they have in common ruled by a supreme power and by reason' (*respublica est familiarum rerumque inter ipsas communium summa potestate ac ratione moderata multitudo*), and he dealt at length with the nature of this *summa potestas* or *majestas*, or, as we call it, sovereignty. But the idea underlying it is simple. Bodin was convinced that a confusion of uncoordinated independent authorities must be fatal to a state, and that there must be one final source and not more than one from which its laws proceed. The essential manifestation of sovereignty (*primum ac praecipuum caput majestatis*), he thought, is the power to make the laws (*legem universis ac singulis civibus dare posse*), and since the sovereign makes the laws, he clearly cannot be bound by the laws that he makes (*majestas est summa in cives ac subditos legibusque soluta potestas*).

We might suppose from this phrase that Bodin intended his sovereign to be an irresponsible supra-legal power, and some of the language in the *Republic* does seem to support that interpretation. But that was not his real intention.[1] For he went on to say that the sovereign is not a *potestas legibus omnibus soluta*; there are some laws that do bind him, the divine law, the law of nature or reason, the law that is common to all nations, and also certain laws which he calls the *leges imperii*, the laws of the government. These *leges imperii*, which the sovereign does not make and cannot abrogate, are the fundamental laws of the state, and in particular they include the laws which determine in whom the sovereign power itself is to be vested and the limits within which it is to be exercised; we should call them today the laws of the constitution. The real meaning of Bodin's doctrine can only be understood if we remember always that the state he is describing is one in which the government is, as he calls it, a *recta* or a *legitima gubernatio*, that is to say, one in which the highest power, however strong and unified, is still neither arbitrary nor irresponsible, but derived from, and defined by, a law which is superior to itself. In that he was following the medieval tradition of the

[1] See on this point McIlwain, *Constitutionalism and the Changing World*.

nature of law, for in the Middle Ages men looked on law not as something wholly man-made; they believed that behind the merely positive laws of any human society there stood a fundamental law of higher binding force embodying the wisdom of the past, and that positive laws must conform to this higher law if they were to have validity. The notion that legitimate power could ever be purely arbitrary is alien to all the legal thought of the Middle Ages, and in this respect Bodin's work made no break with the past. Medieval rulers might, and no doubt often did, behave arbitrarily; but that could not alter the fact that it was still by the law that the rightfulness or otherwise of their conduct must be judged; it was law that made the ruler, not, as later theories of sovereignty have taught us to believe, the will of rulers that made the law. Where Bodin broke away from the medieval tradition of law was in making his sovereign a legislator, for legislation was a function which that tradition did not readily admit; when a medieval ruler made new law men preferred to regard it as an act of interpreting, or of restoring the true construction of, the law as it had been handed down from the past.

In the form in which Bodin propounded the doctrine of sovereignty it raised no special problem for the international lawyer. Sovereignty for him was an essential principle of internal political order, and he would certainly have been surprised if he could have foreseen that later writers would distort it into a principle of international disorder, and use it to prove that by their very nature states are above the law. Bodin

evidently did not think so, for he included in the
Republic a discussion of those very rules for the conduct
of states out of which other writers of his day were
already beginning to build the new science of international law; it certainly never occurred to him that
in what he was writing about sovereignty he was cutting away their foundations. Yet this is what we are
told that the doctrine of sovereignty has done, and
though the story is long and tangled there have been
two main developments which have brought about
this astonishing reversal of its original effect. One is
that sovereignty came later to be identified with absolute power above the law, and the other is that what
was originally an attribute of a personal ruler inside
the state came to be regarded as an attribute of the
state itself in its relations to other states. The causes
that led to these changes lie in the history of the
modern state, and the theory has followed, as it
generally does, in the wake of the facts.

We have seen that Bodin intended his sovereign
to be a constitutional ruler subordinate to the fundamental law of the state. But there had always been
grave weaknesses in the medieval concept of the
fundamental law as a defence against absolutism.
There was no authentic text of this law, and no means
therefore of determining whether a particular ruler
had transgressed it, and even if he had, there was
usually nothing that could be done about it. But
throughout the Middle Ages the power of rulers was
always limited in fact, and so long as that state of
things endured it was possible for men to go on believing

that law did set some limitations on ruling power. In the sixteenth century, however, the barriers against absolutism were giving way, and the consolidation of strong governments with no effective checks on the powers of rulers was breaking down the medieval idea of law as a customary rule which set limits to all human authority and was making it natural to think of law as man-made, the manifestation of a ruler's superior will. The reverence everywhere paid to Roman law encouraged this tendency, for Roman law taught that the will of the prince is law. But in the main it was new political facts that were making of the ruler a supra-legal power, and accustoming men to think of the sovereign not, as Bodin had pictured him, as the ruler by law established, but as the holder of the strongest power in the state, no matter how that power might have been acquired.

This development reached its culmination in the *Leviathan* of Thomas Hobbes, which was published in 1651, and it is interesting to note that Hobbes, like Bodin, was writing with his eyes on the events of his own time; for he, too, had seen a civil war, and for him, as for Bodin, sovereignty was an essential principle of order. Hobbes believed that men need for their security 'a common power to keep them in awe and to direct their actions to the common benefit',[1] and for him the person or body in whom this power resides, however it may have been acquired, is the sovereign. Law neither makes the sovereign, nor limits his authority; it is might that makes the sovereign,

[1] *Leviathan*, ch. xvii.

and law is merely what he commands. Moreover, since the power that is the strongest clearly cannot be limited by anything outside itself, it follows that sovereignty must be absolute and illimitable; 'it appeareth plainly that the sovereign power . . . is as great as possibly men can be imagined to make it.'[1] This, of course, is what in our time we call totalitarianism pure and simple.

One result of identifying sovereignty with might instead of legal right was to remove it from the sphere of jurisprudence, where it had its origin and where it properly belongs, and to import it into political science, where it has ever since been a source of confusion. So long as the sovereign is the highest *legal* authority there is usually no difficulty in identifying him. But to identify the strongest power involves us in an investigation of all those extra-legal forces, political, social, psychological, and so on, which determine how the institutions of the state shall operate in practice. That is a hopeless quest, for as a rule there is no person or body of persons in a society whose will always prevails; in fact, as has been truly said, the real rulers of society are never discoverable. Yet so strong had the hold of sovereignty upon the imaginations of political scientists become that when it became obvious, as it soon did, that the personal monarch no longer fitted the role, they started a hunt for the 'location' of sovereignty, almost as if sovereignty, instead of being a reflection in theory of the political facts of a particular age, were a substance which must surely

[1] Ibid., ch. xx.

be found somewhere in every state if only one looked for it carefully enough. With the coming of constitutional government Locke, and after him Rousseau, propounded the theory that the people as a whole were the sovereign, and in the eighteenth century this became the doctrine which was held to justify the American and the French Revolutions. As a fighting slogan, as a protest against arbitrary government and a demand that government should serve the interests of the governed and not only of the governors, the doctrine of popular sovereignty has had beneficent results, but as a scientific doctrine it rests on a confusion of thought. It tries to combine two contradictory ideas; that of absolute power somewhere in the state, and that of the responsibility of every actual holder of power for the use to which he puts it. It is possible to locate a sovereign in Bodin's sense in a constitutional state, though Bodin went too far in holding that the supreme power of making law must always be concentrated in a single hand; he could not foresee that the device of federation would make it possible to divide that power between different holders without producing chaos in the state.[1] But it is not possible to locate a Hobbesian sovereign in a constitutional state, and the political philosophers failed to see that with the coming of democracy a new theory of the nature of governing power was called for. In any case,

---

[1] Cf. *U.S.* v. *Lanza*, 260 U.S., where Taft C.J. speaks of 'two sovereignties, deriving power from different sources, capable of dealing with the same subject matter [sc. 'prohibition'] within the same territory'.

the whole people cannot be the sovereign in either sense; they do not rule, for the work of government is a skilled and a full-time job which the law cannot avoid entrusting to particular individuals or organs, and as the whole people are incapable of acting as a body, they are not even the strongest power; a politically conscious minority, a military clique, a communist party controlling the police, or a pressure group of some sort, may well be stronger than the people as a whole and better able to make its will prevail. The sovereignty of the people is not even, as soon as we begin to examine its implications more closely, a genuine democratic ideal, for the people can only act by a majority, and a majority rarely is, and never ought to be, all-powerful. No democrat if he is true to his principles can believe that there ought somewhere in the state to be a repository of absolute power, and to say that such a power resides in the people is to deny that either minorities or individuals have any rights except those that the majority allow them. That is totalitarianism, for autocracy is autocracy whoever the autocrat may be.

Still another modern development of the theory of sovereignty has been to give up the attempt to locate absolute power in any specific person or body within the state and to ascribe it to the state itself regarded as a juristic person. Here, again, we can see how changes in the doctrine of sovereignty reflect changes in political facts, for the sovereignty of the state gave expression in theory to the growing strength and exclusiveness of the sentiment of nationality during the nineteenth

century. By so doing it raised a formidable difficulty
for international law. For if sovereignty means absolute power, and if states are sovereign in that sense,
they cannot at the same time be subject to law. International lawyers have tried to escape from the difficulty in various ways which we shall have to consider
later, but if the premises are correct there is no escape
from the conclusion that international law is nothing
but a delusion.

§ 3. *The Influence of the Doctrine of the Law of Nature*

Though the system of international law is modern,
it had, like the modern state itself, a medieval foundation. It was out of the conception of a law of nature
that the early writers on international law developed
their systems, and that foundation, as Sir Frederick
Pollock says, has always and everywhere been treated
as sound except by one insular and unhistorical
school.[1] Modern legal writers, especially in England,
have sometimes ridiculed the conception of a law of
nature, or while recognizing its great historical influence they have treated it as a superstition which the
modern world has rightly discarded. Such an attitude
proceeds from a misunderstanding of the medieval
idea;[2] for under a terminology which has ceased to be
familiar to us the phrase stands for something which
no progressive system of law ever does or ever can dis-
card. Some knowledge of what a medieval writer meant
by the term is necessary if we would understand either
how international law arose, or how it develops today.

[1] *Essays in the Law*, p. 62.   [2] Cf. A. P. d'Entrèves, *Natural Law*.

A long and continuous history,[1] extending at least as far back as the political thought of the Greeks, lies behind the conception; but its influence on international law is so closely interwoven with that of Roman law that the two may here be discussed together. The early law of the primitive Roman city-state was able to develop into a law adequate to the needs of a highly civilized world empire, because it showed a peculiar capacity of expansion and adaptation which broke through the archaic formalism which originally characterized it, as it characterizes all primitive law. In brief, the process of expansion and adaptation took the form of admitting side by side with the *jus civile*, or original law peculiar to Rome, a more liberal and progressive element, the *jus gentium*, so called because it was believed or feigned to be of universal application, its principles being regarded as so simple and reasonable that they must be recognized everywhere and by every one. This practical development was reinforced towards the end of the Republican era by the philosophical conception of a *jus naturale* which, as developed by the Stoics in Greece and borrowed from them by the Romans, meant, in effect, the sum of those principles which ought to control human conduct, because founded in the very nature of man as a rational and social being. In course of time *jus gentium*, the new progressive element which the practical genius of the Romans had imported into their actual law, and *jus naturale*, the ideal law conforming to reason, came to

[1] Cf. Pollock, *Essays in the Law*, ch. ii.

be regarded as generally synonymous. In effect, they were the same set of rules looked at from different points of view; for rules which were everywhere observed, i.e. *jus gentium*, must surely be rules which the rational nature of man prescribes to him, i.e. *jus naturale*, and vice versa. Medieval writers later developed this conception of a law of nature, sometimes elaborating it in ways which appear to the modern mind both fanciful and tedious; but so powerful did its influence on men's minds become that the Church accepted it into the doctrinal system, and St. Thomas Aquinas, for example, taught that the law of nature was that part of the law of God which was discoverable by human reason, in contrast with the part which is directly revealed. Such an identification of natural with divine law necessarily gave the former an authority superior to that of any merely positive law of human ordinance, and some writers even held that positive law which conflicted with natural law could not claim any binding force.

The effect of such a conception as this, when applied to the theory of the relations of the new national states to one another, is obvious, for it meant that it was not in the nature of things that those relations should be merely anarchical; on the contrary they must be controlled by a higher law, not the mere creation of the will of any sovereign, but part of the order of nature to which even sovereigns were subjected. Over against the theory of sovereignty, standing for the new nationalistic separation of the states of Europe, was set the theory of a law of nature denying their irresponsibility and the finality of their independence of one another. No doubt it was impossible to point to any authentic text of this law, and different interpretations of it were possible; but the belief that, in spite of all appearances, the whole universe, and included in it the relations of sovereigns to one another, must be ruled by law, remained. Moreover, the difficulty of discovering the dictates of this law presented itself to a medieval writer with much less force than it does to the modern mind. For he had in fact a special guide ready to his hand in Roman law.

The position of Roman law in Europe in the sixteenth century has an important bearing on the beginnings of international law. There were some countries, such as Germany, in which a 'reception' of Roman law had taken place; that is to say, it had driven out the local customary law and had been accepted as the binding law of the land. In other countries the process had not gone so far as this; but even in these the principles of Roman law were held in great respect and were appealed to whenever no rules of local law excluded them. Everywhere in fact Roman law was regarded as the *ratio scripta*, written reason; and a medieval writer, seeking to expound the law of nature, had only to look about him to see actually operative in the world a system of law which was the common heritage of every country, revered everywhere as the supreme triumph of human reason. Moreover, this law had a further claim to respect from its close association with the Canon Law of the Church.

Thus Roman law reduced the difficulty of finding the contents of natural law almost to vanishing-point; and in fact the founders of international law turned unhesitatingly to Roman law for the rules of their system wherever the relations between ruling princes seemed to them to be analogous to those of private persons. Thus, for example, rights over territory, when governments were almost everywhere monarchical and the territorial notions of feudalism were still powerful, bore an obvious resemblance to the rights of a private individual over property, with the result that the international rules relating to territory are still in essentials the Roman rules of property. It is not difficult, therefore, to see how the belief in an ideal system of law inherently and universally binding on the one hand, and the existence of a cosmopolitan system of law everywhere revered on the other, should have led to the founding of international law on the law of nature. We have to inquire further, however, whether this foundation is valid for us today.

The medieval conception of a law of nature is open to certain criticisms. In the first place, when all allowances have been made for the aid afforded by Roman law, it has to be admitted that it implied a belief in the rationality of the universe which seems to us to be exaggerated. It is true that when medieval writers spoke of natural law as being discoverable by reason, they meant that the best human reasoning could discover it, and not, of course, that the results to which any and every individual's reasoning led him was natural law. The foolish criticism of Jeremy

Bentham: 'a great multitude of people are continually talking of the law of nature; and then they go on giving you their sentiments about what is right and what is wrong; and these sentiments, you are to understand, are so many chapters and sections of the law of nature',[1] merely showed a contempt for a great conception which Bentham had not taken the trouble to understand. Medieval controversialists might use arguments drawn from natural law to support almost any case, but there was nothing arbitrary about the conception itself, any more than a text of Scripture is arbitrary because the Devil may quote it. But what medieval writers did not always realize was that what is reasonable, or, to use their own terminology, what the law of nature enjoins, can rarely receive a final definition: it is always, and above all in the sphere of human conduct, relative to conditions of time and place. We realize, as they hardly did, that these conditions are never standing still. For us as for them, a rational universe, even if we cannot prove it to be a fact, is a necessary postulate both of thought and action; and the difference between our thought and theirs is mainly that we have different ways of regarding the world and human society. When a modern lawyer asks what is reasonable, he looks only for an

[1] *Principles of Morals and Legislation*, ch. ii. But Bentham himself, as Sir Frederick Pollock points out (*History of the Science of Politics*, p. 120), was unconsciously 'as much a dogmatist as any propounder of natural law'. He constructed a universal theory of legislation based on abstract considerations of human motives in general, such as they appeared to him, and without taking the slightest trouble to consult history or specific facts.

answer that is valid now and here, and not for one that is finally true; whereas a medieval writer might have said that if ultimate truth eludes our grasp, it is not because it is undiscoverable, but because our reasoning is imperfect. Some modern writers have expressed this difference by saying that what we have a right to believe in today is a law of nature *with a variable content*.

In the second place, when medieval writers spoke of natural law as able to overrule positive law in a case of conflict, they were introducing an anarchical principle which we must reject. But this was a principle which died hard, and even in the eighteenth century Blackstone could write: 'This law of nature being coeval with mankind and dictated by God himself, is of course superior in obligation to any other. It is binding all over the globe in all countries and at all times; *no human laws are of any validity, if contrary to this*.'[1] In Blackstone, however, such words were mere lip-service to a tradition, and had no effect on his exposition of the law. To hold, however, that unreasonableness can invalidate a rule of law is to confuse the function of legislation with that of ascertaining what existing law is. Law could never perform its proper function of a controlling force in society if courts of law did not hold themselves bound to subordinate their own ideas of what is reasonable to an assumed superior reasonableness in the law; that assumption may not always be well founded, but it is necessary to our social security that it should be acted upon until the law is altered.

[1] *Commentaries on the Laws of England*, Introduction.

These are valid criticisms, but they do not affect the permanent truths in the conception of a law of nature, and though today we generally use a different terminology, we recognize the validity of those truths as fully as ever. For one thing the law of nature stands for the existence of *purpose* in law, reminding us that law is not a meaningless set of arbitrary principles to be mechanically applied by courts, but that it exists for certain ends, though those ends may have to be differently formulated in different times and places. Thus where we might say that our aim is to embody social justice in law (giving to that term whatever interpretation is current in the thought of our time), a medieval thinker might have said that the validity of positive law must be tested by its conformity or otherwise to a law of higher obligation, the law of nature. Natural law, therefore, or a like principle under some other name, is an essential underlying principle of the art of legislation. But that is not all; it is also a principle that is necessarily admitted into the actual administration of law. This is so because the life with which any system of law has to deal is too complicated, and human foresight too limited, for law to be completely formulated in a set of rules, so that situations perpetually arise which fall outside all rules already formulated. Law cannot and does not refuse to solve a problem because it is new and unprovided for; it meets such situations by resorting to a principle, outside formulated law, whose presence is not always admitted. In fact it falls back on the solution which the court or the jury think to be reasonable in all the circumstances. Even a slight acquaintance with the working of the English Common Law shows it perpetually appealing to reason as the justification of its decisions, asking what is a reasonable time, or what is a reasonable price, or what a reasonable man would do in given circumstances. We do not suppose that our answers to those questions will be scientific truths; it is enough if they are approximately just; but on the other hand we do not attempt to eliminate this test of reasonableness by substituting fixed rules, because it would be impossible to do so. But this appeal to reason is merely to appeal to a law of nature. Sometimes, indeed, English law still uses the term 'natural justice', and our courts have to do their best to decide what 'natural justice' requires in particular circumstances, for example, in 1924 the Northern Rhodesia Order in Council, providing for the administration of that protectorate, enacted that in civil cases between natives Rhodesian courts were to be guided by native laws as far as applicable and *not repugnant to natural justice*. The Rhodesian courts will probably experience no difficulty in interpreting this instruction.

'The grandest function of the law of nature', Sir Henry Maine has written, 'was discharged in giving birth to modern international law';[1] and even if such a foundation had not been a sound one, no other would have been possible in the sixteenth century. Afterwards, in the seventeenth and eighteenth centuries, the medieval tradition of a law to which man's rational nature bids him everywhere and always to

[1] *Ancient Law*, ch. iv.

conform became obscured, and later writers returned to another meaning of the term, traces of which are also to be found in Stoic and early Christian writers. They used it to denote a law under which men are supposed to have lived in a *state of nature*, that is to say, in an imaginary pre-political condition of human society which they are supposed to have left behind when they formed themselves into political societies.[1] This development had unfortunate effects on international law, but it will be convenient first to say something of the men whose writings first gave that law systematic form.

§ 4. *The classical writers on International Law*

The recognition of international law as a separate object of study dates from the latter part of the sixteenth century. Earlier writers had written on some of the topics which fall within modern international law, especially on the usages of war and on the treatment of ambassadors; but they did not separate the legal from the theological and ethical, or the domestic from the international, aspects of such questions. Thus side by side with questions such as whether war is ever justified, what causes for going to war are lawful and what unlawful, what means of waging war are permissible, and the like, they discussed questions of tactics, of military discipline, or of the duties of a vassal to help his lord, without feeling that they were treating together topics which properly belonged to different subjects. Theological writers especially were concerned

[1] *Infra*, pp. 36–37, 54.

with the perplexing ethical problems to which the practice of warfare gives rise, and a series of great Spanish Churchmen of the fifteenth and sixteenth centuries made important contributions to the progress of thought on these matters. Perhaps the greatest of these was Francisco de Vitoria, Professor of Theology at Salamanca from 1526 to 1546, whose *Relectiones theologicae*, published after his death, contained, in two courses of lectures, the *Relectiones De Indis* and *De jure belli Hispanorum in Barbaros*, an examination of the title of the Spaniards to exercise domination over the inhabitants of the New World which is remarkable for its courageous defence of the rights of the Indians. In this Vitoria's teaching marks an important step in the expansion of international law into a world system; for it meant that a law which had its rise among the few princes of European Christendom was not to be limited to them or to their relations with one another but was universally valid, founded as it was on a natural law applying equally to all men everywhere. The work of these early Spanish writers has been unfairly neglected, especially in Protestant countries, but in recent years interest in them has been revived and a more just appreciation of their importance is now accorded to them.

Alberico Gentili, commonly known as Gentilis, an Italian Protestant who fled to England to avoid persecution and became professor of Civil Law in Oxford, was perhaps the first writer to make a definite separation of international law from theology and ethics and to treat it as a branch of jurisprudence. 'Let theo-

!ogians hold their peace', he writes, 'in work that belongs to others than they.' His most important work was the *De jure belli* published in 1598. To this book, Gentilis's more famous successor, Hugo de Groot, or Grotius, was, as he himself admitted, greatly indebted, but otherwise it appears to have exercised little influence, and the very name of Gentilis was almost forgotten until recent times.

Grotius was born in Holland in 1583, and died in 1645. Even as a boy he acquired a European reputation for learning, and as a man he became master of every subject to which he turned his interest. He was a lawyer, an historian, a poet, as well as a theologian whose great desire was to see the reunion of the Christian Church. Yet he lived the life, not of a student, but of a man of affairs, practising the law and serving in official positions. He became involved in disputes which were nominally concerned with matters of theology, but in which the real issue was a political one, the question whether the provinces of Holland should form a loose federal union or be consolidated under the House of Orange. Grotius supported the former and the losing cause. After being imprisoned for over two years, he escaped by the devotion of his wife in a box which his captors supposed to contain books, and eventually became ambassador of Sweden at the French Court.

Grotius wrote two works on international law, the *De jure praedae* in 1604, and the *De jure belli ac pacis* in 1625. The former of these, in which he supported the claim of the Dutch East India Company to the capture of a prize from the Portuguese, was never published by him, and was not discovered until 1864. It was then found that a short work which he published anonymously in 1609, the *Mare liberum*, contending, in opposition to the claims of the Portuguese, that the open sea could not be appropriated by any state, had been written as one of the chapters of the *De jure praedae*.

Few books have won so great a reputation as the *De jure belli ac pacis*, but to regard its author as the 'founder' of international law is to exaggerate its originality and to do less than justice to the writers who preceded him; neither Grotius, nor any other single writer, can properly be said to have 'founded' the system. The reputation of the book was not wholly due to its own merits, though these are great; it was partly due to the time and circumstances of its publication. When he wrote it in 1625 Grotius was already so eminent that anything from his pen would have attracted attention. Further, he had the advantage of belonging to the country which in the seventeenth century was in many ways the leading country in Europe. The successful war of liberation by the Dutch against Spain in the previous century had heralded the rise of the modern state system; it had been the first great triumph of the idea of nationality, and the successful assertion of the right of revolt against universal monarchy. In the seventeenth century they were the leaders of European civilization, teaching to other countries not only new methods of commerce but new conceptions of government based on freer institutions and on some measure of religious toleration. When the issue between absolutism and liberty was still doubtful in England, and when everywhere else absolutism was triumphant and destined to remain so until the French Revolution, the Dutch had settled the issue in their own country in favour of liberty. Even some of the qualities which render the book tedious to a modern reader, especially its voluminous citation of authorities from ancient history and the Bible, and its excessively subtle distinctions, commended it to the taste of contemporaries still familiar with the tradition of scholasticism.

Grotius's purpose was practical. He wrote on the laws of war because, as he says:

'I saw prevailing throughout the Christian world a licence in making war of which even barbarous nations should be ashamed; men resorting to arms for trivial or for no reasons at all, and when arms were once taken up no reverence left for divine or human law, exactly as if a single edict had released a madness driving men to all kinds of crime.'[1]

In contrast with this anarchy he proclaimed that even states ought to regard themselves as members of a society, bound together by the universal supremacy of justice. Man, he said, is not a purely selfish animal, for among the qualities that belong to him is an *appetitus societatis*, a desire for the society of his own kind, and the need of preserving this society is the source of natural law, which he defines as:

'The dictate of right reason, indicating that an act, from its agreement or disagreement with the rational and

[1] *Prolegomena*, 28.

social nature of man, has in it moral turpitude or moral necessity, and consequently that such an act is either forbidden or commanded by God the author of nature.'[1]

Besides being subject to natural law, he says, the relations of peoples are subject to *jus gentium*; for just as in each state the civil laws look to the good of the state, so there are laws established by consent which look to the good of the great community of which all or most states are members, and these laws make up *jus gentium*. It is obvious that this is a very different meaning from that which the term bore in the Roman law;[2] there, as we have seen, it stood for that part of the *private* law of Rome which was supposed to be common to Rome and other peoples; whereas in Grotius it has come to be a branch of *public* law, governing the relations between one people and another. It is important, Grotius tells us, to keep the notions of the law of nature and the law of nations (to adopt a mistranslation of *jus gentium* which its new meaning makes almost necessary) distinct; but he is far from doing so himself. Nor was it possible for him to do so, as is apparent from his own statement of how their respective contents are to be discovered. He used, he tells us, the testimony of philosophers, historians, poets, and orators, not because they were themselves conclusive witnesses, but because when they were found to be in agreement, their agreement could only be explained in one of two ways: either what they said must be a correct deduction from the principles of reason, and so a rule of the law of nature; or else it

[1] Book I, ch. i, 10 (1).   [2] *Supra*, p. 17.

must be a matter on which common consent existed, and so a rule of the law of nations. Thus in effect the two terms, as we have already seen, still express the theoretical and the practical sides of the same idea.

Like all thinkers who try to understand the meaning and bases of law, Grotius had to meet the perennial and plausible arguments of those who would identify justice with mere utility. His answer was clear and convincing. Justice, he said, is indeed the highest utility, and merely on that ground neither a state nor the community of states can be preserved without it. But it is also more than utility, because it is part of the true social nature of man, and that is its real title to observance by him.

Grotius's work consisted in the application of these fundamental principles to war; for he says:

'It is so far from being right to admit, as some imagine, that in war all rights cease, that war ought never to be undertaken except to obtain a right; nor, when undertaken, ought it to be carried on except within the bounds of right and good faith. . . . Between enemies those laws which nature dictates or the consent of nations institutes are binding.'[1]

The first book, therefore, inquires whether war can ever be *justum*, lawful or regular; and as Grotius was of opinion that one requirement necessary to make a war lawful was that it should be waged under the authority of one who held supreme power in the state, he was led to inquire into the nature of sovereignty. His treatment of this subject was unsatisfactory and

[1] *Prolegomena*, 25, 26.

confused. By denying that government necessarily exists for the sake of the governed, and treating sovereignty as a proprietary right, a *jus regendi* capable of vesting in sovereigns as fully and by the same titles as rights over corporeal things vest in private persons, Grotius encouraged the unfortunate trend of opinion towards a view of sovereignty as absolute and irresponsible power. He had to admit, too, writing when he did, that wars waged by subordinate feudatory princes who could only be regarded as holding *summa potestas* by a transparent fiction might be lawful, and this made much of his exposition of the subject inconsistent with his own definition. In the second book Grotius dealt with the causes of war, and in effect reduced the causes of lawful wars to two, the defence of person or property and the punishment of offenders. He then proceeded to examine such questions as what constitutes the property of a state, for example, how far the sea may do so, how property is acquired and lost, and other questions which a modern writer would either place under the international law of peace, or exclude from international law altogether. In the third book he dealt with topics which fall under the modern laws of war, that is to say, with the question what acts are permissible and what are forbidden in the conduct of war. Here his plan was not only to state the strict laws of war, but to add what he called *temperamenta*, alleviations or modifications designed to make war more humane.

It is usual in estimating the work of Grotius to speak of its remarkable and instantaneous success; and if it is a proof of success that within a few years of its author's death his book had become a university text-book, that it has often since been appealed to in international controversies, that it has been republished and translated scores of times, and that every subsequent writer treats his name with reverence, however widely he may depart from his teaching, then Grotius must be accounted successful. But if by success is meant that the doctrines of Grotius as a whole were accepted by states and became part of the law which since his time has regulated their relations, then his work was an almost complete failure. It is true that some of his doctrines have since become established law. For instance, the doctrine that the open sea cannot be subjected to the sovereignty of any state and many of the *temperamenta* of war that he suggested have been incorporated into international law; but these particular changes were due at least as much to changes in the character of navigation and in the technique of war respectively as to Grotius. At the heart of his system lay the attempt to distinguish between lawful and unlawful war, *bellum justum* and *bellum injustum*; he saw that international order is precarious unless that distinction can be established, just as national order would be precarious if the law within the state did not distinguish between the lawful and the unlawful use of force. But this distinction never became part of actual international law.

In attempting to establish this distinction Grotius was following a tradition which the classical writers on international law had inherited from the theologians and canonists of the Middle Ages; indeed it goes back as far as to Saint Augustine in the fourth century of the Christian era. But he was well aware of the difficulties of making it prevail in view of the obstinate fact that states persisted in treating the making of war as a matter of policy and not of law. He summed up these difficulties under two main heads.[1] One was that of knowing which of the parties to any particular war had the right on his side; the other was the danger that other states incur if they presume to judge of the rights and wrongs of a war and take action to restrain the wrong-doer. Any scheme for eliminating war has still to grapple with these two difficulties; the first is our modern problem of determining the 'aggressor', and the second is that of 'collective security', of somehow placing behind the law the united force of the society of states, while ensuring at the same time protection to the states which lend their help. Neither Grotius nor the writers who followed him in the seventeenth and eighteenth centuries could see any way of overcoming these difficulties, and he fell back on the lame conclusion that the only practical course was not to ask third states to judge of the lawfulness or otherwise of a war, but to leave that question to the conscience of the belligerents.

It has to be admitted, therefore, that the attempt to establish a distinction in the law between the lawful and the unlawful occasions of making war was largely unreal, and it was retained by most of Grotius's

[1] *De jure belli ac pacis*, iii. 4. 4; and see generally Lauterpacht, *B.Y.I.L.*, 1946, p. 27.

successors more as an ornament to their theme than as a doctrine in which they seriously believed. Finally it disappeared even from theory, and international law came frankly to recognize that all wars are equally lawful.[1] In fact, the foundation of the League of Nations in 1919 marked the first real attempt to falsify this confession of weakness and to embody in actual law the cardinal principle of Grotius's system.

Richard Zouche (1590–1660), Professor of Civil Law in Oxford University and judge of the Court of Admiralty, was a prolific writer on legal subjects, among his works being one on international law, the *Jus et judicium feciale, sive jus inter gentes*, published in 1650. This has been called 'the first manual of international law',[2] for it discusses briefly but clearly almost every part of the subject. Without abandoning the law of nature as one of the bases of international law, Zouche preferred to deduce the law from the precedents of state practice, and he is sometimes regarded as a precursor of the 'positive' school of international lawyers, who regard the practice of states as the only source of law. Zouche introduced one important improvement of method, for he was the first writer to make a clear division between the law of peace and the law of war, and to make the former the more prominent of the two. This was necessary before war could be regarded, as it ought to be, as an abnormal relation between states.

[1] See W. E. Hall, *International Law*, 8th ed., p. 82 and *infra*, p. 397.
[2] Scelle, *Fondateurs de droit international*, p. 322.

Samuel Pufendorf (1632–94), Professor at Heidelberg, and afterwards at Lund in Sweden, published his *De jure naturae et gentium* in 1672, and may be regarded as the founder of the so-called 'naturalist' school of writers. He denied any binding force to the practice of nations and based his system wholly on natural law, but on a natural law in the new and debased form of a law supposed to be binding upon men in an imaginary *state of nature*.[1] There are traces of this conception in Grotius, but it had little influence on his system; for his law of nature was a law of reason directing men at all times, whether organized in political societies or not, and only in this sense has the conception any permanent validity.

Cornelius van Bynkershoek (1673–1743), a Dutch judge, was the author of works on special topics of international law, of which the most important was the *Quaestiones juris publici*, published in 1737. Bynkershoek had an intimate knowledge of questions of maritime and commercial practice, and he has an important place in the development of that side of international law. He belongs to the 'positive' school of writers, basing the law on custom, but holding also that custom must be explained and controlled by reason, which he refers to as *ratio juris gentium magistra*.[2] He held also that the recent practice of states was more valuable evidence of custom than the illustrations from ancient history with which his predecessors had generally adorned their works, since, 'as customs

[1] *Supra*, p. 25; *infra*, p. 54.
[2] *Quaestiones*, Book I, ch. 12.

change, so the law of nations changes';[1] but he attached more weight to the stipulations of particular treaties as evidence of the existence of custom than modern practice would allow.

Emerich de Vattel (1714–69), whose work *Le Droit des gens* was published in 1758, was a Swiss who served in the diplomatic service of Saxony. He intended his work as a manual for men of affairs, and was a popularizer of other men's ideas rather than an original thinker; yet he has probably exercised a greater permanent influence than any other writer on international law, and his work is still sometimes cited as an authority in international controversies. He accepted the doctrine of the *state of nature*; 'nations being composed of men naturally free and independent, and who before the establishment of civil societies lived together in the state of nature; nations or sovereign states must be regarded as so many free persons living together in the state of nature'; and since men are naturally equal, so are states; 'strength or weakness produce in this regard no distinction. A dwarf is as much a man as a giant is; a small republic is no less a sovereign state than the most powerful kingdom'.[2] Thus the doctrine of the equality of states, a misleading deduction from unsound premisses,[3] was introduced into the theory of international law.

According to Vattel the law of nations *in its origin* is merely the law of nature applied to nations, it is not subject to change, and treaties or customs contrary to it are unlawful. But other elements have been

[1] Ibid., *Ad lectorem.*   [2] Introduction.   [2] *Infra*, p. 130.

admitted into the law; for, says Vattel, natural law itself
establishes the freedom and independence of every
state, and therefore each is the sole judge of its own
actions and accountable for its observance of natural
law only to its own conscience. Other states may *request* it to reform its conduct; but what they may
actually *demand* from it is something much less. This
lower standard of *enforceable* duties Vattel calls the
voluntary law of nations, because it is to be presumed
that states have agreed to it, in contrast with the other
element of natural or, as he calls it, *necessary* law. 'Let
each sovereign make the *necessary* law the constant
rule of his conduct; he must allow others to take
advantage of the *voluntary law of nations*' (Book III,
ch. 12).

This exaggerated emphasis on the independence of
states had the effect in Vattel's system of reducing the
natural law, which Grotius had used as a juridical
barrier against arbitrary action by states towards one
another, to little more than an aspiration after better
relations between states; yet for the *voluntary* law,
which was the only part of Vattel's system which had
a real relation to the practice of states, he provided no
sound basis in theory, for he was unable to explain
the source of the obligation of states to observe it.
The results of this unsatisfactory division were unfortunate. For instance, Vattel tells us that by the
necessary law a state has a duty to maintain freedom of
commerce, because this is for the advantage of the
human race; but by the *voluntary* law it may impose
such restrictions upon it as suits its convenience, for its

duties to itself are more important than its duties to others (Book II, ch. 2). By *necessary* law, again, there are only three lawful causes of war, self-defence, redress of injury, and punishment of offences; but by *voluntary* law we must always assume that each side has a lawful cause for going to war, for 'princes may have had wise and just reasons for acting thus, and that is sufficient at the tribunal of the voluntary law of nations' (Book II, ch. 18).

In some respects, however, Vattel's system was an advance on those of his predecessors. He stood for a humaner view of the rights of war. He rejected the patrimonial theory of the nature of government which Grotius had held; 'this pretended right of ownership attributed to princes is a chimera begotten of an abuse of the laws relating to the inheritances of individuals. The state is not, and cannot be, a patrimony, since a patrimony exists for the good of the owner, whereas the prince is appointed only for the good of the state' (I. 5). He recognized in certain circumstances the right of part of a nation to separate itself from the rest (I. 17), a doctrine which partly explains his great popularity in the United States, where a copy of the work was first received in 1775. Professor Albert De Lapradelle has justly written of him that,

'before the great events of 1776 and 1789 occurred, he had written an international law, based on the principles of public law which two Revolutions, the American and the French, were to make effective. . . . Vattel's *Law of Nations* is international law based on the principles of 1789 . . . the projection upon the plane of the law of nations of the great principles of legal individualism. That is what makes Vattel's work important, what accounts for his success, characterizes his influence, and eventually, likewise, measures his shortcomings. Grotius had written the international law of absolutism, Vattel has written the international law of political liberty.'[1]

All the same, the survival of Vattel's influence into an age when the 'principles of legal individualism' are no longer adequate to international needs, if they ever were, has been a disaster for international law. By teaching that the 'natural' state of nations is an independence which does not admit the existence of a social bond between them he made it impossible to explain or justify their subjection to law; yet their independence is no more 'natural' than their interdependence. Both are facts of which any true theory of international relations must take account; the former is a more conspicuous, but not a more real, fact than the latter. It is true that in Vattel's own day the interdependence of states was less conspicuous in international practice than it is today; and this partly excuses the onesidedness of his system. None the less, by cutting the frail moorings which bound international law to any sound principle of obligation he did it an injury which has not yet been repaired.

[1] Introduction to the Carnegie edition of Vattel, 1916.

II

CHARACTER OF THE MODERN SYSTEM

§ 1. *The International Society*

LAW can only exist in a society, and there can be no society without a system of law to regulate the relations of its members with one another. If then we speak of the 'law of nations', we are assuming that a 'society' of nations exists, and the assumption that the whole of the civilized world constitutes in any real sense a single society or community is one which we are not justified in making without examination. In any case the character of the law of nations is necessarily determined by that of the society within which it operates, and neither can be understood without the other.

The law of nations had its origin among a few kindred nations of western Europe which, despite their frequent quarrels and even despite the religious schism of the sixteenth century, had all and were all conscious of having a common background in the Christian religion and the civilization of Greece and Rome. They were in a real sense a society of nations. But the rise of the modern state system undermined the tradition of the unity of Christendom, and eventually gave rise to those sentiments of exclusive nationalism which are rife in the world today. It is true that side by side with this development there has

been an immense growth of the factors that make
states mutually dependent on one another. Modern
science has given us vastly increased facilities and
speed of communications, and modern commerce has
created demands for the commodities of other nations
which even the extravagances of modern economic
nationalism are not able to stifle. If human affairs were
more wisely ordered, and if men were clearer-sighted
than they are in seeing their own interests, it might
be that this interdependence of the nations would
lead to a strengthening of their feelings of community.
But their interdependence is mainly in material
things, and though material bonds are necessary,
they are not enough without a common social con-
sciousness; without that they are as likely to lead to
friction as to friendship. Some sentiment of shared
responsibility for the conduct of a common life is a
necessary element in any society, and the necessary
force behind any system of law; and the strength
of any legal system is proportionate to the strength of
such a sentiment.

Hobbes in the *Leviathan*[1] has described the relations
of states to one another as they appeared to him to be
in a famous passage: 'Kings and persons of sovereign
authority, because of their independency, are in continual jealousies, and in the state and posture of gladi-
ators; their forts, and garrisons, and guns upon the
frontiers of their kingdoms, and continual spies upon
their neighbours; which is a posture of war.' Perhaps
there has never been a time when this description

[1] Ch. 13.

was more true than in our own day, when men were more cruel to one another, and when persecution of those who differ from the majority in race or language or religion was more rife. All this makes it not easy to believe today in the reality of a single world society, and it would be foolish to underrate the difficulties of creating one. Those difficulties indeed have not decreased, but have rather been intensified since the sixteenth century, and there have been two developments in particular which have profoundly affected the fortunes of international law. One has been the expansion of the system from being the law of the small family of nations among which it arose into one that is world-wide and now claims the allegiance of nations which had no part in building it up, and which either have never known, or no longer accept, the fundamental beliefs and sentiments on which it was originally founded. Some of these nations at least are inclined to look on international law as an alien system which the western nations, whose moral or intellectual leadership they no longer recognize, are trying to impose upon them, and in effect they have begun to claim the right to select from among its rules only those which suit their interests or which arise out of agreements to which they have themselves been parties.

The other weakening development just referred to has been a profound change in our ideas of the nature of law. We have seen how international law had its origin in natural law, that is to say, in the belief that nations must be bound to one another by law because it is a principle of nature that this world should be a system of order and not a chaos, and that therefore states, despite their independence, can be no exception to this universal rule. But with the passing of the Middle Ages this view of the nature of law was gradually dethroned by the growth of "positivist theories" according to which all law is nothing but the command of a superior will to an inferior. For international law this modern view of law has been especially unfortunate, but that is a matter to which it will be necessary to return. Here it need only be pointed out that the result of positivism has been to secularize the whole idea of law and thus to weaken the moral foundation which is essential to the vitality of all legal obligation.

There is therefore much in the prospect to discourage those who realize that the strengthening of international law must depend on the strengthening of the bonds that hold states together in an international society. Yet there is one solid ground for hope. We have begun to realize that a world society will not come into existence without conscious human effort. That is a new factor in the problem, for until recently, if we have thought about the question at all, most of us have assumed that international society and international law might be left to grow unaided. We have begun to see, however, that though the problem of world community remains essentially a moral problem, it is also in part a problem of statesmanship, and that international society needs institutions through which its members can learn to work together for common social ends. The League of Nations was the first great experiment with that end in view, and we know that it did not succeed. We are making a second attempt now with the United Nations, and hitherto this too has disappointed our hopes. But it is right that we should remember that only one generation has passed since men began to look on the building of a world community as a practical problem, and less than that since most of us began to see that the problem is really urgent.

§ 2. *The Modern 'Sovereign' State*

The preceding chapter has traced in outline the course of that curious metamorphosis which transformed the doctrine of sovereignty from a principle of internal order, as Bodin and even Hobbes had conceived it, into one of international anarchy. Starting in Bodin as a formal juristic concept, the attribute of a personal monarch entrusted by the constitution with supreme authority over the ordinary laws of the state, sovereignty, under the impulsion of the historical developments which took place in the character of European governments, came to be regarded as power absolute and above the law, and eventually, when it had become impossible to fix the location of such power in any definite person or organ within the state, as the attribute of the personified state itself. The doctrine was developed for the most part by political theorists who were not interested in, and paid little regard to, the relations of states with one another, and in its later forms it not only involved a denial of the possibility of states being subject to any kind of law, but became an impossible theory for a world which contained more states than one.

Writers on international law have attempted in many ingenious ways to reconcile the existence of their subject with the doctrine of the absolute sovereignty of states, but all these devices are in effect variations of the theory of the auto-limitation of sovereignty which is referred to later in this chapter.[1] One formula, for example, is to say that international law is a law of *co-ordination* but not of *subordination*, and even Oppenheim, though he was no believer in absolute sovereignty, yet felt obliged to attribute to international law a specific character not shared by law in general, and tells us that it is usually regarded as a law *between*, but not *above*, the several states.[2] Yet if states are the subjects of international law, as Oppenheim admits that they are, the law must surely be above them, and they must be subordinate to it.

Unfortunately the international lawyer cannot rid his subject of the incubus of the doctrine of sovereignty by showing that it is one of those concepts which, as a great American judge has warned us,[3] become our tyrants rather than our servants when they are treated as real existences and developed with disregard of their consequences to the limit of their logic. We ought to deal with our concepts, he tells us, always as provisional hypotheses to be reformulated and restrained

[1] *Infra*, p. 53.
[2] *International Law*, vol. i, 6th ed., p. 6.
[3] Cardozo, *Paradoxes of Legal Science*, p. 65.

when they have an outcome in oppression and injustice. But sovereignty, however much it may need reformulating as a political doctrine, does stand today for something in the relations of states which is both true and very formidable. It expresses, though in a misleading way, the claims that states habitually make to act as seems good to them without restraint on their freedom. An American Commission which was formed during the last war to study the organization of peace has summarized these claims conveniently.

'A sovereign state' [says the Commission's report] 'at the present time claims the power to judge its own controversies, to enforce its own conception of its rights, to increase its armaments without limit, to treat its own nationals as it sees fit, and to regulate its economic life without regard to the effect of such regulations upon its neighbours. These attributes of sovereignty must be limited.'[1]

Thus for the practical purposes of the international lawyer sovereignty is not a metaphysical concept, nor is it part of the essence of statehood; it is merely a term which designates an aggregate of particular and very extensive claims that states habitually make for themselves in their relations with other states. To the extent that sovereignty has come to imply that there is something inherent in the nature of states that makes it impossible for them to be subjected to law, it is a false doctrine which the facts of international relations do not support. But to the extent that it reminds us that the subjection of states to law is an aim as yet only

[1] *International Conciliation Pamphlet*, 1941.

very imperfectly realized, and one which presents the most formidable difficulties, it is a doctrine which we cannot afford to disregard.

The fundamental difficulty of subjecting states to the rule of law is the fact that states possess power. The legal control of power is always difficult, and it is not only for international law that it constitutes a problem. The domestic law of every state has the same problem, though usually (but not, as the persistence of civil wars proves, invariably) in a form less acute. In any decently governed state domestic law can normally deal effectively with the behaviour of individuals, but that is because the individual is weak and society is relatively strong; but when men join together in associations or factions for the achievement of some purpose which the members have in common the problem of the law becomes more difficult. Union always gives strength, and when the members of these bodies are numerous, when they can command powerful resources, and when they feel strongly that the interests which their combination exists to protect are vital to themselves, they often develop a tendency to pursue their purposes extra-legally, or even illegally, without much regard to the legal nexus which nominally binds them to the rest of the society of which they are a part. In fact, they behave inside the state in a way that is fundamentally similar to, though ordinarily it is less uncompromising than, the way in which sovereign states behave in the international society. Sovereignty is simply the culminating point of a tendency that is apt to recur in the conduct of any

group of human beings which is strong and determined enough to insist on having its own way, and of
all human groups states are the strongest. The problem of subjecting them to law is more difficult than,
but it is essentially similar to, that which confronts
the state in its treatment of powerful associations
within itself.

§ 3. *The Basis of Obligation in Modern International Law*

Traditionally there are two rival doctrines which
attempt to answer the question why states should be
bound to observe the rules of international law.

The doctrine of 'fundamental rights' is a corollary
of the doctrine of the 'state of nature', in which men
are supposed to have lived before they formed themselves into political communities or states; for states,
not having formed themselves into a super-state, are
still supposed by the adherents of this doctrine to be
living in such a condition. It teaches that the principles of international law, or the primary principles
upon which the others rest, can be deduced from the
essential nature of the state. Every state, by the very
fact that it is a state, is endowed with certain fundamental, or inherent, or natural, rights. Writers differ
in enumerating what these rights are, but generally
five rights are claimed, namely self-preservation, independence, equality, respect, and intercourse. It is
obvious that the doctrine of fundamental rights is
merely the old doctrine of the natural rights of man
transferred to states. That doctrine has played a great

part in history; Locke justified the English Revolution by it, and from Locke it passed to the leaders of the American Revolution and became the philosophical basis of the Declaration of Independence. But hardly any political scientist today would regard it as a true philosophy of political relations, and all the objections to it apply with even greater force when it is applied to the relations of states. It implies that men or states, as the case may be, bring with them into society certain primordial rights not derived from their membership of society, but inherent in their personality as individuals, and that out of these rights a legal system is formed; whereas the truth is that a legal right is a meaningless phrase unless we first assume the existence of a legal system from which it gets its validity. Further, the doctrine implies that the social bond between man and man, or between state and state, is somehow less natural, or less a part of the whole personality, than is the individuality of the man or the state, and that is not true; the only individuals we know are individuals-in-society. It is especially misleading to apply this atomistic view of the nature of the social bond to states. In its application to individual men it has a certain plausibility because it seems to give a philosophical justification to the common feeling that human personality has certain claims on society; and in that way it has played its part in the development of human liberty. But in the society of states the need is not for greater liberty for the individual states, but for a strengthening of the social bond between them, not for the clamant assertion of their rights, but for a more insistent reminder of their obligations towards one another. Finally, the doctrine is really a denial of the possibility of development in international relations; when it asserts that such qualities as independence and equality are inherent in the very nature of states, it overlooks the fact that their attribution to states is merely a stage in an historical process; we know that until modern times states were not regarded either as independent or equal, and we have no right to assume that the process of development has stopped. On the contrary it is not improbable, and it is certainly desirable, that there should be a movement towards the closer interdependence of states, and therefore away from the state of things which this doctrine would stabilize as though it were part of the fixed order of nature.

The doctrine of positivism, on the other hand, teaches that international law is the sum of the rules by which states have *consented* to be bound, and that nothing can be law to which they have not consented. This consent may be given expressly, as in a treaty, or it may be implied by a state acquiescing in a customary rule. But the assumption that international law consists of nothing save what states have consented to is an inadequate account of the system as it can be seen in actual operation, and even if it were a complete account of the contents of the law, it would fail to explain why the law is binding. It is in the first place quite impossible to fit the facts into a consistently consensual theory of the nature of international law. *Implied* consent is not a philosophically sound explanation of customary law, international or domestic; a customary rule is observed, not because it has been consented to, but because it is believed to be binding, and whatever may be the explanation or the justification for that belief, its binding force does not depend, and is not felt by those who follow it to depend, on the approval of the individual or the state to which it is addressed. Further, in the practical administration of international law, states are continually treated as bound by principles which they cannot, except by the most strained construction of the facts, be said to have consented to, and it is unreasonable, when we are seeking the true nature of international rules, to force the facts into a preconceived theory instead of finding a theory which will explain the facts as we have them. For example, a state which has newly come into existence does not in any intelligible sense *consent* to accept international law; it does not regard itself, and it is not regarded by others, as having any option in the matter. The truth is that states do not regard their international legal relations as resulting from consent, except when the consent is express, and that the theory of implied consent is a fiction invented by the theorist; only a certain plausibility is given to a consensual explanation of the nature of their obligations by the fact, important indeed to any consideration of the methods by which the system develops, that, in the absence of any international machinery for legislation by majority vote, a *new* rule of law cannot be imposed upon states merely by the will of other states.

But in the second place, even if the theory did not

involve a distortion of the facts, it would fail as an explanation. For consent cannot of itself create an obligation; it can do so only within a system of law which declares that consent duly given, as in a treaty or a contract, shall be binding on the party consenting. To say that the rule *pacta servanda sunt* is itself founded on consent is to argue in a circle. A consistently consensual theory again would have to admit that if consent is withdrawn, the obligation created by it comes to an end. Most positivist writers would not admit this, but to deny it is in effect to fall back on an unacknowledged source of obligation, which, whatever it may be, is not the consent of the state, for that has ceased to exist. Some modern German writers, however, do not shrink from facing the full consequences of the theory of a purely consensual basis for the law; they have inherited from Hegel a doctrine known as the 'auto-limitation of sovereignty', which teaches that states are sovereign persons, possessed of wills which reject all external limitation, and that if we find, as we appear to do in international law, something which limits their wills, this limiting something can only proceed from themselves. Most of these writers admit that a self-imposed limitation is no limitation at all; and they conclude therefore that so-called international law is nothing but 'external public law' (*äusseres Staatsrecht*), binding the state only because, and only so long as, it consents to be bound. There is no flaw in this argument; the flaw lies in the premisses, because these are not derived, as all positivist theory professes to be, from an observation of international facts. The real contribution of positivist theory to international law has been its insistence that the rules of the system are to be ascertained from observation of the practice of states and not from *a priori* deductions, but positivist writers have not always been true to their own teaching; and they have been too ready to treat a method of legal reasoning as though it were an explanation of the nature of the law.

There need be no mystery about the source of the obligation to obey international law. The same problem arises in any system of law and it can never be solved by a merely *juridical* explanation.[1] The answer must be sought outside the law, and it is for legal philosophy to provide it. The notion that the validity of international law raises some peculiar problem arises from the confusion which the doctrine of sovereignty has introduced into international legal theory. Even when we do not believe in the absoluteness of state sovereignty we have allowed ourselves to be persuaded that the fact of their sovereignty makes it necessary to look for some specific quality, not to be found in other kinds of law, in the law to which states are subject. We have accepted a false idea of the state as a personality with a life and a will of its own, still living in a 'state of nature', and we contrast this with the 'political' state in which individual men have come to live. But this assumed condition of states is the very negation of law, and no ingenuity can explain how the two can exist together. It is a notion as false analytically as it admittedly is historically. The truth

[1] Cf. Triepel, *Droit international et droit interne*, p. 81.

is that states are not persons, however convenient it may often be to personify them; they are merely *institutions*, that is to say, organizations which men establish among themselves for securing certain objects, of which the most fundamental is a system of order within which the activities of their common life can be carried on. They have no wills except the wills of the individual human beings who direct their affairs; and they exist not in a political vacuum but in continuous political relations with one another. Their subjection to law is as yet imperfect, though it is real as far as it goes; the problem of extending it is one of great practical difficulty, but it is not one of intrinsic impossibility. There are important differences between international law and the law under which individuals live in a state, but those differences do not lie in metaphysics or in any mystical qualities of the entity called state sovereignty.

The international lawyer then is under no special obligation to explain why the law with which he is concerned should be binding upon its subjects. If it were true that the essence of all law is a command, and that what makes the law of the state binding is that for some reason, for which no satisfactory explanation can ever be given, the will of the person issuing a command is superior to that of the person receiving it, then indeed it would be necessary to look for some special explanation of the binding force of international law. But that view of the nature of law has been long discredited. If we are to explain why any kind of law is binding, we cannot avoid some such assumption as that which the Middle Ages made, and which Greece and Rome had made before them, when they spoke of natural law. The ultimate explanation of the binding force of all law is that man, whether he is a single individual or whether he is associated with other men in a state, is constrained, in so far as he is a reasonable being, to believe that order and not chaos is the governing principle of the world in which he has to live.

§ 4. *The Sources of Modern International Law*

Article 38 of the Statute of the International Court of Justice directs the Court to apply:

(1) International conventions, whether general or particular, establishing rules expressly recognized by the contesting States;

(2) International custom, as evidence of a general practice accepted as law;

(3) The general principles of law recognized by civilized nations;

(4) Subject to the provisions of Article 59,[1] judicial decisions and the teachings of the most highly qualified publicists of the various nations, as subsidiary means for the determination of rules of law.

This is a text of the highest authority, and we may fairly assume that it expresses the duty of any tribunal which is called upon to administer international law.

[1] This article provides that 'the decision of the Court has no binding force except between the parties and in respect of that particular case'.

(a) *Treaties as a source of law*

'Agreement is a law for those who make it, which supersedes, supplements, or derogates from the ordinary law of the land. *Modus et conventio vincunt legem.*'[1] It is natural, therefore, to find that in seeking the law applicable to the facts of a particular case the Court is first directed to inquire whether the general law, under which their rights would otherwise fall to be determined, has been excluded by an agreement between them. There is indeed more scope for the application of this maxim in international than there is in domestic law, for domestic law generally includes a great number of peremptory rules the application of which cannot be excluded by agreement between the parties, whereas in international law almost complete freedom of contract prevails.

Treaties then are clearly a source of law for the parties to them, of 'special' or 'particular' law. But can we go farther and describe them in any sense as a source of 'general' international law? Certainly it is only a special class of treaty which has any claim to be so regarded. The ordinary treaty by which two or more states enter into engagements with one another for some special object can very rarely be used even as evidence to establish the existence of a rule of general law; it is more probable that the very reason of the treaty was to create an obligation which would not have existed by the general law, or to exclude an existing rule which would otherwise have applied.

---

[1] Salmond, *Jurisprudence*, p. 31.

Still less can such treaties be regarded as actually creating new law. The only class of treaties which it is admissible to treat as a source of general law are those which a large number of states have concluded for the purpose either of declaring their understanding of what the law is on a particular subject, or of laying down a new general rule for future conduct, or of creating some international institution. Such treaties are, as will appear in the next chapter, the substitute in the international system for legislation, and they are conveniently referred to as 'lawmaking'; their number is increasing so rapidly that the 'conventional law of nations' has taken its place beside the old customary law and already far surpasses it in volume. These terms are convenient, and they are not inaccurate, for it is not necessary that all the rules of a legal system should be binding on all the members of a community. But even a lawmaking treaty is subject to the limitation which applies to other treaties, that it does not bind states which are not parties to it. Thus, except in the almost impossible event of every state in the world becoming a party to one of these treaties, the law which it creates will not be law for every state. Some writers attempt to meet this difficulty by saying that the law which these treaties create is 'general', though not 'universal', international law; but the terminology is not very happy, nor does it really meet the crux of the difficulty. The real justification for ascribing a law-making function to these treaties is the practical one already referred to, that they do in fact perform the function which legislation performs in a state, though they do so only imperfectly; and that they are the only machinery which exists for the purposive adapting of international law to new conditions and in general for strengthening the force of the rule of law between states. Moreover, there is something artificial in saying, even if it is strictly true in theory, that such important institutions of international life as the Universal Postal Union, or the International Court of Justice, or the United Nations with its multifarious activities, are nothing but contractual arrangements between certain states. We ought to look behind the form of these treaties to their substantial effect.[1]

(b) *Custom as a source of law*

Custom in its legal sense means something more than mere habit or usage; it is a usage felt by those who follow it to be an obligatory one. There must be present a feeling that, if the usage is departed from, some form of sanction will probably, or at any rate ought to, fall on the transgressor. Evidence that a custom in this sense exists in the international sphere can be found only by examining the practice of states; that is to say, we must look at what states do in their relations with one another and attempt to

[1] There is, indeed, now some authority for considering certain classes of treaty provision as creating true 'objective' law. Thus, the International Court has held that the Charter created the United Nations with an "objective" legal personality binding upon non-Members; *infra*, pp. 120–1. Cf. also treaties creating international territorial arrangements, *per* Lord McNair in the Advisory Opinion on the Status of South-West Africa, *I.C.J. Reports*, 1950, pp. 153–7.

understand why they do it, and in particular whether they recognize an obligation to adopt a certain course, or, in the words of Article 38, we must examine whether the alleged custom shows 'a general practice accepted as law'. What this means was explained by the International Court in the *Asylum* case:[1]

'The Colombian Government must prove that the rule invoked by it is in accordance with a constant and uniform usage practised by the States in question, and that this usage is the expression of a right appertaining to the State granting asylum, and a duty incumbent on the territorial State.'

The evidence of custom may obviously be very voluminous and also very diverse. There are multifarious occasions on which persons who act or speak in the name of a state do acts or make declarations which either express or imply some view on a matter of international law. Any such act or declaration may, so far as it goes, be some evidence that a custom, and therefore that a rule of international law, does or does not exist; but, of course, its value as evidence will be altogether determined by the occasion and the circumstances. States, like individuals, often put forward contentions for the purpose of supporting a particular case which do not necessarily represent their settled or impartial opinion; and it is that opinion which has to be ascertained with as much certainty as the nature of the case allows. Particularly

[1] *I.C.J. Reports*, 1950, p. 276; see also I. C. MacGibbon in *B.Y.I.L.*, 1957.

important as sources of evidence are diplomatic correspondence; official instructions to diplomatists, consuls, naval and military commanders; acts of state legislation and decisions of state courts, which, we may presume, will not deliberately contravene any rule regarded as a rule of international law by the state; and opinions of law officers, especially when these are published, as they are in the United States.

In applying the forms of evidence which have been enumerated above in order to establish the existence of an international custom what is sought for is a general recognition among states of a certain practice as obligatory. It would hardly ever be practicable, and all but the strictest of positivists admit that it is not necessary, to show that every state has recognized a certain practice, just as in English law the existence of a valid local custom or custom of trade can be established without proof that every individual in the locality, or engaged in the trade, has practised the custom. This test of *general* recognition is necessarily a vague one; but it is of the nature of customary law, whether national or international, not to be susceptible of exact or final formulation. When a system of customary law is administered by courts, which perpetually reformulate and develop its principles, as has happened in the English Common Law, its uncertainty is so much reduced that it is hardly, if at all, greater than the uncertainty which attaches to enacted or to codified law; but the clarifying influence of courts is only beginning to be felt in international law. It is therefore even less possible to formulate its principles dogmatically than to formulate those of a national system of law. The difference, however, is not one between uncertainty and certainty in formulation, but merely between a greater and a less degree of uncertainty.

The growth of a new custom is always a slow process, and the character of international society makes it particularly slow in the international sphere. The progress of the law therefore has come to be more and more bound up with that of the law-making treaty. But it is possible even today for new customs to develop and to win acceptance as law when the need is sufficiently clear and urgent. A striking recent illustration of this is the rapid development of the principle of sovereignty over the air.[1]

(c) *The general principles of law*

Article 38 of the Statute of the Court directs it to refer to 'the general principles of law recognized by civilized nations'.[2] The phrase is a wide one; it includes, though it is not limited to, the principles of private law administered in national courts where these are applicable to international relations. Private law, being in general more developed than international law, has always constituted a sort of reserve store of principles upon which the latter has been in the habit of drawing. Roman law, as we have seen,

[1] *Infra*, p. 218.

[2] The significance of this important paragraph in the Statute is examined in Lauterpacht, *Private Law Sources and Analogies of International Law*, and in Bin Cheng, *The General Principles of Law as applied by International Courts and Tribunals*.

was so drawn upon by the early writers on international law, and the process continues, for the good reason that a principle which is found to be generally accepted by civilized legal systems may fairly be assumed to be so reasonable as to be necessary to the maintenance of justice under any system. Prescription, estoppel, *res judicata*, are examples of such principles. International law, however, does not borrow from this source by importing private law institutions lock, stock, and barrel with a ready-made set of particular rules; it rather looks to them for an indication of a legal policy or principle.[1]

Paragraph (c) then introduces no novelty into the system, for the 'general principles of law' are a source to which international courts have instinctively referred in the past. But its inclusion is important as a rejection of the positivist doctrine, according to which international law consists solely of rules to which states have given their consent. It is an authoritative recognition of a dynamic element in international law, and of the creative function of the courts which administer it.

(d) *Judicial precedents*

These are described in Article 38 of the Statute as a 'subsidiary means for the determination of rules of law'. Strictly speaking, as Article 59 expressly states, an international decision is binding only upon the parties to the case and in respect of that particular

[1] *Per* Lord McNair, *International Status of South-West Africa, I.C.J. Reports*, 1950, p. 148.

case. Precedents are not therefore binding authorities in international law, but the English theory of their binding force merely elevates into a dogma a natural tendency of all judicial procedure. When any system of law has reached a stage at which it is thought worth while to report the decisions and the reasoning of judges, other judges inevitably give weight, though not necessarily decisive weight, to the work of their predecessors. Until recently there has been only a restricted scope for the operation of this tendency in international law for the reason that international adjudications have been relatively few, and reports have not been very readily accessible. This state of things is changing rapidly, and judicial precedents are taking their proper place in the system; indeed, Judge Lauterpacht has said[1] that the practice of referring to its previous decisions has become one of the most conspicuous features of the Judgments and Opinions of the Court. The change is a beneficial one; it is creating for international law an ampler stock of detailed rules, testing its abstract principles by their fitness to solve practical problems, and depriving it of the too academic character which has belonged to it in the past. No rule exists to determine the value of any particular precedent, and the decisions of national courts dealing with matters of international law may be helpful, as well as those of international courts; but the decisions of the International Court of Justice and of its predecessor the Permanent Court

[1] *The Development of International Law by the International Court* (1958), p. 9.

of International Justice are accorded more weight than any others.

(e) *Text-writers*

These again are a 'subsidiary means for the determination of rules of law'. The function of text-writers in the international system is in no way peculiar; it is a misapprehension to suppose that they have or claim any authority to make the law. Actually they render exactly the same services as in any other legal system. One of those services is to provide useful evidence of what the law is. This function is universally recognized, and it has been expressed by Mr. Justice Gray, delivering the judgment of the Supreme Court of the United States, in these words:

'International law is part of our law, and must be ascertained and administered by the courts of justice of appropriate jurisdiction, as often as questions of right depending upon it are duly presented for their determination. For this purpose, where there is no treaty, and no controlling executive or legislative act or judicial decision, resort must be had to the customs and usages of civilized nations; and as evidence of these, to the works of jurists and commentators who by years of labour, research, and experience have made themselves peculiarly well acquainted with the subjects of which they treat. Such works are resorted to by judicial tribunals, not for the speculations of their authors concerning what the law ought to be, but for trustworthy evidence of what the law really is.'[1]

[1] *Paquete Habana* (1899), American Prize Cases, p. 1938.

Another function of text-writers is referred to by Mr. Justice Gray when he speaks of their 'speculations concerning what the law ought to be', for their writings may help to create opinion which may influence the conduct of states and thus indirectly in the course of time help to modify the actual law. Whether the speculations of any particular author are likely to have this active influence depends mainly on his prestige, and on the persuasiveness with which he presents his arguments. But it is important not to confuse these two functions, the providing of evidence of what the law is, and the exercise of influence on its development.

(f) *The place of 'reason' in the modern system*

In our discussion of natural law we saw that no system of law consists only of formulated rules, for these can never be sufficiently detailed or sufficiently foreseeing to provide for every situation that may call for a legal decision; those who administer law must meet new situations not precisely covered by a formulated rule by resorting to the principle which medieval writers would have called natural law, and which we generally call reason. Reason in this context does not mean the unassisted reasoning powers of any intelligent man, but a 'judicial' reason, which means that a principle to cover the new situation is discovered by applying methods of reasoning which lawyers everywhere accept as valid, for example, the consideration of precedents, the finding of analogies, the disengagement from accidental circumstances of the principles underlying rules of law already established. This source of new rules is accepted as valid and is constantly resorted to in the practice of states, both in the decisions of international tribunals and in the legal arguments conducted by foreign offices with one another, so that a positivism which refuses to accept it is untrue to its own premisses. It is thus referred to in an interesting passage in an award of the Claims Tribunal which was set up by an agreement between the United States and Great Britain in 1910:

'Even assuming that there was . . . no treaty and no specific rule of international law formulated as the expression of a universally recognized rule governing the case . . ., it cannot be said that there is no principle of international law applicable. International law, as well as domestic law, may not contain, and generally does not contain, express rules decisive of particular cases; but the function of jurisprudence is to resolve the conflict of opposing rights and interests by applying, in default of any specific provision of law, the corollaries of general principles, and so to find . . . the solution of the problem. This is the method of jurisprudence; it is the method by which the law has been gradually evolved in every country resulting in the definition and settlement of legal relations as well between States as between private individuals.'[1]

The admission of this element in the judicial process is indeed inevitable if we are to avoid the untenable conclusion that international law contains lacunae or 'gaps' which may conceivably oblige a court, instead

[1] Case of the *Eastern Extension, etc. Telegraph Co. Ltd*. Nielsen's Report, p. 75, quoted in Cory, *Compulsory Arbitration*, p. 226.

of declaring the rights of the parties on the facts before it, to pronounce a *non liquet*, that is to say, to declare that in default of any rule applicable to the case the point at issue 'is not clear' and therefore cannot be decided. Such a situation does not in fact arise in international, any more than it arises in domestic, litigation. It does not arise, because international law, like any other system of law, is, in a formal, though of course not in any other, sense a 'perfect' system; it can provide a solution for any issue submitted to a court, and it can do this because it accepts the practice by which the judge is required to 'find' a rule of law which is applicable to the case before him.[1] Lord Mansfield, perhaps the greatest judge who ever sat on the English bench, doubtless had the same principle in mind when he wrote: 'The law of nations is founded on justice, equity, convenience, and *the reason of the thing*, and confirmed by long usage.'[2]

§ 5. *The Legal Character of International Law*

It has often been said that international law ought to be classified as a branch of ethics rather than of law. The question is partly one of words, because its solution will clearly depend on the definition of law which we choose to adopt; in any case it does not affect the value of the subject one way or the other, though those who deny the legal character of international law often speak as though 'ethical' were a depreciatory

---

[1] For a different view see Professor Stone in *B.Y.I.L.*, 1959, p. 124.
[2] For the occasion and reference see Pollock, *Essays in the Law*, p. 64.

epithet. But in fact it is both practically inconvenient and also contrary to the best juristic thought to deny its legal character. It is inconvenient because if international law is nothing but international morality, it is certainly not the whole of international morality, and it is difficult to see how we are to distinguish it from those other admittedly moral standards which we apply in forming our judgments on the conduct of states. Ordinary usage certainly uses two tests in judging the 'rightness' of a state's act, a moral test and one which is somehow felt to be independent of morality. Every state habitually commits acts of selfishness which are often gravely injurious to other states, and yet are not contrary to international law; but we do not on that account necessarily judge them to have been 'right'. It is confusing and pedantic to say that both these tests are moral. Moreover, it is the pedantry of the theorist and not of the practical man; for questions of international law are invariably treated as legal questions by the foreign offices which conduct our international business, and in the courts, national or international, before which they are brought; legal forms and methods are used in diplomatic controversies and in judicial and arbitral proceedings, and authorities and precedents are cited in argument as a matter of course. It is significant too that when a breach of international law is alleged by one party to a controversy, the act impugned is practically never defended by claiming the right of private judgment, which would be the natural defence if the issue concerned the morality of the act, but always by attempting to prove that no rule has been violated. This was true of the defences put forward even for such palpable breaches of international law as the invasion of Belgium in 1914, or the bombardment of Corfu in 1923.

But if international law is not the same thing as international morality, and if in some important respects at least it certainly resembles law, why should we hesitate to accept its definitely legal character? The objection comes in the main from the followers of writers such as Hobbes and Austin, who regard nothing as law which is not the will of a political superior. But this is a misleading and inadequate analysis even of the law of a modern state; it cannot, for instance, unless we distort the facts so as to fit them into the definition, account for the existence of the English Common Law. In any case, even if such an analysis gave an adequate explanation of law in the modern state, it would require us to assume that that law is the only true law, and not merely law at a particular stage of growth or one species of a wider genus. Such an assumption is historically unsound. Most of the characteristics which differentiate international law from the law of the state and are often thought to throw doubt on its legal character, such, for instance, as its basis in custom, the fact that the submission of parties to the jurisdiction of courts is voluntary, the absence of regular processes either for creating or enforcing it, are familiar features of early legal systems; and it is only in quite modern times, when we have come to regard it as natural that the state should be constantly making new laws and enforcing existing ones, that to identify law with the will of the state has become even a plausible theory. If, as Sir Frederick Pollock[1] writes, and as probably most competent jurists would today agree, the only essential conditions for the existence of law are the existence of a political community, and the recognition by its members of settled rules binding upon them in that capacity, international law seems on the whole to satisfy these conditions.

§ 6. *Some Defects of the System*

But it is more important to understand the nature of the system than to argue whether it ought to be called law or something else. The best view is that international law is in fact just a system of customary law, upon which has been erected, almost entirely within the last two generations, a superstructure of 'conventional' or treaty-made law, and some of its chief defects are precisely those that the history of law teaches us to expect in a customary system. It is a common mistake to suppose that of these the most conspicuous is the frequency of its violation. Violations of law are rare in all customary systems, and they are so in international law. The explanation of that fact is simple, and so too is the explanation of the common belief to the contrary. For the law is normally observed because, as we shall see, the demands that it makes on states are generally not exacting, and

---

[1] *First Book of Jurisprudence*, p. 28.

on the whole states find it convenient to observe it; but this fact receives little notice because the interest of most people in international law is not in the ordinary routine of international legal business, but in the occasions, rare but generally sensational, on which it is flagrantly broken. Such breaches generally occur either when some great political issue has arisen between states, or in that part of the system which professes to regulate the conduct of war. But our diagnosis of what is wrong with the system will be mistaken if we fail to realize that the laws of peace and the great majority of treaties are on the whole regularly observed in the daily intercourse of states. And this is no small service to international life, however far it may fall short of the ideal by which we rightly judge the achievements of the system. If we fail to understand this, we are likely to assume, as many people do, that all would be well with international law if we could devise a better system for enforcing it; but the weakness of international law lies deeper than any mere question of sanctions. It is not the existence of a police force that makes a system of law strong and respected, but the strength of the law that makes it possible for a police force to be effectively organized. The imperative character of law is felt so strongly and obedience to it has become so much a matter of habit within a highly civilized state that national law has developed a machinery of enforcement which generally works smoothly, though never so smoothly as to make breaches impossible. If the imperative character of international law were equally strongly felt, the institution of definite international sanctions would easily follow.

A customary system of law can never be adequate to the needs of any but a primitive society, and the paradox of the international society is that, whilst on the material side it is far from primitive, and therefore needs a strong and fairly elaborate system of law for the regulation of the clashes to which the material interdependence of different states is constantly giving rise, its spiritual cohesion is, as we have already seen, weak, and as long as that is so the weakness will inevitably be reflected in a weak and primitive system of law.

Among the most serious shortcomings of the present system are the rudimentary character of the institutions which exist for the making and the application of the law, and the narrow restrictions on its range. The institutions which do exist will be described in the next chapter. But we may note here that there is no legislature to keep the law abreast of new needs in the international society; no executive power to enforce the law; and although certain administrative bodies have been created, these, though important in themselves, are far from being adequate for the mass of business which ought to be treated today as of international concern. There exist also convenient machinery for the arbitration of disputes and a standing court of justice, but the range of action of these is limited because resort to them is not compulsory.

The restricted range of international law is merely

the counterpart of the wide freedom of independent action which states claim in virtue of their sovereignty, and, as we have seen, it is because the demands that international law makes on states are on the whole so light that its rules in general are fairly well observed. The system is still at what we may describe as the *laissez-faire* stage of legal development. The conduct of a state does not fall under international law merely because it may affect the interests of other states; this may be true and yet the matter in question may fall within what is called the 'domestic jurisdiction' of a single state. For example, legislation restricting immigration is not a matter which affects the interests only of the countries of immigration; it creates serious difficulties for countries which have a surplus of population, and where economic life has come to depend on emigration facilities. This latter fact, however, is irrelevant from a legal point of view, for immigration, though it is only one side of a problem of great international concern, the problem of the migration of population, is a matter which international law leaves each country to determine for itself. Other illustrations of matters which at present international law leaves to 'domestic jurisdiction' are the manner in which a state chooses to treat its own subjects, its choice of a form of government, its naturalization laws, and yet its action on any of these matters may easily have repercussions on the interests of other states. An even more serious limitation on the range of international law is that practically the whole sphere of international economic relations, except where mutual concessions have been arranged by treaty, belongs to domestic jurisdiction. Tariffs, bounties, preferences, raw materials, markets and the like are matters which often underlie the rivalries of modern states and provide the causes, if not the occasions, of their disputes; yet international law can very rarely interpose its regulating influence here. Law will never play a really effective part in international relations until it can annex to its own sphere some of the matters which at present lie within the 'domestic jurisdictions' of the several states; for so long as it has to be admitted that one state may have its reasonable interests injuriously affected by the unreasonable action of another, and yet have no legal basis for complaint, it is likely that the injured state, if it is strong enough, will seek by other means the redress that the law cannot afford it. At the best the present state of things leads to the maintenance by powerful states of policies outside the law, conceived in their own interests, and paying only so much regard to the interests of the other states as prudence dictates. As things are, such policies cannot even be wholly condemned, because the interests which they protect are often perfectly reasonable interests such as a really adequate system of law would recognize and safeguard; but, unfortunately, there is at present no security that these policies will be confined to the protection of the *reasonable* interests of the states concerned.

It is a natural consequence of the absence of authoritative law-declaring machinery that many of the principles of international law, and even more the detailed application of accepted principles, are uncertain. But on the whole the layman tends to exaggerate this defect. It is not in the nature of any law to provide mathematically certain solutions of problems which may be presented to it; for uncertainty cannot be eliminated from law so long as the possible conjunctions of facts remain infinitely various. Although therefore the difference between international law and the law of a state in this respect is important it is one of degree and not of kind, and it tends to be reduced as the practice of resorting to international courts, which are able to work out the detailed practical implication of general principles, becomes more common. The difficulty of formulating the rules of international law with precision is a necessary consequence of the kinds of evidence upon which we have to rely in order to establish them.

But even graver than any of the particular sources of weakness referred to above is the tolerance which the system has hitherto perforce extended to the persistence of war. We have seen[1] how the classical writers attempted to establish a distinction between *bellum justum* and *bellum injustum*, and that the facts were too strong for this distinction to endure since states persisted in using war as an instrument, not of the law, but of their national policies, and most modern international lawyers have felt bound to admit, in the words of Hall already quoted, that 'international law has no alternative but to accept war, independently

[1] *Supra*, pp. 33 et seq.

of the justice of its origin, as a relation which the parties to it may set up if they choose'. This is doubtless the more realistic view, but it is also an acknowledgement of defeat, and it is certain that if international law is ever to become one of the pillars of a stable international order states must place behind it a power that will enable it to make and maintain the most elementary of all legal distinctions, that between the legal and the illegal use of physical force. Fitfully, and so far without any assured prospect of success, the present generation has set itself to essay this task.

Whether from a review of all these shortcomings we ought to conclude that international law is a failure depends upon what we assume to be its aim. It has not failed to serve the purposes for which states have chosen to use it; in fact it serves these purposes reasonably well. The layman hears little of international law as a working system, for most of its practice goes on within the walls of foreign offices, which on principle are secretive; and even if the foreign offices were inclined to be more communicative the layman would not find what they could tell him very interesting, any more than he would normally be interested in the working of a solicitor's office. For in fact the practice of international law proceeds on much the same lines as that of any other kind of law, with the foreign offices taking the place of the private legal adviser and exchanging arguments about the facts and the law, and later, more often than is sometimes supposed, with a hearing before some form of international tribunal. The volume of this work is considerable, but most of it is not sensational, and it only occasionally relates to matters of high political interest. That does not mean that the matters to which it does relate are unimportant in themselves; often they are very important to particular interests or individuals. But it means that international law is performing a useful and indeed a necessary function in international life in enabling states to carry on their day-to-day intercourse along orderly and predictable lines. That is the role for which states have chosen to use it and for that it has proved a serviceable instrument. If we are dissatisfied with this role, if we believe that it can and should be used, as national law has begun to be used, as an instrument for promoting the general welfare in positive ways, and even more if we believe that it ought to be a powerful means of maintaining international peace, then we shall have to admit that it has so far failed. But it is only fair to remember that these have not been the purposes for which states have so far chosen to use it.

§ 7. *Proposals for Codification*

A method often advocated for the improvement of international law is that it should be codified. A code, it is argued, would provide a systematic arrangement of the law, would make its provisions clearer and more easily ascertainable, would remove uncertainties, and fill up existing lacunae. It is true that no code ever does or can attain these ends completely. When a code is made, it is never possible to foresee all the situations to which it will have to be applied; and in any case, even if that were possible, it would not be desirable to give the law a form so detailed and precise as to exclude the need for adapting it to new situations by the ordinary processes of judicial interpretation. But that is only to say that neither a code nor any other device can ever make the application of law to facts a merely automatic process.

The difficulties of any process of codification vary with the nature of the materials on which the drafts-man has to work, that is to say, with the state of the law as it exists before codification is undertaken. If the existing law is on the whole well settled, if it already exists in the form, for example, of customary rules generally accepted, or of judicial precedents, or of particular acts of legislation, the work of the draftsman is mainly one of orderly arrangement; he is not required to concern himself with the substance or policy of the law, but only with the form of its presentation. It is true that even in this case the work must involve some element of law-creation, for the draftsman must exercise some discretion in eliminating minor inconsistencies and uncertainties and in filling up lacunae. But this side of his work is only incidental to his main task, which is to state the law in a form clearer and more convenient than that in which it has hitherto existed, and that is a task which can appropriately be entrusted to lawyers.

This type of codification is common enough in municipal systems of law. But the codification of international law would be a very different task. The

international codifier could not limit his attention to
the form of the law; he would inevitably be concerned
throughout with its substance. He would have to
choose between competing rules, to fill up gaps on
which the law is uncertain or silent, and to give precision to abstract general principles of which the practical application is unsettled; in short the codification
of international law is only possible to the extent that
political decisions can be obtained as to the law which
the code is to contain. In circumstances such as these
codification ceases to be a technical task which can
be entrusted to lawyers; it becomes a political matter,
a task of law creation, and the contents of the code can
be settled only if governments can agree upon them.

How difficult it may be to secure such agreement
was shown at a Codification Conference convened by
the League of Nations at The Hague in 1930. Three
subjects were before the Conference, the law of
nationality, of territorial waters, and of responsibility
for damage done in the territory of a state to foreigners.
The preparatory work had been thorough, and the
Conference was entered on with high hopes. It was
a dismal failure. Agreements were reached on only a
few minor points of the law of nationality, and even
these were ratified afterwards by very few states.
Some of the preparatory work was of permanent
value, for it contained the answers given by governments to a questionnaire asking for their views on the
present state of the law. But on the whole the Conference probably did more harm than good. When
governments are asked to bind themselves to a pro-

posed formulation of some rule of law they inevitably ask themselves whether they may not some day find it desirable to challenge the rule as formulated, or they refrain from accepting it because it forms part of a draft containing other provisions to which they object; in either case the result of their refusal may be to throw doubt on something which has hitherto been generally regarded as an established rule of customary law.

The League's enthusiasm for codification wilted after the failure of the 1930 Conference. The Charter of the United Nations, however, revitalized the movement for codification by providing that the General Assembly should 'initiate studies and make recommendations for the purpose of encouraging the progressive development of international law and its codification' (Article 13). The fruit of this provision was the establishment of the International Law Commission in 1948 with a special Statute to regulate its organization and functioning.[1] The Commission consists of twenty-one[2] 'persons of recognised competence in international law' elected by the General Assembly which is expected to ensure that the Commission as a whole is representative of the main forms of civilization and of the principal legal systems of the world. The Statute distinguishes between (a) the development of international law, i.e. 'the preparation of draft conventions on subjects which have not yet been regulated by international law or in regard to

[1] See Sohn, *Basic Documents of the United Nations* (1956), p. 31.
[2] Originally 15.

which the law has not yet been sufficiently developed in the practice of States', and (b) its codification, i.e. 'the more precise formulation and systematisation of rules of international law in fields where there already has been extensive state practice, precedent and doctrine'. The Commission is to promote both these purposes and those who drafted the Statute recognized that there is no clear-cut line between them and that in any work of 'codification' gaps may have to be filled in or amendments made to take account of new conditions.

When the Commission is engaged essentially in 'progressive development' of any branch of the law, its work can acquire legal force only through the medium of an international agreement; accordingly, in that case the Statute contemplates that the Commission shall produce a draft convention and the General Assembly then decide whether steps shall be taken to bring about the conclusion of an international agreement. When, however, the Commission's task is essentially one of 'codification', the Statute envisages two other possible conclusions to its work: (a) simple publication of its Report and (b) a resolution of the General Assembly adopting all or part of the Report. Here the Statute reflects a widely held view[1]—that scientific restatements of the law by a group of eminent and independent international lawyers may offer greater possibilities of making pro-

[1] See Sir Cecil Hurst, 'A Plea for the Codification of International Law on New Lines', in *Grotius Society Transactions, 1946*; R. Y. Jennings, *B.Y.I.L.*, 1947, p. 201.

yeah!

gress in codification than attempts to produce texts agreed and ratified by governments. Such restatements, while theoretically of no authority, would be expected by their intrinsic merit to gain acceptance as a definitive formulation of the branch of the law in question and to be given application in state practice and in the jurisprudence of international tribunals. And, clearly, if a restatement were to be endorsed by the General Assembly in a resolution, it would have the greatest possible influence, even although technically it lacked the legal authority of an international convention. By the use of the restatement technique it was hoped to free the process of codification as far as possible from the influence of individual national policies and claims such as caused the failure of the 1930 Conference.

The Commission has now been at work for over ten years. In 1949 it adopted a provisional list of fourteen subjects considered suitable for codification: (1) Recognition of States; (2) Succession of States and Government; (3) Jurisdictional immunities of States and their property; (4) Jurisdiction with regard to crimes committed outside national territory; (5) Régime of the high seas; (6) Régime of territorial waters; (7) Nationality; (8) Treatment of aliens; (9) Right of asylum; (10) Law of treaties; (11) Diplomatic intercourse and immunities; (12) Consular intercourse and immunities; (13) State responsibility; and (14) Arbitral procedure. The Commission decided to give priority to the Law of treaties, Arbitral procedure, and the Régime of the high seas, and was later asked by the General Assembly to add the Régime of territorial waters and Diplomatic intercourse and immunities to the priority list. Up to date the Commission has taken up, and carried to varying points of completion, nine out of the fourteen subjects on its provisional list. In addition, it has dealt with a number of matters assigned to it by the General Assembly: (a) Draft declaration on the rights and duties of States; (b) Formulation of the principles of the Nuremberg Charter; (c) Draft code of offences against the peace and security of mankind; (d) Definition of aggression; (e) International criminal jurisdiction; and (f) Reservations to Multilateral conventions. It has also been asked by the General Assembly to undertake, 'as soon as it considers advisable', the codification of the law of asylum and a study of 'historic waters'.

In its early years the Commission, whose members serve only on a part-time basis, was perhaps slowed up by being called on to deal with too many matters at the same time; but it now has to its credit a number of draft conventions or codes submitted to the General Assembly. Its elaborate code of arbitral procedure proved to be too progressive for the taste of the General Assembly, but retains a certain value as a model code of procedure. The political stresses of the cold war have prevented the Commission's work on crimes against peace and other aspects of international criminal law from being carried to completion; and opinion concerning the effect of reservations to multilateral conventions has been found to be too divided for precise rules on this subject yet to be embodied in a code. On the other hand, the Commission's work on the law of the sea—both the high seas and territorial waters—met with a very large measure of acceptance at the Geneva Conferences of 1958 and 1960 and the Commission may justly claim a large share of the credit for the resulting Conventions which represent a major contribution to the codification and development of this part of international law. Another draft Convention—on diplomatic intercourse and immunities—has been adopted by a diplomatic conference at Vienna in 1961.

Experience has confirmed the impossibility of drawing a sharp distinction between 'codification' and 'progressive development'. The distinction still has a certain importance, since a project for 'progressive development' can only be initiated by the General Assembly, whereas the Commission itself may initiate 'codification'. But the Commission has not differentiated between the two processes in its handling of a subject. Experience has also shown that even when the operation is essentially one of codification some States will begin to question apparently established rules and political factors come into play. Indeed considerable pessimism is expressed in some quarters as to the prospects of codification under present conditions, when the Communist bloc challenge customary rules which do not suit them and the new States of Africa and Asia are inclined to question customary law developed from the practice of European states. These are certainly factors which militate

against rapid and spectacular advances in the codification of international law. But they increase rather
than diminish the importance of the International
Law Commission as an instrument for promoting
agreement upon rules of international law. For whatever criticisms may be made of the work of the Commission, it is primarily through the Commission, if at
all, that we may hope to see the divergences in some
measure harmonized and more stable foundations
laid for the law of the new international society now
emerging.

§ 8. *The Application of International Law in Municipal Courts*[1]

The accepted doctrine is that international law is
part of our law, and one practical consequence of this,
which has been called the doctrine of 'Incorporation',
is that international law for a British court is not a
foreign law. When British courts have to deal with an
issue which depends on a rule of foreign law, the rule
has to be proved as a fact by evidence like any other
fact, but as international law is part of the law of the
land the courts will take judicial notice of it.

The earliest recorded judicial statement of the doctrine of incorporation is a dictum of Lord Chancellor
Talbot in *Barbuit's Case*[2] in 1735, where he is reported
to have said 'the law of nations in its fullest extent is
and forms part of the law of England'. But there is

[1] See the articles of Professor Dickinson in *A.J.I.L.*, vol. xxvi,
p. 239, and of Professor Lauterpacht in *Grotius Society Transactions*,
1939, p. 52.   [2] *Cas. t. Talbot*, 281.

nothing in the report to suggest that the Lord Chancellor thought that he was introducing a new principle; he seems to have been merely stating one that was already well established in the law. Probably for the origin of the doctrine we must remind ourselves of the original conception of international law as simply the law of nature applied to the relations between sovereign princes, and of the fact that the Common Law too professed to be an embodiment of reason. It was natural therefore that judges should think of the two kinds of law not as two unrelated systems, but as the application to different subject-matters of different parts of one great system of law. However that may be, the doctrine survived after natural law theories of the basis of international law had ceased to be fashionable in the nineteenth century, and were succeeded by the positivist view that the law is founded on the consent of states express or implied; the only change was that the doctrine was given a somewhat different formulation. It was formulated by Lord Chief Justice Alverstone in 1905 in the case *West Rand Mining Co.* v. *The King*[1] in these terms: 'Whatever has received the common consent of civilized nations must have received the assent of our country, and that to which we have assented along with other nations in general may properly be called international law, and as such will be acknowledged and applied by our municipal tribunals when legitimate occasion arises for those tribunals to decide questions to which doctrines of international law may be relevant.' A more recent

[1] [1905] 2 K.B. 391.

statement to the same effect is one by Lord Atkin delivering the advice of the Privy Council in *Chung Chi Chung* v. *The King*:[1] 'The courts acknowledge the existence of a body of rules which nations accept among themselves. On any judicial issue they seek to ascertain what the relevant rule is, and, having found it, they will treat it as incorporated into the domestic law.'

The doctrine then has been established in our law for at least 200 years, but it is subject to certain qualifications which we shall have to admit.

One of these is that under the British Constitution an Act of Parliament is paramount; international law is part of the common law, and in a British court any rule of the common law must yield before an Act of Parliament. The point arose in 1906 in the Scottish case of *Mortensen* v. *Peters*,[2] where the appellant, a Danish national, had been fined for trawling in the Moray Firth outside the three-mile limit under an Act which made it an offence for 'any person' to trawl in those waters. It was argued that Parliament could not have intended those words to apply to a foreigner, but the Court said:

'In this Court we have nothing to do with the question whether the legislature has or has not done what foreign powers may consider a usurpation in a question with them. Neither are we a tribunal sitting to decide whether an Act of the legislature is *ultra vires* as in contravention of generally acknowledged principles of international law. For us an Act of Parliament is supreme, and we are bound

[1] [1939] A.C. 160.   [2] 14 *S.L.R.* 227, *per* Lord Dunedin.

to follow its terms. . . . It is a trite observation that there is no such thing as a standard of international law extraneous to the domestic law of a kingdom to which appeal may be made. . . . International law, so far as this court is concerned is the body of doctrine regarding the international rights and duties of states which has been adopted and made part of the law of Scotland.'

An American court used similar language in the case of *Over the Top* in 1925:[1] 'International practice is law only in so far as we adopt it, and like all common or statute law it bends to the will of Congress.' There is, however, a presumption that neither Parliament nor Congress will intend to violate international law, and a statute will not be interpreted as doing so if that conclusion can be avoided. In *Mortensen* v. *Peters* the Court was not satisfied that the offence alleged had been committed outside Scottish territorial waters, and it is believed that there is no case in British reports in which a court has felt bound by a statute to override a rule which it regarded as a rule of international law.

A second qualification of the doctrine of incorporation is that a treaty, though internationally binding, does not thereby alone become part of the law of the land under the British Constitution. The making of treaties is a prerogative power which the executive may exercise without the concurrence of the legislature, so that if a treaty were *ipso facto* to become part of our domestic law it would mean that the executive could legislate for the country. Under the American

[1] 5 *Federal Reporter*, 838.

Constitution the rule is different, for a treaty is 'the supreme law of the land . . . anything in the constitution or laws of any State notwithstanding'; but the American Constitution associates one House of the legislature, the Senate, with the executive, the President, in the making of treaties. *Walker* v. *Baird*[1] illustrates the British rule. The commander of a naval vessel, acting under orders to enforce a convention with France for regulating the lobster fisheries off Newfoundland, had seized certain lobster factories of the plaintiff, but it was held that this did not excuse the invasion of private rights. There are possibly some exceptional cases in which the Crown, without legislative confirmation, can make treaties which will bind individuals and affect their rights, but the general rule is clear. In practice the Cabinet system, by ensuring that executive and legislature will work together, normally prevents any conflict between British treaty obligations and the law of the land from arising.

A third qualification arises from the practice of British courts in accepting information from the executive, instead of taking evidence in the ordinary way, on matters which they regard as falling within the executive sphere. In such cases the responsibility for ensuring that the Court's decision conforms to international law rests with the executive and not with the court. For example, if the executive informs the court that Britain has recognized Barataria as an independent state, or that such and such persons

[1] [1892] A.C. 491.

constitute its government, the court will not inquire whether Barataria does or does not satisfy the inter-national requirements of a state, or whether the persons designated are really acting as a government. The doctrine of 'act of state' also may have the effect of precluding the courts from judging in accordance with what they believe to be the rules of international law, for by that doctrine an alien, resident abroad, who has been injured by some act authorized or adopted by the Crown, has no remedy in British courts; his remedy, if any, is by diplomatic action taken by his own government.[1]

A fourth qualification of the doctrine of incorpora-tion is one that no national court can avoid. It is that a national court can only apply its own version of what the rule of international law is, and that how-ever objectively it may try to approach a question which raises an issue of international law, its views will inevitably be influenced by national factors. The Scottish Court case put this very frankly in the pas-sage from *Mortensen* v. *Peters* which has been quoted above, and it is interesting to contrast that passage with one from the judgment of Lord Stowell in the case of *The Maria*.[2]

'The seat of judicial authority,' [he said] 'is indeed locally here . . . but the law itself has no locality. . . . It is the duty of the person who sits here to determine this question exactly as he would determine the same question

[1] The doctrine of 'act of state', however, does not apply in the case of an alien on British territory; *Johnstone* v. *Pedlar*, [1921] 2 A.C. 262.
[2] 1 C. Rob. 340.

if sitting in Stockholm. . . . If I mistake the law in this matter, I mistake that which I consider, and which I mean should be considered, as the universal law upon the question.'

But when we remember that the question upon which Lord Stowell was deciding concerned the resistance to visit and search by a British warship on the part of a Swedish ship sailing under convoy, and that the right of convoy was one on which the British and Swedish views were at that time diametrically opposed, it is hard to believe that Lord Stowell really thought that a Swedish judge, sitting in Stockholm, would have been likely to decide the case in the way in which he proposed to decide it himself. The English doctrine of precedents also has to some extent the effect of obscuring for an English court the fact that international law, being a customary law, is developed by agencies which include, but are not limited to, the English courts. For English courts hold themselves bound to apply English rules about the force of precedents to questions of international law in exactly the same way as they apply them to questions of domestic law, and if there is an English precedent available, no amount of foreign authority will displace it. English courts sometimes seem to the lawyers of other countries to be applying purely English law when they themselves profess to be applying international law.[1]

Professor Dickinson has summed up the doctrine of incorporation in its modern form in these words:

[1] Cf. Lord Stowell in *The Recovery*, 6 C. Rob. 341.

'It is the modern Anglo-American doctrine that the national rule on a question of international concern shall be derived, in the absence of a controlling statute, executive decision, or judicial precedent, from relevant principles of international law to which the nation has given its implied or express consent. The rule thus derived is none the less a rule of national law because it is derived from an international source. Nor does the reference to the nation's implied or express consent state one of the doctrine's essential elements. It merely acknowledges the prevailing positivist theory which founds international law upon consent. When the positivist theory has been supplanted by another theory, the reference to consent may disappear. As it is actually applied therefore the Anglo-American doctrine of incorporation is fundamentally sound.'

The doctrine is a beneficial one, since under it municipal courts both treat international law as authoritative in its own right and deny that it has any specific quality distinguishing it from the law which they apply. Furthermore, it is a doctrine which has appealed to lawyers in other countries and has been adopted, with some variations, in the constitutions of a large number of other states.

III

THE LEGAL ORGANIZATION
OF INTERNATIONAL
SOCIETY

§ 1. *The Beginnings of International Constitutional Law*

UNTIL very modern times government has been regarded as a purely national function, and intercourse between states has taken place through national officials. This is still the general rule. Every state, for example, has a department of the national government corresponding to the Foreign Office; and the foreign offices of the world are linked together by the practice of 'legation', or sending of representatives to other states. Since the sixteenth century the practice of maintaining standing legations in other countries has been general, but envoys are still sometimes sent for special purposes as well. A diplomatic agent abroad is appointed by 'letters of credence' from his own government, and these he presents to the head of the government to which he is 'accredited'. A state may decline to receive any particular representative, may ask for his recall, or even dismiss him; but any of these is a serious step which should not be taken except for good reason. This, however, and most of the other matters relating to diplomacy, with the exception of the immunities[1] to which diplomatic persons are

[1] *Infra*, p. 255.

entitled by international law, belong to the sphere of international comity rather than to law.

But diplomacy of this kind is only an instrument for conducting the business of one state with another, and not for conducting *general* international business in which a number of states have an interest. This latter kind of business has vastly increased in extent and importance in modern times, and states have had to recognize that in many departments of government none of them can serve the interests of its own people in the best way unless it arranges to co-ordinate its action with that of other states. This development began about the middle of the nineteenth century, and led to the creation of institutions which, while they cannot yet be regarded as giving a 'constitution' to the international society, may not unfairly be described as a beginning of its constitutional law.

These institutions operate by organizing co-operation between the national governments and not by superseding or dictating to them, and they are, therefore, probably not so much the beginnings of an international 'government', though the term is often convenient, as a substitute for one. Their consideration, however, invites the same questions as those which arise in the study of any other legal system, and it is proper to ask how far and in what manner they perform for international law the functions which governmental institutions perform for the law of a state, that is to say, the functions of legislation, of execution and administration, and of judicature.

§ 2. *International Legislation*

An international legislature, in the sense of a body having power to enact new international law binding on the states of the world or on their peoples, does not exist. The very notion that international law requires any deliberate amendment is, indeed, quite a modern one. The international community has been content to rely for the development of its law on the slow growth of custom, and perhaps the first recognition of the need of any consciously constructive process in building up the law was the declaration by the Congress of Paris in 1814 in favour of freedom of navigation on international rivers. This declaration was not very effective, but it was important as showing that in the conference the international community had obtained a sort of rudimentary legislative organ. Little use was made of conferences for this purpose until the latter half of the nineteenth century, but after the Conference of Paris in 1856, at which a famous Declaration dealing with the laws of maritime warfare was agreed to, quasi-legislation by conference became fairly frequent.

The movement took different forms. In part it was inspired by the humane desire to mitigate the horrors of war; examples of this are the Geneva Conventions for ameliorating the condition of the sick and wounded, the first in 1864, and most of the Hague Conventions of 1899 and 1907. It took another form in the foundation of the international administrative system which is referred to in the next section. Lastly,

conferences have often been used for the settlement
of *special* political questions by action which is really
legislative in character, although it generally preserves
the forms of mere mediation between supposedly
sovereign states. Instances are, the Conference of
London which established the independence of Belgium in 1831; the Conference of London which
established that of Luxembourg in 1867; the Congress
of Berlin, 1878, which dealt with the affairs of Turkey
and the Balkan States; the Conference of Algeciras
which dealt with Morocco in 1906. On these and
other occasions states, or more often the Great Powers,
have asserted a right to decide, by their collective
action, questions in which they all felt themselves to be
interested, without much regard to the alleged rules
of international law concerning intervention, which
are based upon a theory of the independence of every
sovereign state which is liable to be disregarded in an
international crisis. There is no doubt that the conference used in this way has frequently been the means
of preventing wars.

The process of changing the law by means of conventions reached at international conferences has obvious disadvantages if we compare it with the work
of an ordinary legislative body. The conference is not
a continuous body; it meets for some special purpose
and then dissolves. The conventions at which it
arrives have no binding force over states which do
not accept them, and unfortunately states, through
apathy, through the pressure of some domestic
interest, or for some other reason, often fail to ratify

even those conventions which their representatives have signed. But more serious than the difficulties which arise from the defective nature of international legislative machinery is the psychological difficulty of mobilizing public opinion behind proposals for international legislation. Only a small minority of the people of any country are continuously interested in international affairs, and the domestic claims upon the time and energies of statesmen are so numerous that they are not easily induced to take up proposals of reform for which there is no very insistent demand. Almost any proposal for international change by agreement involves some sacrifice or apparent sacrifice of particular interests, and in the general ignorance of the issues at stake the sacrifice is easily made to appear greater than the compensating advantage. But despite all these difficulties the volume of international legislation is already considerable. Judge Hudson[1] has estimated that during the half-century 1864–1914, 257 international conventions of a legislative kind were entered into, and that during the years 1919–29, that is to say, in the first eleven years after the foundation of the League of Nations, there were no less than 229. These figures naturally include, as does the statute book of any legislature, many instruments not in themselves very important, but they are significant of a promising change in the management of international affairs.

The formation of the League of Nations greatly stimulated the practice of international legislation.

[1] *International Legislation*, vol. i, p. xxxvi.

In pre-League days, when a matter was thought to call for international regulation, it had to be taken up as a piece of business unrelated to other matters of a similar kind; a special conference would be summoned through the slow-moving channels of diplomacy, a secretariat improvised, and perhaps a special organ created to give effect to the decisions of the conference after it had broken up. The League provided a permanent organization which could be used for taking up any matter that states had decided to regulate internationally, which could collect the relevant information on which to base an agreement, and could supervise the working of an agreement if one should be concluded. In this aspect of its work the League was simply a standing conference system, and for no idealistic reasons but merely as a matter of practical convenience the modern world can hardly conduct its international relations without such a system. Not only are there many functions which states cannot perform efficiently unless they act together—one of the most obvious is the control of disease, of which the germs recognize no frontiers—but even their more intimately domestic policies, especially in economic matters, have become more and more dependent for their success on some assurance that other nations will not adopt policies which will defeat their objects. In short, the field of action within which any one state can work out its socially desirable purposes without taking account of what other states are doing, or are likely to do, is for various reasons contracting. New technological developments in industry and transport are making the economy of every country, even of the greatest and most nearly self-sufficing, ever more sensitive to what happens in other countries. A change, too, in our ideas of the proper functions of government has greatly increased the sphere of state activity at the expense of that of private individuals, and this has converted into international business between governments much that was formerly only the concern of private individuals.

This growing modern interdependence of states makes the problem of developing international law more urgent, but unfortunately it does not necessarily make it easier. When the ideological differences between states are as deep as they are today, the frequent and public contacts between states which follow from the provision of institutions for encouraging their collaboration may have exactly the opposite effect. Such institutions, as Soviet Russia has made only too clear, offer a convenient sounding-board for virulent and continuous invective, and may therefore only serve to aggravate an already dangerous situation. When states do not even share in a common desire to work together, it might be better that for the time being they should cease to go through the motions of co-operation.

§ 3. The Executive and Administrative Functions

The international system has no central organ for the enforcement of international legal rights as such, and the creation of any such general scheme of sanctions is for the present a very distant prospect.

But the most urgent part of the problem of enforcement is the subjection to law of the use of force by states, and in modern times two notable experiments, in the Covenant of the League of Nations and the Charter of the United Nations, have been made with this end in view. These two experiments have followed different lines. The system of the Covenant relied on the fulfilment by the members of undertakings which they had severally given to take certain prescribed measures against an aggressor, but it did not set up a supra-national authority; the organs of the League could be used for co-ordinating the actions of the individual members, but they could not issue directions as to the action these members were to take. On the other hand, the Charter has created for the first time an authority which, at least according to the letter of its constitution, is to exercise a power of this supra-national kind, though how far the Charter has made that power effective is a question which it will be necessary to examine later.[1]

This absence of an executive power means that each state remains free, subject to the limitations on the use of force to be discussed later,[2] to take such action as it thinks fit to enforce its own rights. This does not mean that international law has no sanctions, if that word is used in its proper sense of means for securing the observance of the law; but it is true that the sanctions which it possesses are not systematic or centrally directed, and that accordingly they are precarious in their operation. This lack of system is

[1] *Infra*, Ch. VIII, § 6.   [2] *Infra*, Ch. IX.

obviously unsatisfactory, particularly to those states which are less able than others to assert their own rights effectively.

But the difficulties of introducing any radical change into the present means of enforcing international law are extremely formidable. The problem has little analogy with that of the enforcement of law within the state, and the popular use of such phrases as an 'international police force' tends to make it appear much simpler than it really is. Police action suggests the bringing to bear of the overwhelming force of the community against a comparatively feeble individual law-breaker, but no action of that sort is possible in the international sphere, where the potential law-breakers are states, and the preponderance of force may even be on the law-breaking side. Even in a federation, as the experience of the United States has shown, the problem of enforcing the law against a member state has not been easy to solve.

The administrative function, like the executive, is not provided in the international system with any centralized organ, but in the latter half of the nine-teenth century a number of separate institutions with specialized administrative functions were created. They arose not from any idealistic theory of inter-national relations, but from the compelling force of circumstances; in one department of administration after another experience showed that government could not be even reasonably efficient if it continued to be organized on a purely national basis. The first such institutions were the International Telegraphic

Union formed in 1865 and the Universal Postal Union formed in 1874, and there are now many others. These bodies differ in their constitution, but the Postal Union is the most successful example of the type. This was not achieved until efforts to carry on foreign postal services by a number of separate treaties between pairs of states had revealed the hopeless inefficiency, from a business point of view, of adhering to theories of independence in such a matter as postage, and it was resisted in almost every country, both as an infringement of sovereignty and as involving an abandonment of the principle by which every state, as far as it can, tries to 'make the foreigner pay' the expenses of its government. It consists of a Congress which meets at intervals, in which each state, including some colonies of the larger states, has one vote. The Congress has power to alter the rules of the Union by a majority vote, and although alterations have to be ratified by the governments, ratification has become a formality, since a refusal to ratify would involve leaving the Union, and no state can afford to do that. Besides the Congress, the Union has a permanent Bureau at Bern, which, amongst other functions, collects and distributes information, and acts as a clearing-house for settling accounts. In the intervals between Congresses, the Bureau may receive proposals for altering the rules of the Union; it then proceeds to collect the votes of the states upon them, and the alteration may take effect without any meeting.

A less advanced type of the public international union is seen in the Copyright Union, formed in 1886, under which the rights of authors, composers, and others in their works are protected in foreign countries. This has a permanent Bureau at Bern, but no governing Congress; it operates under conventions which are revised from time to time by specially summoned conferences of states. There are also many instances in which the modern movement towards international co-operation in the field of administration has taken the form not of creating an international organ, but of an agreement to co-ordinate national laws or to introduce uniform methods into the national administration, for example, a Convention for the protection of submarine cables of 1884, the Automobile Convention of 1904, and a Convention of 1910 for the suppression of the White Slave Traffic.

These are a few out of the many experiments in international administrative co-operation which have been made in the last two generations under the impulse of difficulties which were incapable of being solved by methods of government organized on the traditional theory that each state is a sovereign and separate unit. States are no longer separate units in such matters as commerce, labour, art, morals, inventions, health; and slowly and as yet very imperfectly they are being compelled to recognize that they cannot be altogether separate units in the political or economic fields. The creation of the League of Nations in 1919 was therefore not the introduction of a wholly new principle into international life, but the logical outcome of a movement which had been gathering force for many years.

§ 4. *The League and the United Nations*

The Covenant defined the objects of the League as being 'to promote international co-operation and to achieve international peace and security'. The Charter contains a statement of 'Purposes and Principles' which goes into greater detail than the Covenant, but these are also in substance the objects of the United Nations. In fact in this matter the architects of any international organization which is to be general in its scope have no real choice; peace, and co-operation between nations for the promotion of peace and for other purposes are the two great objectives at which they are bound to aim. Inevitably, therefore, the similarities between the League and the United Nations are many and fundamental. But there are important differences too, for the Charter was intended to correct certain defects, or what were believed to be defects, in the Covenant, and it is easier to assess the value of the Charter if it is examined against the background of the Covenant. The League has ceased to exist, but it has left a legacy of experience which the student of international relations cannot afford to neglect.

The principle on which the League was founded was simple and consistent. It was an association of independent but co-operating states, and its institutions were intended as means for making it as easy as possible for these states to work together. The members retained their sovereignty, but they had all agreed to do and not to do certain things in the exercise of their sovereign rights. Thus the Covenant did not contain even the beginnings of a system of international government in the strict sense of that word. 'The League' was hardly more than a name for describing the members collectively; it was not an organic union, and there was hardly anything that it could do in a corporate capacity. Throughout the Covenant it was not 'the League', but the 'members of the League', that were to act in certain ways, and everything depended upon their being ready and able to fulfil the obligations which they had undertaken. An institution constituted on these lines was bound to be, as a body, weak, and though there were political motives which made the substitution of the United Nations for the League inevitable, it was also hoped that by shaping the United Nations on different lines this weakness might be corrected.

A necessary corollary of the co-operative principle on which the League was founded was the so-called 'rule of unanimity'; in general, decisions of the Assembly or the Council of the League required the agreement of all the members represented at a meeting. There were certain exceptions to this rule, especially one providing that when the Council was reporting on a dispute and making recommendations for its settlement the votes of parties to the dispute were not to be counted. But, apart from the exceptions, it is a mistake to suppose that the rule of unanimity was bound to paralyse, or that in fact it did paralyse, the working of the League; it did not have that effect because successful working did not depend on the ability of the organs of the League to reach decisions, but, as has just been mentioned, almost entirely on the willingness of the members severally to fulfil the obligations which they had undertaken in the Covenant. The real effect of the rule was to make it impossible for a majority of other states to increase or vary a state's obligations without its own consent, in short, to safeguard the co-operative basis of their association; it did not confer on a dissenting state a right to veto the action of the others.

The principal organs of the League were the Assembly, consisting of representatives of all the members, the Council, with the Great Powers as permanent members and others, eleven in number in the last days of the League, elected by the Assembly, and the Secretariat. The Covenant allotted a few functions to the Assembly and a few others to the Council, but generally it did not differentiate between the functions of these two bodies; either of them could deal with any 'matter within the sphere of action of the League or affecting the peace of the world'. It thus left them free to adjust their relations in the light of experience, and that is what they did. The Council, being a smaller body and meeting more frequently, was better able to act in an emergency; it came to be regarded as a sort of executive committee of the Assembly, working out the details and supervising the administration of policies which the latter had adopted in general terms. The arrangement illustrates a quality which characterized the whole Covenant. Its authors realized that they were

launching an untried experiment, and they refrained
from cramping its future development by too precise
and detailed prescriptions of the powers and duties
of the League; they were content to give it the bare
outlines of the constitution which it needed for a start
on its career. In this respect the Charter, which has
111 articles against the 26 of the Covenant, provides
a striking contrast, and its attempt to provide for all
contingencies has already led to frequent legalistic
debates such as rarely arose under the Covenant.

The United Nations has six principal organs, the
General Assembly, the Security Council, the Economic and Social Council, the Trusteeship Council,[1]
the International Court of Justice,[2] and the Secretariat. The Charter distinguishes between the functions of the General Assembly and the Security
Council by placing on the latter the 'primary responsibility' for the maintenance of peace, and precluding the former, whose functions in other respects
are very wide and general, from dealing with that
subject in a way that might embarrass the Security
Council. But the effect of this differentiation is in
some respects unfortunate; it separates matters which
are not intrinsically separable, for those that are
given to the General Assembly, social and economic
matters, for example, are often the underlying causes
of the frictions which endanger international peace;
and by limiting the Security Council to questions of
security it leaves that body with little work of a constructive character, and so makes more difficult the

[1] *Infra*, p. 185.   [2] *Infra*, p. 351.

growth of a feeling of corporate responsibility among the members like that which developed and proved of great value in the Council of the League.

The specific functions of the General Assembly, which consists of all the members of the Organization, are to discuss any matter within the scope of the Charter and to make recommendations thereon either to the members of the United Nations or to the Security Council or to both, but this is subject to the proviso that it must refer to the Security Council any question relating to international peace on which action is necessary, and that it may not make any recommendation on a dispute or situation which is being dealt with by the Security Council. The General Assembly also approves the budget of the Organization and apportions the expenses among the members. It takes its ordinary decisions by a majority vote, but if a question is 'important' a two-thirds majority of the members present and voting is required, and these 'important' questions include recommendations with respect to the maintenance of peace, the election of all non-permanent members of the three Councils, the admission, suspension, and expulsion of members, the budget, and any other question which by a bare majority the General Assembly decides ought to be considered as 'important'. The introduction of majority voting is a departure from the usual practice of international bodies, including that of the League, but here the innovation has not the vital importance that we shall see it has in the constitution of the Security Council.

That is because, apart from its control over the budget, all that the General Assembly can do is to discuss and recommend and initiate studies and consider reports from other bodies. It cannot *act* on behalf of all the members, as the Security Council does, and its decisions are not directions telling the member states what they are or are not to do. In principle its functions are similar to those of the Assembly of the League, and like that body it must rely on co-operation among the members and not on power, for it has no powers.

The Security Council consists of five permanent members--China, France, the U.S.S.R., the United Kingdom, and the United States, and six other members elected by the General Assembly for a term of two years. Its functions are laid down in Article 24 of the Charter in these terms:

'In order to ensure prompt and effective action by the United Nations, its members confer on the Security Council primary responsibility for the maintenance of international peace and security, and agree that in carrying out its duties under this responsibility the Security Council acts on their behalf. In discharging these duties the Security Council shall act in accordance with the purposes and Principles of the United Nations.'

The Charter then refers to certain 'specific powers' granted to the Security Council to enable it to discharge its duties; most of these relate to its action in the pacific settlement of disputes and with respect to threats to the peace, and it will be necessary to return to these later.[1] Article 25 then provides that

[1] *Infra*, p. 381.

'The members of the United Nations agree to accept and carry out the decisions of the Security Council in accordance with the present Charter.'

It is clear that these provisions confer on the Security Council powers which far exceed those possessed by any of the organs of the League, or by any of the other organs of the United Nations. They are powers greater than have ever before been exercised by any international body, and they constitute the most far-reaching of the innovations which the Charter has introduced into international organization.

It was impossible, however, to give this binding effect to the Security Council's decisions without making the method by which its decisions were to be reached a matter of crucial importance, and it soon appeared that the Great Powers or at least some of them would not consent to be bound by decisions which were arrived at without their concurrence. They refused to accept a system of voting under which they might be outvoted, and in the system which was eventually accepted and embodied in the Charter they insisted on a privileged position. Decisions of the Security Council require the affirmative votes of seven members, but these seven votes must include the concurring votes of all the five permanent members. Consequently each of the five Great Powers has a veto on decisions, and despite the apparently vast extent of the powers of the Security Council, this veto has always to be borne in mind in estimating their real significance.

There are two exceptions to this rule of voting;

they are that decisions on matters of procedure may be made by the votes of *any* seven members, and that when a member is a party to a dispute which the Security Council is investigating that member must abstain from voting. But procedural matters are naturally the less important matters, and moreover the question whether a particular matter is or is not procedural is not itself a question of procedure, and a permanent member can use its veto on that preliminary question.[1] Then again there can naturally only be a 'party to a dispute' if a 'dispute' exists, and the question whether there is or is not a dispute is one on which the veto can be used. There is also a distinction in the Charter between a 'dispute' and 'a situation which might lead to international friction and give rise to a dispute', and when the Security Council is investigating a 'situation', there is nothing to prevent a permanent member, however deeply it may be involved, from using the veto.

The veto is the price that the United Nations has paid in obtaining an organ invested with power to decide and act in a corporate capacity, and it is already clear that the price has been a high one. So long as we are considering political organization in the abstract, a body that has power to act on behalf of all the members of an organization is more likely, other things being equal, to ensure, as the Charter says, 'prompt and effective action' than one which can only *recommend* the members to act in a certain

[1] This is the so-called double veto; see Leo Gross, *Harvard Law Review*, 1953, p. 251.

way. But abstract principles in politics are dangerous guides. No political institution can work unless it is adapted to the special conditions of its society, and it is no more possible to conjure away the weaknesses of the present loose society of independent states by endowing it with institutions appropriate to a society of a more advanced type than it is to turn a nation into a democracy by giving it a democratic constitution. The founders of the United Nations seem to have assumed that the reason why the League had not been strong enough for its task was that the Covenant had based it on a wrong principle; it was essential, they thought, to have an organization which could act as a corporate body. If so, this was to misunderstand the cause of the League's weakness; it was not the Covenant that made it weak, but the frailty of the bonds that hold the society of states together, and the Covenant merely reflected this unfortunate fact.

International institutions cannot be raised from the co-operative to the organic level until we have a society of states which is far more closely bound together than are the states of today, until, in short, nations have the same sort of confidence in one another's intentions and policies and the same absence of fundamental diversity of interests that the states of a federation must have if their union is to endure. In the world as it is today the insistence of the Great Powers on their veto cannot be considered altogether unreasonable. As the British official commentary on the Charter says,[1] 'power should be com-

[1] Cmd. 6666, p. 16.

mensurate with responsibility, and it is on the Great Powers that the Charter places the main responsibility'. It is not unreasonable, therefore, that when a decision of the Security Council may have major political consequences, especially when it may lead to enforcement measures to give it effect—and it was probably assumed that only in such cases would the veto actually be used—the Great Powers should refuse to allow this burden to be thrust upon them by some majority of less interested smaller powers. The fault lies not in the veto, but in the effect that the Charter has given to the decisions of the Security Council; if its decisions were to have the effect that the Charter gives them, the veto was inevitable and reasonable. But the result of insisting that only a body that had power to make binding decisions could act effectively has been to give us a Council that can seldom decide or act.

The Security Council might still have been a reasonably effective body in cases not directly involving the Great Powers, if the veto had not been used so frequently by the Soviet Union for purely political motives to stifle investigation by the Council or to make its own point of view prevail. As it was, the Council proved in the majority of cases quite unable, owing to the veto, to discharge its responsibility under the Charter for keeping the peace. Then came the Korean war and underlined at once the gravity of the dangers resulting from the frustration of the Council by the veto and the potentialities of collective action by members under the aegis of the United

INTERNATIONAL ORGANIZATION 115

Nations for repelling aggression. On the outbreak of
hostilities in 1950, owing to the deliberate absence of
the Soviet delegate from the Council, it was able to
pass three important resolutions which, *inter alia*,
'determined' the existence of an armed attack by
North upon South Korea, called for the withdrawal
of North Korean forces, and recommended member
states to assist South Korea in repelling the attack
and to put their forces under a single command flying
the flag of the United Nations. Soon afterwards,
realizing its mistake, the Soviet Union returned to
the Council and, although unable by means of the
veto to stop the action already begun under the three
resolutions, blocked the taking of any further Council
decisions in regard to Korea; and the situation was
only remedied later by removing the question of
Korea from the agenda of the Security Council to that
of the General Assembly. Meanwhile, with the lesson
of Korea before it, the Assembly had adopted three
resolutions, known as the Uniting For Peace Resolutions, the principal of which established new procedures to enable the Assembly itself to fill the gap in
the Charter system of collective security left by the
impotence of the Council. Under this Resolution, if
the Council, because of a veto by a permanent member, fails to exercise its primary responsibility for
maintaining peace, in any case where there appears
to be a threat to the peace, breach of the peace, or act
of aggression, the Assembly is immediately to consider the matter with a view to making appropriate
recommendations to members for collective measures,

including armed force, to maintain or restore peace;
if the Assembly is not in session at the time it may
be summoned to an emergency special session at
the request either of *any seven members* of the Council
or of a majority of the members of the United
Nations.[1] Under its normal voting rules laid down in
the Charter, decisions of the Assembly concerning
recommendations with respect to the maintenance of
peace, as previously noted,[2] are taken by a two-thirds
majority, so that, if there is a large measure of agreement amongst members in regard to the rights and
wrongs of a case, the Assembly cannot be prevented
from expressing its opinion and registering decisions.
These decisions have the force only of 'recommendations' and do not bind members to undertake the
measures recommended, however strong is the moral
effect of a decision by so large a majority of the whole
body of the United Nations. The Uniting For Peace
Resolution is, therefore, a return to the co-operative
system of the Covenant which has been forced upon
the United Nations by the impotence of the Council.

The validity of the Uniting for Peace Resolutions
was challenged by the Communist states on the
grounds that under the Charter: (*a*) the General
Assembly may not make any recommendation on a
dispute or situation which is being dealt with by the
Security Council, unless the latter so requests; (*b*) any

[1] The Resolution contains further provisions concerning the
establishment of a peace observation commission and a collective
measures committee and earmarking of armed forces by members
which are referred to in Ch. VIII below.

[2] *Supra*, p. 109.

question relating to the maintenance of peace on which *action* is necessary must be referred by the Assembly to the Council; and (c) the power to make a determination as to the existence of any threat to the peace, breach of the peace or act of aggression is specifically conferred upon the Council. The answer given was that the Charter, by conferring upon the Council primary responsibility for the maintenance of peace, does not relieve either individual members or the United Nations as a whole of their obligations and responsibilities under the Charter to maintain peace; accordingly, if the Council does not exercise its primary responsibility, the Assembly may take up the matter; Article 51 specifically reserves to all members their 'inherent right of individual or collective self-defence' and there is nothing in the Charter to preclude members from organizing the exercise of their rights under this Article within the framework of the Organization; nor, in the absence of any determination by the Council, is there anything in the Charter to take away the right of individual member states to make their own appreciations of a threat to the peace, breach of the peace or act of aggression. Whatever may be the relative merits of these arguments, the Uniting for Peace Resolution has already been acted on several times by the General Assembly and has become, without doubt, an integral part of the constitution of the United Nations. Special Emergency Sessions of the Assembly were convened under the Resolution to deal with the Suez and Hungarian incidents in 1956, the Lebanon and Jordan crises in 1958, and the Congo crisis in 1960; and it was in conformity with its new conception of its responsibilities under the Resolution that the Assembly pronounced Communist China to be an aggressor with respect to Korea in 1951. The Council retains its legally established primacy in the maintenance of peace and the earlier stages of the Lebanon, Jordan, and Congo crises were in fact handled by the Council; but so long as the cold war remains intense, it is likely to be the Assembly which plays the chief role.

The Economic and Social Council consists of eighteen members elected by the General Assembly, and it is virtually a committee of that body. Its primary function is the promotion of economic and social progress, of international cultural and educational co-operation, and of respect for human rights and fundamental freedoms. It initiates studies in these fields, and makes recommendations on them to the General Assembly, to the members of the United Nations, or any of the international organizations, like the Food and Agriculture Organization (F.A.O.) and the World Health Organization (W.H.O.), known as 'Specialized Agencies'. It may also itself prepare draft conventions and call international conferences on matters within its competence. Not the least important of its functions is that of co-ordinating the activities of the Specialized Agencies through which international co-operation in so many vital fields is now achieved. This function is expressly given to the Economic and Social Council by the Charter, which also empowers it to enter into agreements with any of the Agencies in order to bring the agency into relationship with the United Nations. It may arrange for representatives of the Agencies to participate in its deliberations and *vice versa*, and for reports to be made to it by the Agencies. This does not mean that the Council directs or controls the work of the Specialized Agencies, which retain their autonomy. But it does co-ordinate and guide the activities of a large number of important international administrative bodies.

The Secretariat is practically an international civil service, and it is as necessary to effective international co-operation as a national civil service is to a national government. Its head is the Secretary-General, appointed by the General Assembly on the recommendation of the Security Council. He may bring before the Security Council any matter which he thinks may threaten the maintenance of peace, and in recent years the Council and Assembly have given him important executive roles to play, e.g. in connexion with the truce in Palestine, the United Nations Emergency Force in Egypt, the clearance of the Suez Canal and the Congo.[1] Neither he nor any member of his staff may seek or receive instructions from any government or from any authority outside the United Nations. The members, too, for their part, have undertaken to respect the international character of the Secretariat and not to influence its members in the discharge of their functions.

[1] See pp. 388–93 below.

New members are admitted to the United Nations by the General Assembly upon the recommendation of the Security Council. A member against which preventive or enforcement action has been taken by the Security Council may be suspended, and a member which has persistently violated the principles of the Charter may be expelled, by the same process. The Charter can be amended by a two-thirds vote in the General Assembly, but this majority must include all the permanent members of the Security Council. It follows that a decision on any of these questions can be prevented by the veto of any one permanent member of the Security Council.

The International Court of Justice has considered the juridical nature of the United Nations in an Advisory Opinion on *Reparation for Injuries Suffered in the Service of the United Nations*.[1] After the murder of Count Bernadotte while serving on a United Nations commission in Israel the General Assembly asked the Court to advise whether in the event of an agent of the United Nations suffering injury in circumstances involving the responsibility of a state the United Nations as an organization has the capacity to bring an international claim against the state responsible with a view to obtaining reparation. The Court was of opinion that the states which set it up, representing as they did the vast majority of the members of the international community, had the power, in conformity with international law, to bring into being an entity possessing objective international personality

[1] *I.C.J. Reports*, 1949, p. 174.

and not merely personality recognized by themselves alone. That does not mean that the United Nations is a state and still less that it is a super-state, or that its rights and duties are the same as those of a state. It means that it is a subject of international law and capable of possessing international rights and duties and of maintaining its rights by bringing international claims. What its rights and duties are depends upon its purposes and functions as specified or implied in its constituent documents and developed in practice, and it is clear that these could not be effectively discharged if they involved the concurrent action on the international plane of the foreign offices of the members.

§ 5. *The Specialized Agencies*

The Charter, while it invests the United Nations with the general task of promoting progress and international co-operation in economic, social, health, cultural, educational, and related matters, contemplates that these tasks will be mainly fulfilled not by organs of the United Nations itself but by autonomous international organizations established by inter-governmental agreements outside the United Nations. There are now many such international agencies having functions in many different fields, e.g. in posts, telecommunications, railways, canals, rivers, sea transport, civil aviation, meteorology, atomic energy, finance, trade, education and culture, health and refugees. Some are virtually world-wide in their membership, some are regional or otherwise limited in their membership. The Charter provides that those agencies which have 'wide international responsibilities' are to be brought into relationship with the United Nations by agreements entered into between them and the Economic and Social Council,[1] and are then to be known as 'specialized agencies'. Apart from F.A.O. and W.H.O., already mentioned, they include the Universal Postal Union (U.P.U.), International Telecommunications Union (I.T.U.), World Meteorological Organization (W.M.O.), International Civil Aviation Organization (I.C.A.O.), International Maritime Consultative Organization (I.M.C.O.), International Bank for Reconstruction and Development (The Bank), International Monetary Fund (The Fund), The International Atomic Energy Authority (I.A.E.A.), International Labour Organization (I.L.O.), United Nations Educational, Scientific and Cultural Organization (U.N.E.S.C.O.), and the International Refugee Organization. The Specialized Agencies being autonomous bodies outside the United Nations, their membership is not confined to members of the United Nations.

The International Labour Organization.

The I.L.O. is an agency with a peculiar structure which gives it a particular interest. It was founded as an independent body by the peace treaties of 1919, but was linked to the League to some extent; although non-members of the League might also be-

[1] These agreements require the approval of the General Assembly.

long, all members of the League were automatically members of the I.L.O. Now, a member of the United Nations is not automatically a member of the I.L.O., but is entitled to become one by accepting unconditionally the provisions of its constitution. Other states have to gain admission by a two-thirds vote. The I.L.O. consists of (1) a General Conference of representatives, meeting at least once a year; and (2) a permanent Labour Office.

The Conference is composed of four members from each state, two being government delegates, and two non-government delegates representing employers and workpeople respectively. The latter are nominated by their governments, but they must be chosen in agreement with the industrial organizations which are most representative of employers and workpeople in the respective countries; and the Conference may refuse to admit a delegate whom it deems not to have been nominated in accordance with this provision. The delegates vote individually, the non-government having equal rights with the government delegates. This is a point of great interest to the theory of international relations; for the General Conference is a tentative recognition of the fact, which has long been apparent in every international sphere except the political, that interests of international concern do not necessarily follow, but often cross, the boundary lines of territorial states. Obviously, however, its constitution was framed on the assumption that the industrial organizations represented would be independent of their own governments, and objection has been taken to recognizing the credentials of the employers' and workpeople's representatives of totalitarian states for which the tripartite classification of the members has obviously no meaning. At present, however, they are being accepted.

Decisions of the Conference are either draft Conventions, or Recommendations for national legislation. Either of these requires a two-thirds majority for adoption, and although states are not bound to ratify a convention or to accept a recommendation, they must bring them before whatever authority in their respective countries is competent to deal with them by ratification or legislation or otherwise. It should be noted that this so-called 'ratification' differs from the ordinary ratification of a treaty which has been negotiated and signed by plenipotentiaries.[1] The draftsmen of a Labour convention are not representatives of states, but the members of the General Conference; there is no stage of signature as in ordinary treaties, and the choice before the states is between acceptance or rejection of the draft as the Conference frames it. Reservations would violate the rights of the non-governmental members of the Conference and are therefore inadmissible. States must make an annual report on the measures which they take to give effect to conventions which they have ratified, and associations of employers or workers may make representations to the Labour Office of the failure of a state to observe a convention, and the Governing Body of the Office may ask the state

[1] *Infra*, p. 319.

to reply to the complaint and may publish the representation and the reply if any. If such a complaint is made by another state, the Governing Body may refer it to a Commission of Inquiry constituted out of a standing panel of employers, workers, and independent persons, which prepares a report and recommendations on the matter; the state affected may appeal against the recommendation to the International Court of Justice, whose decision on the matter is final.

The Labour Office, which is the secretariat of the Organization, is controlled by a Governing Body of forty persons, twenty representing governments, ten elected by the employers' and ten by the workers' delegates to the Conference. Each of the ten countries of 'chief industrial importance' nominates one of the governmental representatives, and the other ten are chosen from other states. Its functions are to collect and distribute information on all subjects relating to the international adjustment of industrial life and labour, to examine subjects which it is proposed to bring before the Conference, and to conduct such special investigations as the Conference may order.

IV

STATES

§ 1. *General Notion of States in International Law*

A STATE is an *institution*, that is to say, it is a system of relations which men establish among themselves as a means of securing certain objects, of which the most fundamental is a system of order within which their activities can be carried on. Modern states are territorial; their governments exercise control over persons and things within their frontiers, and today the whole of the habitable world is divided between about a hundred of these territorial states. A state should not be confused with the whole community of persons living on its territory; it is only one among a multitude of other institutions, such as churches and corporations, which a community establishes for securing different objects, though obviously it is one of tremendous importance; none the less it is not, except in the ideology of totalitarianism, an all-embracing institution, not something from which, or within which, all other institutions and associations have their being; many institutions, e.g. the Roman Catholic Church, and many associations, e.g. federations of employers and of workers, transcend the boundaries of any single state. Nor should a state be confused with a nation, although in modern times many states are organized on a national basis, and although also the terms are sometimes used interchangeably, as in the title 'United Nations', which is actually a league of states, and even in the term 'inter*national* law'; a single state, e.g. the Indian Republic, may include many nations, or a single nation may be dispersed among many states, as the Poles were before 1919. Further, the term 'state' is relative, for there may be states within a state. Whether a smaller entity, having certain institutions of self-government but contained within a larger, should be called a state or not, is generally felt to depend upon the extent of its powers; but there can be no exact rule. A state of the American Union is invariably called a state, whereas an English county is not; a province of Canada, which has powers intermediate between these two, might or might not be so called. It is not, however, with all the institutions which in common parlance are called states that international law is concerned, but only with those whose governmental powers extend to the conduct of their external relations. Whether a state has such powers or not is a question of fact which must be answered by examining its system of government; the terminology which is used in the classification of composite states, or states which are 'composed of' other states, is an unsafe guide, both because different writers use the same terms in different senses, and also because the possible variations of state organization and inter-state relations, ranging as they do from mere alliance for temporary purposes to complete amalgamation or subordination, are so many that a permanently valid classification is impossible. But it is usual today to distinguish a *federal state*, that is to say, a union of states in which the control of the external relations of all the member states has been permanently surrendered to a central government so that the only state which exists for international purposes is the state formed by the union, from a *confederation of states*, in which, though a central government exists and exercises certain powers, it does not control all the external relations of the member states, and therefore for international purposes there exists not one but a number of states. Thus the United States since 1787, the German Republic from 1918 to 1933, and the Swiss Confederation since 1848, each form a single federal state, whereas the United States from 1778 to 1787, and the German Confederation from 1820 to 1866, were confederations of many states. This distinction would be convenient if it were always observed, but unfortunately it is not; for example, the Swiss Republic is always styled a *confederation*. But even so it would be difficult to classify all the states to which the classification is relevant definitely under one or other of the two heads; for example, the German Empire from 1870 to 1918 was in essence a federal state, but in form it retained some traces of a confederation of states, since Bavaria and some of the other member states were separately represented in foreign countries for certain limited and mainly honorary purposes.

§ 2. *Independent*[1] *and Dependent States*

The states with whose relations international law is primarily concerned are those which are 'independent' in their external relations; it is also to some extent concerned with a few states which 'depend' on other states in the conduct of those relations in a greater or less degree. This simple fact that there exist 'dependent' as well as 'independent' states is sufficient to show that independence cannot be a fundamental right of states as such, even if there were no other objections to the doctrine of fundamental rights. The proper usage of the term 'independence' is to denote the status of a state which controls its own external relations without dictation from other states; it contrasts such a status with that of a state which either does not control its own external relations at all, and is therefore of no interest to international law, like the State of New York, or controls them only in part. The exact significance of the term appears most clearly in such a phrase as 'declaration of independence', whereby one state throws off its control by, or its dependence on, another.

Independence is merely a descriptive term; it has no moral content. It may or may not be morally right or socially desirable that an actually independent state should remain independent, or that some community should break away from an existing state

[1] The dissenting opinion of M. Anzilotti in the case of the *Austro-German Customs Union* before the Permanent Court contains a useful discussion of the meaning of 'independence'. (1931 Series A/B, No. 41, pp. 57–58.)

and form an independent state of its own. To insist on a 'right', and particularly on a 'natural right' of independence, suggests that for a state to pass from the condition of independence to that of dependence, as the American states did when they formed the Union, necessarily involves a moral loss, instead of a mere change of legal status to be judged according to the circumstances of the case. Further, it should be noted that 'independence' is a negative term; we cannot legitimately infer from it anything whatsoever about the positive rights to which a state may be entitled. In particular, we have no right to argue as though an independent state had a right to determine its own conduct without any restraint at all; 'independence' does not mean freedom from law, but merely freedom from control by other states. Unfortunately, such a method of argument is very common; the associations of sovereignty have become attached in the popular mind to the notion of independence, and the word is often used as though it meant freedom from any restraint whatsoever, and appealed to as a justification for arbitrary and illegal conduct. The temptation to mistake catchwords for arguments is strong in all political controversy; it is especially dangerous in the controversies of states.

§ 3. *The Doctrine of the Equality of States*[1]

The doctrine of equality was introduced into the theory of international law by the naturalist writers.

[1] Cf. Dickinson, *Equality of States in International Law*, and Baker in *B.Y.I.L.*, 1923-4.

They argued that as men in the 'state of nature', that is to say, before their entry into the political state, were equal to one another, and as states are still in a 'state of nature', therefore states must be equal to one another. The argument, however, is based on unsound premisses, and in its natural meaning the conclusion is contradicted by obvious facts, for by whatever test states are measured—size, population, wealth, strength, or degree of civilization—they are not equal, but unequal to one another. When, therefore, this doctrine requires us to believe that states are equal in law despite these obvious inequalities in other respects, we are bound to ask what are the practical consequences which are supposed to follow from this legal equality, and when we do that we shall find it difficult to find any consequence which does not equally follow from, and is not better explained by, the fact that states are independent. That at least seems to be true of the list of four consequences which Oppenheim tells us follow from the doctrine of equality of states: they are (a) that when a question arises which has to be settled by consent, every state has a right to a vote and to one vote only; (b) that the vote of the weakest state has as much weight as the vote of the most powerful; (c) that no state can claim jurisdiction over another; and (d) that the courts of one state do not as a rule question the validity of the official acts of another state in so far as those acts purport to take effect within the latter's jurisdiction.[1] These are all true statements of the law,

[1] *International Law*, 8th ed., vol. i, § 115.

but no theory of equality is needed to explain or justify them.

But the doctrine of equality is worse than merely redundant, for it may easily become seriously misleading. If it merely means that the rights of one state, whatever they may be, are as much entitled to be protected by the law as the rights of any other, that is to say, if it merely denies that the weakness of a state is any excuse in law for disregarding its legal rights, then the statement is true, but obvious. But it is not true if it means, as it is easily understood to mean, that all states have equal rights, any more than it is true that all Englishmen have equal rights in English law, though they are all equally entitled to have whatever rights they have upheld by the law. Politically the Great Powers have long exercised a primacy among states, and both in the Covenant and the Charter this has been converted into a legal primacy. Some states again are under protectorates; some formerly had their territorial jurisdiction limited by the system of Capitulations; some have legal obligations towards minorities among their own subjects from which other states are free. If it is said that all states *ought* to have equal rights whether they actually do or not, then the doctrine ceases to be merely innocuous and becomes mischievous. That argument was advanced at the Hague Conference of 1907, when a scheme for setting up an international court of justice was wrecked by the refusal of some of the smaller powers to accept anything less than equal representation for all states on the court. It is desirable that the society of states should become a better organized society than it has been in the past, but it would be obstructive of progress that every state, large or small, should claim an equal voice in every new co-operative enterprise. The cry of 'one state, one vote' in the management of affairs which the society of states decides are of general international concern is a quite spurious application of a nominally democratic principle.[1]

§ 4. *Types of Dependent States*

Primarily, as we have seen, international law deals with the relations of independent states to one another. It is also to some extent concerned with certain other states, which, though partly controlled by another state, still maintain some relations with states other than that which controls them. This relation of dependency is sometimes described as a *protectorate*, sometimes as a *suzerainty*, but it is difficult to give precise juristic signification to either term; the degree of control on one side and of dependency on the other may vary indefinitely, and in any case it must be deduced from the events or treaties which created the relation, and not from the term used to describe it. This was laid down in 1923 by the Permanent Court in the following terms:[2]

'The extent of the powers of a protecting state in the

[1] Thus the system of voting in the General Assembly (*supra*, p. 109) gives a very unfair influence to the smaller powers, especially in budgetary matters.

[2] The case of the *Nationality Decrees in Tunis and Morocco* (1923, Series B. 4, p. 27).

territory of a protected state depends, first, upon the treaties between the protecting state and the protected state establishing the protectorate, and, secondly, upon the conditions under which the protectorate has been recognized by third powers as against whom there is an intention to rely on the provisions of these treaties. In spite of common features possessed by protectorates under international law, they have individual legal charac- teristics resulting from the special conditions under which they were created, and the stage of their development.'

A relation of dependency sometimes exists between two states in fact, but for political reasons is not avowed either as a protectorate or a suzerainty. Thus the United States at one time exercised far-reaching control over some of the nominally independent states of Central America; prior to the adoption of the 'Good Neighbour' policy these countries suffered one or more periods of American military government and a practically complete control of their foreign rela- tions. A similar *de facto* protectorate by Great Britain over Egypt also existed from 1882 until 1914, when a protectorate was openly declared.

The danger of deducing the legal incidents of the relation from the term by which it is described was illustrated in the discussion which preceded the South African War of 1899.[1] The question between Great Britain and the South African Republic, so far as it was a legal one, was whether the latter state had carried out the terms of the Convention of Pretoria, 1881, as modified by the Convention of London,

[1] Cf. Westlake, *Collected Papers*, p. 442.

1884. But the controversy was confused and embittered by arguments attempting to show that Great Britain was entitled to rights of control other than those expressly stipulated for, because the former convention had described the relation then set up as a 'suzerainty'. With this should be contrasted the treatment of the matter in the judgment of Dr. Lushington in the case of *The Ionian Ships* (1855; 2 Spinks, 212). During the Crimean War these ships, the property of Ionian citizens, were brought in for adjudication on a charge of trading with the enemy; but the owners claimed that their country was at peace with Russia, and their trade therefore lawful. The Treaty of Paris, 1815, had declared 'the United States of the Ionian Islands' to be an independent state under the protection of Great Britain, and Dr. Lushington treated the question whether Ionians were British subjects as turning not on any general principle, but on the construction of the relations established by the particular treaty. In the result he held that the Islands were a separate state not automatically involved in the wars of Great Britain; that Great Britain had the right under the Treaty to make war and peace on their behalf, but that on this occasion she had not exercised it; the ships were, therefore, not liable to condemnation.[1]

At the present time there appears to be no instance

[1] Professor H. A. Smith (*Great Britain and the Law of Nations*, vol. i, p. 68) shows that this decision conflicted with the view held in diplomatic and executive quarters, and that there are grave objections to holding that a protected state can be neutral when the protecting power is at war.

of a relation between states which is described as a suzerainty. The term was applied to the relation between Great Britain and the South African Republic, and also to that between Turkey and Bulgaria from 1878 to 1909, but it seems likely to disappear from diplomatic terminology. Instances in which the existence of a protectorate over a state of European civilization is openly avowed are also at present few and unimportant; Andorra is under the joint protectorate of France and Spain, San Marino under that of Italy, and Monaco under that of France. There still exist a few protectorates over states of Oriental civilization, such as that of the United Kingdom over Bahrain, but the growth of national sentiment in all parts of the world makes any extension of the status unlikely.

In contrast with these types of dependent states the status of 'neutralization' involves no impairment of independence. A neutralized state is merely one whose integrity has been permanently guaranteed by international treaty, conditionally on its maintaining a perpetual neutrality except in its own defence. Switzerland was neutralized by the Treaty of Vienna, 1815, and the provision was reaffirmed by the Treaty of Versailles, 1919. Belgium and Luxembourg, which were neutralized by the Treaties of London of 1831 and 1867 respectively, ceased to have that status after the war of 1914. Switzerland is very tenacious of her status and scrupulous in performing its obligations; she joined the League of Nations only on the understanding that she would not be required to take part in military action or to permit the passage of foreign troops over her territory. For fear of prejudicing her neutrality she has not sought to become a member of the United Nations. Austria, on the other hand, which was neutralized in 1955 by agreement with the Great Powers, applied to become and has been admitted a member.

§ 5. *Commencement of the Existence of a State*

A new state comes into existence when a community acquires, with a reasonable probability of permanence, the essential characteristics of a state, namely an organized government, a defined territory, and such a degree of independence of control by any other state as to be capable of conducting its own international relations. Occasionally a new state has been formed in territory not previously under the rule of any state; as when in 1836 Boers from Cape Colony founded the South African Republics, or when in 1847 negroes from the United States founded the Liberian Republic. But generally in modern times a new state has been formed by the division of an existing state into more states than one.

Whether or not a new state has actually begun to exist is a pure question of fact; and as international law does not provide any machinery for an authoritative declaration on this question, it is one which every other state must answer for itself as best it can. Sometimes the circumstances make the answer obvious; as when the union between Sweden and Norway was dissolved by agreement in 1905, and each of these countries commenced a separate international existence. But often the question is both difficult and delicate, especially when part of an existing state is forcibly endeavouring to separate itself from the rest; for a premature recognition of the independence of the revolting part would be an unwarrantable intervention in the internal affairs of the other state. It is impossible to determine by fixed rules the moment at which other states may justly grant recognition of independence to a new state; it can only be said that so long as a real struggle is proceeding, recognition is premature, whilst, on the other hand, mere persistence by the old state in a struggle which has obviously become hopeless is not a sufficient cause for withholding it.

The legal significance of recognition is controversial. According to one view it has a 'constitutive' effect; through recognition only and exclusively a state becomes an international person and a subject of international law.[1] But there are serious difficulties in this view. The status of a state recognized by state A but not recognized by state B, and therefore apparently both an 'international person' and not an 'international person' at the same time, would be a legal curiosity. Perhaps a more substantial difficulty is that the doctrine would oblige us to say that an unrecognized state has neither rights nor duties at international law, and some of the consequences of accepting that conclusion might be startling. We should have to say, for example, that

[1] Oppenheim, *International Law*, 8th ed., vol. i, § 71.

an intervention, otherwise illegal, would not have been illegal in Manchukuo, or that if Manchukuo had been involved in war, she would have been under no legal obligation to respect the rights of neutrals. Non-recognition may certainly make the enforcement of rights and duties more difficult than it would otherwise be, but the practice of states does not support the view that they have no legal existence before recognition.[1]

The better view is that the granting of recognition to a new state is not a 'constitutive' but a 'declaratory' act; it does not bring into legal existence a state which did not exist before. A state may exist without being recognized, and if it does exist in fact, then, whether or not it has been formally recognized by other states, it has a right to be treated by them *as* a state. The primary function of recognition is to acknowledge as a fact something which has hitherto been uncertain, namely the independence of the body claiming to be a state, and to declare the recognizing state's readiness to accept the normal consequences of that fact, namely the usual courtesies of international intercourse. It is true that the present state of the law makes it possible that different states should act on different views of the application of the law to the same state of facts. This does not mean that their differing interpretations are all equally correct, but

[1] See on this point Jaffé, *Judicial Aspects of Foreign Relations*, at p. 98. When Jewish airmen shot down British aeroplanes over Egypt in January 1949 the British Government at once informed the government of the Jewish state, which at that time Britain had not recognized, that they would demand compensation.

only that there exists at present no procedure for determining which are correct and which are not. The constitutive theory of recognition gains most of its plausibility from the lack of centralized institutions in the system, and it treats this lack not as an accident due to the stage of development which the law has so far reached, but as an essential feature of the system. It is in fact one more relic of absolutist theories of state sovereignty.

In practice non-recognition does not always imply that the existence of the unrecognized state is a matter of doubt. States have discovered that the granting or withholding of recognition can be used to further a national policy; they have refused it as a mark of disapproval, as nearly all of them did to Manchukuo; and they have granted it in order to establish the very independence of which recognition is supposed to be a mere acknowledgement, as when in 1903 the United States recognized Panama only three days after it had revolted from Colombia or when in 1948 the United States recognized Israel within a few hours of its proclamation of independence.[1]

[1] In regard to the recognition of Israel, Mr. W. R. Austin, the representative of the United States on the Security Council, asserted the political character of the act of recognition in the most unequivocal terms: 'I should regard it as highly improper for me to admit that any country on earth can question the sovereignty of the United States of America in the exercise of that high political act of recognition of the *de facto* status of a state. Moreover, I would not admit here, by implication or by direct answer, that there exists a tribunal of justice or of any other kind, anywhere, that can pass upon the legality or the validity of that act of my country.' (*New York Times*, 19 May 1948.)

The recognition of a new state as independent must be distinguished from the recognition as belligerent of a part of a state in rebellion against its legitimate government. In normal circumstances the existence of a rebellion within a state is a domestic matter with which other states have no concern, but it sometimes takes a form in which this attitude of detachment can no longer be fairly demanded of them. Two conditions must be satisfied before an outside state is justified in acting. In the first place, the operations must have reached the dimensions of an actual war; that is to say, the rebels must be organized under a government which controls a certain territory of its own, which sees that the laws of war are observed by its troops, and in general which is acting for the time being like the government of an independent state at war. There need be no assurance of this government's permanence, for that is clearly a matter which can only be determined by the issue of the war. In the second place, the course of the war must be such that other states cannot simply stand aside from it. This may happen even if hostilities are confined to the land; for example, the troops of one party may cross the frontier of a neighbouring state and thus compel that state to decide whether or not to intern them, which would be to recognize them as belonging to an army at war. When the war extends to the sea, it is almost inevitable that any state which possesses a mercantile marine will be compelled to make a decision for or against the recognition of the belligerency of the rebels, since it will have to decide whether or not to allow the exercise against its own subjects of the rights which the existence of a maritime war gives to belligerents. If it allows their ships to be searched for contraband goods or captured for breaking a blockade, it thereby does in effect recognize the existence of a regular war, because nothing but war could render those acts permissible: if it refuses, it may have to back its refusal by force and thus be drawn into the war. Its position would be intolerable if it could be required to allow belligerent rights only to the legitimate government and to refuse them to the rebels, since that would be to force it to take sides in the quarrel. In such circumstances, therefore, other states are within their rights in declaring themselves neutral in the struggle, and since there can be no neutrals unless there are two belligerents, such a declaration is equivalent to a recognition of the belligerency of both parties.

The effect of a recognition of belligerency is that the state giving it demands and accepts for itself all the consequences which follow from the existence of a regular war; it claims the rights of a neutral, and accords the rights of a belligerent to the warring parties. Further, the act is also advantageous to the state against which the rebellion is made, since it is relieved thereby of responsibility for the acts of its own rebellious subjects towards other states. But the effects of the recognition are purely provisional; it puts both belligerent parties in the position of states; but only for the purposes and for the duration of the war. It differs radically, therefore, from a recognition of the revolting part of a state as independent. None the less, the granting of recognition of belligerency to rebels is a step often resented by the state to which they belong, and its judgment of the propriety of the recognition is likely to differ from that of the recognizing state. The choice of the time for granting recognition is therefore a delicate matter. The test has been already indicated; recognition is justified when an actual war is being waged and when the state granting it is, or seems likely to be, forced into a position where it cannot avoid taking some action, either recognition or refusal of recognition, in relation to the war.[1]

[1] In the Spanish Civil War of 1936-9 foreign states, for political reasons which differed in the case of different states, did not formally recognize the belligerency of the contending parties. But it was found impossible to carry out consistently a policy which refused to recognize the patent fact that a war in the fullest sense was being waged. For example, the Non-Intervention Agreement, by which a large number of states undertook to forbid their nationals to export munitions to either party, was either a recognition of the fact of war, or it was, as the legitimate Spanish Government alleged, a highly unfriendly act towards that government. Britain, too, though refusing to allow either side to exercise belligerent rights against British ships on the high seas, declined to protect them in Spanish territorial waters where, on the hypothesis that no war was being waged, it was equally unlawful to molest them. Other anomalies to which the policy of non-recognition led are given in an article, 'Some Problems of the Spanish Civil War', by Professor H. A. Smith, in *B.Y.I.L.*, 1937, p. 17. His conclusion is that the accepted rules which govern the attitude of foreign powers in a civil war are the fruits of experience, and have proved effective in the past in confining such wars within the limits of the countries in which they have broken out. He doubts whether any temporary advantage can in the long run outweigh the harm which is done by the disregard of well-tried principles.

§ 6. *Continuity and Termination of the Existence of a State*

The government of a state must not be identified
with the state itself, but between states intercourse is
only possible if each has a government with which the
others may enter into relations and whose acts they
may regard as binding on the state itself. What form
of government a state should adopt, and whether it
should replace an existing government by a new one,
are domestic matters with which other states are not
concerned. But they are concerned to know whether
the person or persons with whom they propose to
enter into relations are in fact a government whose
acts will be binding at international law upon the
state which they profess to represent.

The law regarding this question has been clearly
stated in an award of Chief Justice Taft in an arbitration between Great Britain and Costa Rica in 1923.[1]
Great Britain claimed that certain British companies
had acquired certain rights against Costa Rica by
contracts entered into with one Tinoco. It appeared
that in 1917 Tinoco overthrew the existing government of Costa Rica and established a new constitution which lasted till 1919, when the old constitution
was restored; and that in 1922 the restored government passed legislation nullifying all engagements
entered into by Tinoco's government. The Chief
Justice held that if Tinoco's government was the
actual government of Costa Rica at the time when
the rights were alleged to have been acquired, the

[1] Reported in *A.J.I.L.*, 1924, p. 147.

restored government could not repudiate the obligations which his acts had imposed on the state of Costa
Rica. He further said that this question must be
decided by evidence of the facts. It was immaterial
that by the law of Costa Rica Tinoco's government
was unconstitutional. Even the objection put forward by Costa Rica that many states, including
Great Britain herself, had never recognized Tinoco's
government, was only relevant as suggesting, though
it did not prove, that that government had not been
the actual government of Costa Rica; but since
Tinoco 'was in actual and peaceable control without
resistance or conflict or contest by any one until a
few months before the time when he retired', he held
that his acts were binding upon Costa Rica. On the
further question of the merits of the companies' claims,
his decision on the whole favoured that state.

This decision therefore shows that a state is bound
internationally by the acts of the person or persons
who in actual fact constitute its government. This
is sometimes expressed by saying that a new government 'succeeds' to the rights and. obligations of its
predecessor, but the expression is a loose one, because
international rights and obligations belong to states
and not to governments, and a new government 'succeeds' to them only in the sense that it becomes the
government of a state to which they are attached. It
follows, therefore, that the identity of a state is not
affected by changes in the form or the persons of its
government, or even by a temporary anarchy, as in
China or Mexico in recent years. But constitutional

changes may make it difficult for other states to know who, if any one, is in a position to bind the state, and may thus give rise to the problem of deciding whether or not they will recognize a new government. The recognition of a new government is not to be confused with the recognition of a new state, but it raises problems in some respects similar. In both cases a premature recognition is an intervention in the domestic affairs of another state, and in both the question which other states have to decide is one of fact. Again, recognition of a government, although the conditions on which it should be accorded are also defined by international law, is equally capable of being used as an instrument of policy; for example, the United States has at times, especially under President Wilson, refused to recognize new governments which have been set up by force in Central America, and at present many states are refusing to recognize the communist government of China. But to refuse to recognize facts because they are unpleasant is apt to be inconvenient, and such a policy is difficult to carry out consistently for long or against any but weak states, as those states which refused to recognize the government of the Soviets, including the United States itself, eventually discovered.

Recognition either of a state or a government may be recognition *de jure* or *de facto*. The latter meets the case where a state, either because the position is obscure or for political reasons, is reluctant to recognize definitely some entity claiming to be a state or government, but yet finds it necessary for practical reasons to enter into some sort of official relations. Recognition *de facto* is provisional; it means that the recognizing government offers for the time being to enter into relations, yet ordinarily without cordiality, and without the usual courtesies of diplomacy. But the terminology is misleading in more ways than one. It is not the act of recognition that is *de jure* or *de facto*, but the state or the government, as the case may be, that is recognized as existing either *de jure* or *de facto*. Moreover, it is not clear what law, international or national, is supposed to be referred to when a situation is said to be recognized *de jure*. Neither of these makes good sense. If a state or a government does actually exist, then, *for the purposes of international law*, it necessarily exists *de jure*; that law is not concerned to ask how the state or the government has come into existence. On the other hand, the recognizing state is not concerned with the question whether the state of things which it is recognizing is legal by the national law of another state; for the recognizing state it is irrelevant that a new state may have come into existence by civil war, or that a government may be a revolutionary government.

Non-recognition of a foreign government is more than a refusal to enter into relations. From 1917 to 1921 Great Britain refused to recognize the Soviet Government. In 1921 she recognized that government as the *de facto*, and in 1924 as the *de jure*, government of Russia. In 1927 she broke off diplomatic relations with it. That action did not mean that she ceased to recognize the Soviet Government as the government of Russia; she merely declined to deal with that government. It has, however, been pointed out[1] that non-recognition as practised today (that is to say, when it is used for some ulterior political purpose, and not because the stability of the government in question is really a matter of doubt) differs very little from the breaking off of diplomatic relations, and this seems to be true so far as the international consequences of either are concerned; and that it may be largely a matter of chance, depending on whether it is a new or an old government which displeases us, which will be used.[2]

On the declaratory view of the nature of recognition

[1] Cf. Jaffé, loc. cit., p. 148.

[2] The Foreign Secretary stated the principles acted on by the British Government in the House of Commons on 21 March 1951:

'The question of the recognition of a State or government should be distinguished from the question of entering into diplomatic relations with it, which is entirely discretionary. On the other hand it is international law which defines the conditions under which a government should be recognized *de jure* or *de facto*, and it is a matter of judgement in each particular case whether a regime fulfils the conditions. The conditions under international law for the recognition of a new regime as the *de facto* government are that the new regime has in fact effective control over most of the State's territory and that this control seems likely to continue. The conditions for the recognition of a new regime as the *de jure* government of a State are that the new regime should not merely have effective control over most of the State's territory, but that it should in fact be firmly established. His Majesty's Government consider that recognition should be accorded when the conditions specified by international law are in fact fulfilled and that recognition should not be given when these conditions are not fulfilled. The recognition of a government *de jure* or *de facto* should not depend on whether the character of the regime is such as to command His Majesty's Government's approval.' (See *The International Law Quarterly*, 1951, p. 387.)

its granting or withholding does not, *so far as international law is concerned*, affect the status in law of the state or government to which it is accorded or from which it is withheld. But recognition has important effects, at any rate according to English and American views, in the administration of the domestic law of the recognizing state. The representatives and the property of a foreign state or government are immune from legal process, and the validity of such a government's acts in its own country cannot be questioned in our courts; but our courts regard it as a matter for the Executive and not for themselves to determine whether an entity claiming to be a state, or persons claiming to be a government, ought to be treated as a state or government for these purposes. For the courts, therefore, recognition may be said to have in a sense a 'quasi-constitutive' effect. If, for instance, the Tinoco case had come before an English court, it would have been obliged to hold that as its government had never recognized Tinoco, he never was the government of Costa Rica and therefore his acts had never bound that state; but for an arbitrator administering international law, which was Chief Justice Taft's function, British recognition or non-recognition could not be the factor determining Tinoco's status. In *Luther* v. *Sagor* the English courts had to deal with a claim to certain timber which had been the property of the plaintiff company in Russia; it had been confiscated by legislation of the Soviet Government, sold by them, and subsequently brought to England by the purchaser. At the time when the case was heard by

Roche J. the British Government had not recognized
the Soviet Government, and he accordingly gave
judgment for the plaintiffs. But before the case was
heard by the Court of Appeal the Soviet Government
had been recognized with restrospective effect as a *de
facto* government, and the Court therefore reversed
the decision of Roche J., holding that the Soviet
legislation had been effective to pass the title in the
timber.[1]

Luther v. *Sagor* shows that the English courts will
acknowledge as valid the legislation of a foreign
government recognized by Great Britain, even
though the recognition is only *de facto*. Further, the
House of Lords has held, in the case of the *S.S.
Arantzazu Mendi*,[2] that General Franco's government, at a time during the Spanish Civil War when
it was recognized by Britain 'as a government which
at present exercises *de facto* administrative control
over the larger portion of Spain', could not be im-
pleaded in an English court. For these two purposes
therefore English courts evidently regard the legal
effects of *de jure* and *de facto* recognition as identical.
The chief and perhaps the only point of difference
appears to be that the *de jure* government will be held
to represent the state in question and, in principle,
to be entitled to any of its property not actually in
the possession or control of a rival *de facto* government.[3]

---

[1] [1921] 1 K.B. 456, and 3 K.B. 532.   [2] [1939] A.C. 256.
[3] *Gdynia Ameryka Linie* v. *Boguslawski*, [1953] A.C. 11; *Civil Air
Transport Inc.* v. *Central Air Transport Corporation*, [1953] A.C. 70.

A change in the extent of a state's territory has in principle no effect on its international identity, but in practice difficult cases may occur. Thus when two states become united, it may not always be easy to determine whether one of the two has annexed the other, or whether both have merged their separate identities so as to form a single new state. For instance, it might seem natural to regard Italy as a new state formed by the union of the several independent states of the Italian Peninsula, but in fact she regards herself as, and has been accepted as being, the kingdom of Piedmont territorially enlarged by annexation of the other Italian states.[1] On the other hand, a Californian court has held that Yugoslavia is not the old kingdom of Serbia enlarged, but a new state which came into existence after the First World War.[2]

Recently, when Egypt and Syria joined together to form the United Arab Republic, the case was treated as an amalgamation—a merger—of the two states into a single unit representing both of them.[3] When an existing state breaks up into more than one it may similarly be difficult to say whether the old state has been extinguished and its place taken by two or more new states, or whether the old state continues to exist with its territory reduced by the separation from it of a new state or states. The republic of Austria, created after the First World War, was probably a new state, and not the empire of Austria-Hungary with a new

[1] See, for example, the case of *Gastaldi* v. *Lepage Hemery*, Ann. Dig., 1929–30, Case No. 43.
[2] *Artukovic* v. *Boyle*, A.J.I.L., 1953, p. 319.   [3] *Infra*, p. 156.

form of government and a reduced territorial extent. On the other hand, the present Turkish Republic seems to be regarded as a continuation of the Turkish Empire, in spite of the many new states which have been carved out of its former territories.[1]

In all cases of the transfer of territory from one state to another, whether the event involves the extinction of a state or not, the point of chief legal interest is to determine the effect, if any, of the transfer on the international rights and duties of the states concerned.[2] This question is often regulated by the provisions of a treaty of cession, but unless so regulated it does not admit of a simple answer, and the problems which it raises cannot be solved by assuming a general principle of 'state succession' and then proceeding to deduce its consequences. 'Succession' is primarily a principle of private law, and suggests that the extinction of a state is in some sense comparable to the death of an individual. But states do not die in any literal sense; their population and their territory do not disappear, but merely suffer political change. Moreover, succession is a notion taken from the law of property; and it is easy to be misled by the suggestion that something analogous to the transfer of property takes place when people and territory cease to form part of one state and begin to form part of another. It is safer to proceed by examining the actual practice of states to see how far any fixed rules

[1] See *Ottoman Debt Arbitration*, *Ann. Dig.*, 1925–6, Case No. 57.
[2] For a full treatment of this involved subject see D. P. O'Connell, *The Law of State Succession* (1956).

have been formed on this matter. We may treat it under the heads of treaties, membership of international organizations, property, contracts, and wrongs.

Treaty rights and obligations, in general, do not attach to the territories of the contracting parties but to the states—the legal persons—which have concluded the treaty. So, when considering the effect of a change in the sovereignty of territory on treaty rights and obligations, the key to the matter is to have regard to the personalities of the contracting states and to see if these have in any material way changed their identity.[1] The mere cession of a piece of territory from one state to another does not affect the treaty rights or obligations of either. What happens is simply that the territory passes out of the treaty system of the ceding state into that of the new sovereign. Nor are treaty rights and obligations affected when part of an existing state breaks off and becomes a new state; they remain with the old state, and the new state—a new legal person—starts its career without any. Further, when a state ceases to exist, its treaties generally cease with it. This is admitted in the case of political treaties, e.g. treaties of alliance; and there is very little authority for the suggestion that non-political treaties pass to the state or states which take the place of the extinguished state. Thus in 1896 when France annexed Madagascar she applied the French tariff, disregarding certain trading rights to which Great Britain and the United

[1] Hall, *International Law*, 8th ed., p. 114.

States were entitled by treaties with the Queen of Madagascar; and Japan acted in the same way when she annexed Korea in 1910.

One class of treaty is alleged to constitute an exception to the general rule, although even this is not certain. There are treaties, sometimes called 'dispositive' treaties, which are regarded as impressing a special character on the territory to which they relate, and creating something analogous to the servitudes or easements of private law; and there is authority for saying that when a state takes over territory affected by a treaty of this kind it takes over not the mere territory itself, but the territory with rights and obligations attached to it. A treaty of neutralization or one regulating customs zones or the use of a river are examples of such treaties.[1]

Membership of international organizations is in the last analysis a question of being or becoming a party to a treaty. It is therefore only logical that in considering the effect of a change of sovereignty upon membership of international organizations the principle that the personality of the contracting state is the key to membership should be applied, as it has been, in cases of secession and dismemberment. Thus, when the Irish Free State broke away from Great Britain and established itself as a separate state, it was required to apply for admission as a new member of the League of Nations, while the United Kingdom

[1] See *The Free Zones case* (1932, Series A/B, No. 46, p. 144); *The Wimbledon*, 1923, Series A, No. 1; and McNair, *Law of Treaties*, Chap. XIV.

STATES 155

continued in its former membership, its legal personality unchanged, though its territory had been reduced. Similarly, under the United Nations the
states arising from the constitutional changes introduced in British and French territories, Burma,
Ceylon, Ghana, Vietnam, Guinea, &c., have all been
regarded as new legal persons needing a vote of admission to make them members of the United
Nations. The first and decisive precedent under the
United Nations was the somewhat special double
dismemberment operation which gave rise to the
two independent states of India and Pakistan.
'India', comprising the territory both of India and
Pakistan, had been a member of the League and an
original member of the United Nations. Although not
fully independent of Great Britain, she had been
recognized as possessing a distinct international personality. In 1947 India became fully independent and
at the same time split into two. The United Nations
Secretariat advised that, although 'India' had undergone a fundamental constitutional change, this
change had not altered her legal personality or her
status as a member of the United Nations. Pakistan,
on the other hand, must be considered to have broken
off from 'India' and to be an entirely new state not
entitled to be considered a member without a vote
of admission. Although this opinion met with some
criticism, it was adopted by the majority and the new
India was accepted as already a member while
Pakistan was admitted as a new member.

The reverse process—the joinder of two existing

states so as to constitute a single state—is less common, but a very interesting example is to be found in the formation of the United Arab Republic in 1958. Egypt and Syria were both already members of the United Nations and the new Republic addressed a Note to the Secretary-General declaring that it now considered itself to be a single member. Similar Notes were addressed to numerous other organizations of which both states had been members. The upshot was that the United Arab Republic was accepted by the United Nations and by the other organizations as an existing member not requiring a fresh vote of admission despite the fact that the Republic, politically and legally, was clearly a new state. The case appears to have been treated as the fusion of two international persons into one person representing both of them—a merger of two memberships into one. What view would have been taken if only Egypt or only Syria had previously been a member of the United Nations is an interesting question.

State property situated within a transferred territory, such as public buildings, government funds in the banks, or state railways, passes to an annexing state; or, if a state ceases to exist, then all its property, wherever situated, passes to the state to which the sovereignty over its territory has passed. In *Haile Selassie* v. *Cable & Wireless Co. Ltd.*[1] the Emperor Haile Selassie had obtained judgment in the Chancery Division for a sum of money owing by the company to the government of Ethiopia, at a time when

[1] [1939] Ch. 182; cf. *U.S.* v. *McRae* (1869) L.R. 8 Eq. 69.

he was still recognized by the British Government as the *de jure* ruler of Ethiopia; but before the case came on in the Court of Appeal the British Government had recognized the King of Italy as the *de jure* Emperor of Ethiopia, and it was held that the judgment must be reversed, the right to the debt having become vested in the King. The same principle was applied after the American Civil War to property of the Confederate Government situated in England, when the British Government handed over to the United States the Confederate cruiser *Shenandoah*, which had taken refuge in Liverpool.

How far an annexing state takes over the contractual liabilities of a state whose territory it annexes is a question of much difficulty. Oppenheim[1] was of opinion that 'the recent practice of states ... tends to establish as a rule of international law the duty of a successor state, whether the succession arises upon cession or annexation or dismemberment, to respect the acquired rights of private persons whether proprietary, contractual, or concessionary'. On the other hand, an English court in *West Rand Central Gold Mining Co.* v. *The King*[2] adopted a contrary but

[1] Oppenheim, *International Law*, vol. i, 4th ed., p. 168 (note).

[2] [1905] 2 K.B. 391. The case is open to many criticisms, and the actual decision did not require so sweeping a generalization. Moreover, the case was a petition of right in which the suppliant, an English company, sought to recover from the Crown the value of gold seized by the government of the former South African Republic. The case decides that an English court can give no relief in such a case, but it does not necessarily follow that if the company dispossessed of the gold had been a foreign company the Crown would have been under no international liability.

equally extreme position, and declared that 'the conquering sovereign can make any conditions he thinks fit respecting the financial obligations of the conquered country, and it is entirely at his option to what extent he will adopt them'. The former of these views is probably in advance of, but the latter is certainly behind, the actual state of international law on this matter.

The Permanent Court more than once had occasion to refer to the question, though it did not formulate any comprehensive rule; probably no rule applying indifferently to contractual rights and liabilities of all kinds is to be expected. In the case of the *German Settlers in Poland*,[1] after declaring that 'private rights acquired under existing law do not cease on a change of sovereignty', the Court upheld as against Poland the rights of certain German settlers in the territory transferred from Prussia after the First World War. These settlers held their lands upon a special form of contract with the Prussian State which entitled them on certain conditions to a transfer of the full ownership thereof, and the contracts were upheld notwithstanding the fact that they had originally been made for the purpose of strengthening the German at the expense of the Polish element in the territory which had since become part of Poland. In the case of the *Mavrommatis Palestine Concessions*[2] the Court held that the administration of Palestine was bound to respect certain concessions granted by Turkey to a Greek subject for

[1] (1923) Series B , No. 6.
[2] (1925) Series A, Judgment No. 5.

works to be carried out at Jerusalem. The Court has not had to deal with the assumption by a successor of the public debt of an annexed state, or of a proportionate part where part only of a state's territory is transferred. On this matter practice has varied, though it seems to be tending towards the acceptance of at any rate some liability. Sometimes an annexing state has recognized a legal obligation to accept liability; Italy appears to have done so when she took over from Austria the local debt of Lombardy in 1860. Sometimes it has taken over part of a state's general debt on annexing territory, although the debt was not charged on the territory; thus Prussia took over part of the Danish debt when she annexed Schleswig-Holstein in 1866. Sometimes it has accepted partial liability without admitting any legal obligation to do so; Great Britain acted in this way after the South African War. Possibly the solution of the matter is to be found by considering the nature of the contract, and particularly whether the identity of the original contracting state is or is not a material element in it. Thus it is generally assumed that an annexing state is not bound to take over a public debt incurred for the purpose of financing a war against itself. On the other hand, in a concession contract for the execution of works of public utility, as in the *Mavrommatis* case, or in a sale of lands, as in the *German Settlers* case (apart from the political purpose in that case, which the Court disregarded), the identity of the contracting state is immaterial. But it must be admitted that this distinction is not definitely formulated in the cases.

The liability of an annexing state for the wrongful acts of the state whose territory is annexed was considered by an Anglo-American Claims Tribunal in the *Robert E. Brown Claim.*[1] Before the annexation of the South African Republic by Great Britain the government of President Kruger had dismissed the Chief Justice of the Republic from office and reduced the courts to a state of dependence on the government. The Tribunal found that in consequence of this state of 'legal anarchy' Robert E. Brown, an American citizen, had suffered a denial of justice in connexion with certain gold-mining claims. On the United States preferring Brown's claim against Great Britain as the successor to the South African Republic, the Tribunal held that the liability under international law for the torts of the defunct state does not pass to a state acquiring territory by conquest which is under no obligation to take steps to right a wrong that may have been committed by its predecessor. In the *Hawaian Claims*[2] the Tribunal applied the same principle to the case of a voluntary cession— the voluntary coalition of the Hawaian Republic with the United States—declining to hold the United States liable for the wrongful imprisonment of British subjects by the Hawaian Republic. On the basis of these precedents many writers declare it to be a general rule that liability for a tort is automatically extinguished if the wrongdoing state ceases to exist. In a recent Award, however, the Permanent

[1] (1923) *R.I.A.A.*, vol. 6, p. 120.
[2] (1925) *R.I.A.A.*, vol. 6, p. 157.

Court of Arbitration doubted the existence of any
such general rule and appeared to think that liability
for wrongs to private individuals may not be extinguished on a voluntary coalition or a voluntary dismemberment of two states.[1]

[1] The *Lighthouses Arbitration* between France and Greece, *I.L.R.*,
1956, pp. 81–93.

V

THE TERRITORY OF STATES

§ 1. *Territorial Sovereignty*

AT the basis of international law lies the notion that a state occupies a definite part of the surface of the earth, within which it normally exercises, subject to the limitations imposed by international law, jurisdiction over persons and things to the exclusion of the jurisdiction of other states. When a state exercises an authority of this kind over a certain territory it is popularly said to have 'sovereignty' over the territory, but that much-abused word is here used in a rather special sense. It refers here not to a relation of persons to persons, nor to the independence of the state itself, but to the nature of rights over territory; and in the absence of any better word it is a convenient way of contrasting the fullest rights over territory known to the law with the minor territorial rights to be later mentioned. Territorial sovereignty bears an obvious resemblance to ownership in private law, less marked, however, today than it was in the days of the patrimonial state, when a kingdom and everything in it was regarded as being to the king very much what a landed estate was to its owner. As a result of this resemblance early international law borrowed the Roman rules for the acquisition of property and adapted them to the acquisition of territory, and these rules are still the foundation of the law on the subject.

§ 2. *Modes of Acquiring Territory*

The sovereignty of territory may be acquired by occupation, prescription, cession, conquest, and accretion.

Occupation is a means of acquiring territory not already forming part of the dominions of any state. Since all the habitable areas of the earth now fall under the dominion of some state or other, future titles by occupation are not likely to be frequent, but the law of the matter is still important because the occupations of the past often give rise to the boundary disputes of the present. The principles of law are fairly well settled; the difficulty generally arises in applying them to the facts, which may go back for centuries. In the leading case on the subject, the *Legal Status of Eastern Greenland*,[1] the Permanent Court traced the facts back to the tenth century A.D.

The dispute arose out of the action of Norway in proclaiming the occupation of certain parts of East Greenland in 1931. Denmark thereupon asked the Court to declare the Norwegian proclamation invalid, on the ground that the area to which it referred was subject to Danish sovereignty, which extended to the whole of Greenland. The Court pointed out that the Danish claim was based merely upon continued display of authority and that such a claim involves two elements, 'the intention or will to act as sovereign, and some actual exercise or display of authority'.[2] In these words the Court were affirming

[1] (1933) Series A/B, No. 53.
[2] Professor Ross, however, seems to be correct in saying that the

the well-established principle that occupation, in order to create a title to territory, must be 'effective' occupation, that is to say, it must be followed up by action, such as, in a simple case, the planting of a settlement or the building of a fort, which shows that the state not only desires to, but can and does, control the territory claimed. The Court were satisfied on the evidence that at any rate after a certain date, 1721, Denmark's *intention* to claim title to the whole of Greenland was established. But the areas in dispute were outside the settled areas of Greenland, and it was necessary therefore for the Court to examine carefully the evidence by which Denmark tried to satisfy the second necessary element in occupation, namely the exercise of authority. On this they pointed out that the absence of any competing claim by another state (and until 1931 no state other than Denmark had ever claimed title to Greenland) is an important consideration; a relatively slight exercise of authority will suffice when no state can show a superior claim. They held, too, that the character of the country must be regarded; the arctic and in-accessible nature of the uncolonized parts of Green-land made it unreasonable to look for a continuous or intensive exercise of authority. Denmark was able to show numerous legislative and administrative acts purporting to apply to the whole of Greenland, trea-

subjective requirement of the 'will to act as sovereign' in addition to the objective display of authority is 'an empty phantom', a sort of vestigial relic of the *animus possidendi* of Roman law. *International Law*, p. 147.

ties in which other states, by agreeing to a clause excluding Greenland from their effects, had apparently acquiesced in her claim, and in recent years an express recognition of it by many states. The Court held that in the circumstances this was sufficient evidence to establish her title to the whole of the country. The area which Norway claimed in 1931 was therefore not at that time a *terra nullius* capable of being acquired by her occupation.

On principle the area to which the legal effects of an occupation extend should be simply the area effectively occupied, and this is a question of fact. But politically a strict adherence to this principle is impracticable; a state which has effectively occupied a certain area may reasonably intend to extend it, or it may be that the security of the area occupied would be threatened if another state should occupy adjacent unoccupied territory. Hence states have usually claimed title to an area greater than that effectively occupied, and though the claims have often been extravagant the law recognizes some extension as reasonable. Hall states the matter fairly when he says that 'a settlement is entitled, not only to the lands actually inhabited and brought under its immediate control, but to all those which may be needed for its security, and to the territory which may fairly be considered to be attendant upon them'.[1]

From the requirement that occupation must be 'effective' it follows that mere discovery of an unappropriated territory is not sufficient to create a title,

[1] *International Law*, 8th ed., p. 129.

for discovery alone does not put the discoverer in a position to control the territory discovered, however he may desire or intend to do so. But on this point the law makes a concession and allows the strict rule of effective occupation to be qualified by the doctrine of 'inchoate title'. Since an effective occupation must usually be a gradual process it is considered that some weight should be given to mere discovery, and it is regarded therefore as giving an 'inchoate title', that is to say, a temporary right to exclude other states until the state of the discoverer has had a reasonable time within which to make an effective occupation, or a sort of option to occupy which other states must respect while it lasts.

The effects of discovery were discussed by the arbitrator (M. Huber) in the *Island of Palmas* award.[1] The United States, as successor of Spain, claimed an island which lies half-way between the Philippines and the Dutch East Indies, mainly on the ground of its discovery in the sixteenth century. The arbitrator held that even if the international law of that century recognized mere discovery as giving a title to territory (though there is very little reason for thinking that it did), such a title could not survive today, when it is certain that discovery alone, without any subsequent act, does not establish sovereignty; whilst if the title originally acquired was 'inchoate' (as according to the modern doctrine it would be) it had not been turned into a definitive title by an actual and durable taking of possession within a reasonable time. It

[1] Text in *A.J.I.L.*, 1928, p. 867.

THE TERRITORY OF STATES

could not therefore on either view prevail over the continuous and peaceful display of authority, which the evidence satisfied him had been exercised by Holland.

Prescription as a title to territory is ill defined and some writers deny its recognition altogether. International law does appear, however, to admit that, by a process analogous to the prescription of municipal law, lo_ig possession may operate either to confirm the existence of a title the precise origin of which cannot be shown or to extinguish the prior title of another sovereign. This was certainly the opinion of Hall, who said: 'Title by prescription arises out of a long continued possession, where no original source of proprietary right can be shown to exist, or where possession in the first instance being wrongful, the legitimate proprietor has neglected to assert his right, or has been unable to do so.'[1] Indeed, many territorial titles and many frontiers are accepted by international law today simply because they have existed *de facto* for a long time; they exemplify the maxim *e facto oritur jus*, which is at the root of prescription in all systems of law.

In the absence of definite evidence that the possession began as a wrongful assumption of a sovereignty already belonging to another state, peaceful and continuous possession raises a presumption that the original assumption of sovereignty was in conformity with international law and has the effect of consolidating the claimant's title. Possession of

[1] *International Law* (8th ed.), p. 143.

territory consists in the exercise or display of state authority in or in regard to the territory in question. In the *Island of Palmas Arbitration*[1] M. Huber spoke of the acquisition of sovereignty by way of continuous and peaceful display of state authority as 'so-called prescription' and also said that 'the continuous and peaceful display of territorial sovereignty (peaceful in relation to other states) is as good as a title. In the *Minquiers and Ecrehos* case[2] between the United Kingdom and France both parties sought to trace their claims to sovereignty from titles said to exist in medieval times so that, as the Court pointed out, the case was not concerned with the 'occupation' of a *terra nullius*. Even so, the Court treated the historical evidence as to possession of the two groups of islands as decisive of the sovereignty which it awarded to the United Kingdom on the basis of the latter's exercise of state functions with regard to them. Again, even in the *Eastern Greenland* case, which is commonly referred to as the leading case on 'occupation', the Court emphasized that Denmark did not found her claim upon any 'particular act of occupation' but alleged a title 'founded on the peaceful and con-tinuous display of state authority'; and it awarded the sovereignty to Denmark on the basis of the latter's display of state authority with regard to the whole of Greenland during successive periods of history.

In fact, it is neither very easy nor very necessary to draw a precise line between an ancient title de-rived from an original 'occupation' and one founded

[1] *A.J.I.L*, 1928, pp. 909 and 876.   [2] *I.C.J. Reports*, 1953, p. 47.

simply on long and peaceful possession. For in the *Island of Palmas* case M. Huber emphasized that proof of an original taking of possession is not enough and that possession must be maintained by display of State authority; and, on the other hand, both he in that case and the Court in the *Eastern Greenland* case pointed out that proof of peaceful possession in the most recent period before the rival claimant attempts to assume the sovereignty is sufficient by itself to establish a title to the territory—without proof of a long historic possession. The truth seems to be that peaceful display of state authority is by itself a valid title to sovereignty and that proof either of an original act of occupation or of the long duration of a display of state authority is important primarily as confirming the peaceful and non-adverse character of the possession. Peaceful display of state authority over a long period excludes the existence of any valid prior title in another state and makes it unnecessary to rely upon the principle of extinctive prescription by long adverse possession.

The principle of extinctive prescription under which the passage of time operates ultimately to bar the right of a prior owner to pursue his claim against one who, having wrongfully displaced him, has continued for a long time in adverse possession is recognized in almost all systems of municipal law and it appears equally to be admitted by international law. In the *British Guiana Boundary Arbitration*[1] between Great Britain and Venezuela the parties to the dis-

[1] (1904) *B.F.S.P.*, vol. 99, pp. 930–2.

pute agreed that the Tribunal should apply the following rule: 'Adverse holding or prescription during a period of fifty years shall make a good title. The Arbitrators may deem exclusive political control of a district, as well as actual settlement thereof, sufficient to constitute adverse holding or to make title by prescription.' The principle appears also to have been recognized by the International Court in the *Anglo-Norwegian Fisheries* case[1] as a method whereby a coastal state may acquire exclusive sovereignty over areas of seas which under general international law would be part of the high seas, although the Court did not in that case consider the principle to be applicable because it held that Norway's claim was not in conflict with general international law. Long possession in order to have the effect of extinguishing a prior title to sovereignty must be continuous, public, and peaceful; i.e. a continuous, public, and undisturbed exercise or display of state authority must be shown. It is a nice question as to exactly how far diplomatic and other paper forms of protest by the dispossessed state suffice to 'disturb' the possession of the interloper so as to prevent the latter from acquiring a title by prescription. Paper protests may undoubtedly be effective for a certain length of time to preserve the claim of the dispossessed state. If, however, the latter makes no effort at all to carry its protests farther by referring the case to the United Nations or by using other remedies that may be open to it, paper protests

---

[1] *I.C.J. Reports*, 1951, p. 130; see also *Direct United States Cable Co.* v. *Anglo-American Telegraph Co.* (1877), 2 A.C. 394.

will ultimately be of no avail to stop the operation of prescription. Thus it was largely for the purpose of avoiding any risk of the extinguishment of its claims by prescription that in 1955 the United Kingdom filed a unilateral application with the International Court challenging alleged encroachments by Argentina and Chile on the Falkland Islands Dependencies.

Cession is a mode of transferring the title to territory from one state to another. It results sometimes from a war, sometimes from peaceful negotiations; it may either be gratuitous, or for some consideration, as when Denmark sold the Danish West Indies to the United States in 1916.

Conquest is the acquisition of the territory of an enemy by its complete and final subjugation and a declaration of the conquering state's intention to annex it. In practice a title by conquest is rare, because the annexation of territory after a war is generally carried out by a treaty of cession, although such a treaty often only confirms a title already acquired by conquest. A modern instance of title by conquest is that of Roumania to Bessarabia in the period between the two World Wars.

There is an obvious moral objection to the legal recognition of a title by conquest, but it is no greater than the moral objection to the recognition of an enforced cession of territory. That the latter has in the past conferred a valid legal title is undeniable, and it would have been idle for the law to have accepted the effects of force when the formality of a forced assent had followed and not otherwise. The attitude of the

law towards both these titles has been merely a corollary, but a necessary corollary, of its inability to regulate the use by states of armed force. So long as war
continues to be used as an instrument of national
policy, it will continue to produce the same results as
it has in the past, and one of those results will be the
annexation of territory.

It was proposed in 1932 by Mr. Stimson, then
American Secretary of State, and his proposal has
come to be known as the *Stimson Doctrine of Non-
Recognition*, that states should refuse to recognize 'any
situation, treaty or agreement which may be brought
about contrary to the covenants and obligations of
the Pact of Paris'. Thereby, he said, ' a caveat will
be placed upon such actions which, we believe, will
effectively bar the legality hereafter of any title or
right sought to be obtained by pressure or treaty
violation'. The Assembly of the League also passed
a resolution to the same effect.

Unfortunately the legal consequences which Mr.
Stimson foresaw for his doctrine are by no means
sure. If non-recognition should leave unchanged the
facts of which it marks disapproval, it would result in
a discordance between the law and the facts which
in the long run would merely advertise the impotence
of the law. Within three years of the League Resolution Italy had conquered Ethiopia, and most of the
League states had decided that it was expedient to
recognize that Ethiopia had become Italian territory.
The truth is that international law can no more
refuse to recognize that a finally successful conquest

does change the title to territory than municipal law can a change of régime brought about by a successful revolution. What have hitherto been the legal consequences of successful war cannot in the long run be avoided by any change in the law, or any well-intentioned convention of states which does not also register a change in their practice in respect of war.

Accretion is the addition of new territory to the existing territory of a state by operation of nature, as by the drying up of a river or the recession of the sea. It is of minor importance and the detailed rules on the matter need not here be considered.

§ 3. *Dependent Territories*

(a) *Colonies and Colonial Protectorates*

Colonies are lands acquired by treaty of cession, annexation, prescription, or conquest, which become dependent possessions of the acquiring state without being brought constitutionally under the state's own system of government.

In the latter half of the nineteenth century the appetites of the colonizing states of Europe for new territory in Africa outran their powers of digestion, and they introduced forms of staking out their claims in territories where for one reason or another they were for the time being unable or unwilling to make an effective occupation. One such device was the 'colonial protectorate', the word 'protectorate' here describing a relation between a state and a native community not sufficiently civilized to be regarded as a state, and not, as heretofore, a relation of dependence between two states. For the most part these new protectorates were established by agreements more or less voluntary with the native chiefs, and they generally led to full annexation. In the meantime it claimed to exclude any other state from making an occupation, or from maintaining any direct relations with the protected communities; conversely it accepted a somewhat vague obligation to maintain a reasonable degree of security for foreign subjects and property within the protected territory. But it is probable that the distinction between one of these protectorates and a colony is one of constitutional, rather than of international, law. When, for example, a few years ago we annexed the Kenya Protectorate as a colony, the change had, internationally, no legal significance. Constitutionally, the most important difference is that the inhabitants of a protectorate do not take the nationality of the protecting state.

Prior to the establishment of the United Nations a state's government of its colonial territories was considered to be as much a matter within its own domestic jurisdiction as the government of its metropolitan territory. Under Article 23 (e) of the Covenant, it is true, members of the League undertook 'to secure just treatment of the native inhabitants of territories under their control'. But this clause did not meet with any development or any specific application in the practice of the League, and provided little basis for saying that the administration of colonial territories was a matter of 'international concern'. At the instance of Australia and the United Kingdom, however, there was inserted into the Charter as Chapter XI a 'Declaration Regarding Non-Self-Governing Territories' which has in some measure made the administration of non-self-governing colonies a matter of international concern. Under Article 73 members of the United Nations having responsibilities for the administration of territories whose peoples have not yet attained a full measure of self-government 'recognise the principle that the interests of the inhabitants of these territories are paramount' and 'accept as a sacred trust the obligation to promote to the utmost' their well-being. As part of this obligation they undertake to ensure the political, economic, social, and educational advancement of colonial peoples, to develop self-government, to take due account of their political aspirations, and to assist them in the development of their free political institutions according to the particular circumstances and stage of advancement of each territory. In contrast with Chapters XII and XIII which deal with trusteeship territories, Chapter XI does not speak of 'administration' or 'supervision' of colonial territories by the United Nations; does not provide for reports from the administering Power or for accepting petitions from the inhabitants or for visits to the territories; does not speak of any *functions* of the United Nations with respect to colonial territories; and does not designate any organ of the United Nations to discharge any responsibilities of the United Nations with respect to them. All that Chapter XI does contain in the way of procedural machinery is an obligation imposed by Article 73 (e) to 'transmit regularly to the Secretary-General *for information purposes* . . . statistical and other information of a technical nature relating to economic, social, and educational conditions in the territories', and the history of the drafting of Chapter XI shows that it was no accident that political information was omitted from this provision. Nevertheless, the ink was scarcely dry upon the Charter before India and other states were proposing that a special committee of the General Assembly, composed on the same pattern as the Trusteeship Council, should be established on a permanent basis with the function of exercising 'supervision and control' of non-self-governing territories on behalf of the United Nations and that political and constitutional information should be included in the information transmitted by the administering state. These proposals produced a sharp reaction from the administering states, some of whom maintained that Chapter XI was never intended to be more than a declaration of policy—a statement of aims—by the administering states, conferring no power on the United Nations to intervene in any way in the administration of colonial territories.

A mere comparison of the provisions of Chapters XI with those of Chapters XII and XIII appears strongly to confirm that the Charter intended to put non-self-governing colonial territories on a quite different footing from trusteeship territories. In consequence, proposals to hear petitions or evidence from individuals or to send a visiting mission to the territory, such as have sometimes been made by members, would appear to go well beyond the intentions of the Charter. On the other hand, the use of the word 'declaration' in international instruments is by no means inconsistent with the acceptance of legal obligations and the key words of Article 73 '*accept as a sacred trust the obligation*' are undoubtedly words which *prima facie* connote legal obligation. In face of this language it is difficult to believe that the provisions of Article 73, like the human rights provisions of Articles 55 and 56, do not create true legal obligations for Members, even although no machinery was provided for their application.

Moreover, as the United Kingdom Government itself pointed out, the General Assembly is specifically authorized by Article 10 to discuss any matter within the scope of the Charter so that it is difficult to deny it the right to discuss any point arising out of information concerning a non-self-governing territory provided under Article 73. Nor can it be denied that Article 22 empowers the General Assembly to 'establish such subsidiary organs as it deems necessary for the performance of its functions'. But, having regard to the silence of Article 73 as to the 'functions' of the United Nations with respect to non-self-governing territories, it is debatable whether Article 22 authorizes the General Assembly to establish a subsidiary committee on the lines of the Trusteeship Council to examine into and report upon the administration of colonial territories.

The General Assembly has not tested the legal position by asking the International Court for an advisory opinion. Instead, a somewhat uneasy compromise has been reached between the points of view of the administering states and of the protagonists for United Nations supervision of colonial territories. A special Committee, composed of the administering states and an equal number of other states, was established on an annual basis up to 1949 when it was appointed for a three-year period and has since been regularly renewed for further three-year periods. If still criticized by some administering states as going beyond the Charter, the Committee appears to have become an established subsidiary organ of the United Nations. Its terms of reference are (*a*) to examine the Secretary-General's summaries and analyses of the information transmitted by the administering states together with any relevant papers emanating from the Specialized Agencies,[1] and (*b*) to make 'such procedural recommendations as it may deem fit and such *substantive* recommendations as it may deem desirable relating to functional fields generally *but not with respect to individual territories*'. The Committee is thus restricted to making pronouncements on general policy and general principle with respect to non-self-governing territories. Even so, its debates and, still more, the debates in the Assembly on its report, have provided the occasion for onslaughts on the colonial system and for much prejudiced criticism by states whose own methods of government and

[1] *Supra*, pp. 121-5.

economic and social standards fall below those of the colonial régimes which they criticize. In this way Chapter XI may have done something to promote the wrong form of political agitation in colonial territories and premature demands for independence. On the other hand, by driving the administering states to explain their own problems and policies, Chapter XI has both prevented them from giving too much emphasis to gradualness in the political evolution of their territories and has helped to spread a wider understanding of the difficulties of promoting responsible self-government in politically under-developed territories. At any rate, the United Kingdom and other administering states, while maintaining that the Charter places them under no obligation to provide political information, have thought it to be in their best interests to supply it.

Another important and controversial point is whether the General Assembly has a say in the question whether any particular territory is or is not a 'non-self-governing territory' within the meaning of Chapter XI. Some administering states have strongly taken the position that the decision rests exclusively with the state concerned and that any pronouncement upon the point by the Assembly amounts to an intervention in internal constitutional matters. Thus, Spain and Portugal have declined to treat any of their overseas territories as falling within Chapter XI on the basis that their respective constitutions make the territories an integral part of the metropolitan state. The United Kingdom, while applying Chapter XI to the great majority of its dependent territories, has also asserted the right to determine the question for itself without the concurrence of the General Assembly. The same problem arises when a non-self-governing territory is claimed to have attained either 'full self-government' or 'independence' and to have thus passed out of the régime of Chapter XI. The General Assembly has asserted a competence to determine whether or not political changes in a territory justify the administering state in ceasing to transmit information under Chapter XI. In 1948 it resolved that administering states should communicate to the Secretary-General information concerning any political changes alleged to render Chapter XI no longer applicable. The administering states have conformed to this resolution but they do not concede that the Assembly has the competence to decide the question. When notifying the Secretary-General of a change, they state that information under Chapter XI will no longer be transmitted without waiting for the Assembly's view; Denmark so acted in the case of Greenland, the Netherlands in the cases of Surinam and the Antilles, the United States in the cases of Puerto Rico, Hawaii, and Alaska, France in the case of numerous territories of the French Union. This has not stopped the Assembly from debating particular cases, such as Puerto Rico, Surinam, and the Antilles at some length.

The difference of opinion between the administering states and the majority in the Assembly as to the scope of the legal régime created by Chapter XI remains unresolved. The practical effect, however, of inserting Chapter XI in the Charter has clearly been to render administering states politically accountable in some measure to the General Assembly with respect to their non-self-governing territories.

(b) *Trust Territories*

After the First World War, article 22 of the Covenant of the League of Nations created a new status for the territories surrendered by Germany and Turkey to the Principal Allied and Associated Powers which were 'inhabited by peoples not yet able to stand by themselves'. The guiding principle of the new institution was declared to be that the well-being of these peoples forms a 'sacred trust of civilization'; and this trust was to be carried out by placing them under the 'tutelage' of different members of the League as 'mandatories on behalf of the League'.

This system of mandates has now been replaced under the Charter of the United Nations by the International Trusteeship system, but the objectives of the new system are much the same as those of the old. The substantial objective is 'to promote the political, economic, social, and educational advancement of the inhabitants of the trust territories, and their progressive development towards self-government or independence as may be appropriate to the particular circumstances of each territory and its peoples and the freely expressed wishes of the peoples concerned, and as may be provided by the terms of each trusteeship agreement'.

The status of the authority administering a trust
territory resembles in some respects a protectorate,
but it is a 'responsible' protectorate in which the
protecting power has obligations as well as rights both
towards the inhabitants of the territory and towards
the United Nations. There is to be 'equal treatment
in social, economic and commercial matters for all
members of the United Nations and their nationals,
and also equal treatment for the latter in the administration of justice', but this is not to prejudice the
fundamental objectives of the system. Most of the
mandates allowed the military training of the natives
only for local defence and police purposes; in trust
territories the administering authority may use
volunteer forces not only for these purposes, but also
in carrying out its own obligations towards the
Security Council.

A territory can only enter the trusteeship system by
an individual agreement, and there are three kinds of
territory to which the system may be applied. They
are: (*a*) Territories previously held under mandate;
the surviving mandated territories have now, with
the exception of South-West Africa, been placed
under trusteeship by their mandatories. (*b*) Territories detached from enemy states as a result of the
Second World War; this has been applied to Italian
Somaliland, which has been placed under Italian
trusteeship, and to certain Pacific islands detached
from Japan. (*c*) Territories voluntarily placed under
the system by the states responsible for their administration, in which case the administering authority

may be either one or more states, or the United
Nations itself. There have not so far been any trusteeships of this category.

The present position concerning the mandate of
South-West Africa has been dealt with by the International Court of Justice in no less than three advisory opinions. In the first[1] the Court held that under
the Charter the Union of South Africa is not obliged
to place the territory under trusteeship but is itself
not competent to modify the status of the territory
except with the agreement of the United Nations;
that meanwhile the territory remains subject to the
international obligations attaching to the mandate
under the League; that the supervisory functions of
the League have passed to the United Nations so that
the Union is now bound to submit annual reports
to the General Assembly; and that the supervision
exercised by the General Assembly should not exceed
in degree that which applied under the mandate
system and should conform as far as possible to the
procedure followed by the Council of the League.
On the General Assembly proposing to apply the
two-thirds majority voting rule to questions concerning the mandate, the Union objected that under the
League unanimity was required for decisions concerning the mandate. The Court in a second Opinion[2]
upheld the view of the General Assembly, saying in
effect that, the voting procedure of an international
organization being part of its constitution, it is the
voting rules of the Charter, not of the Covenant,

[1] *I.C.J. Reports*, 1950, p. 128.   [2] *I.C.J. Reports*, 1955, p. 67.

which now apply to the Assembly's decisions concerning the mandate. Meanwhile, the General Assembly had set up a special Committee on South-West Africa to exercise its right of supervision, but the Union, refusing to accept the Court's view that the right of supervision had passed to the United Nations, declined to co-operate in any way with this Committee. The latter was therefore driven to examine into and report on the position in the territory on the basis of any material that came to its hand. This included petitions from inhabitants of the territory, and the General Assembly then asked the Court whether the oral hearing of petitioners would be permissible under the principles which the Court had laid down in its first Opinion. Again, the General Assembly was upheld by the Court.[1] It was true that oral hearings had not in fact been given to petitioners under the League system; but the Council of the League had possessed the competence to authorize such oral hearings if it had thought fit, and this competence had now passed to the General Assembly. Since the grant of oral hearings would put the Committee in a better position to judge the merits of petitions it could not be said to add to the burden of the Mandatory Power. Furthermore, the need to grant oral hearings had arisen directly out of the refusal of the Union to give effect to the first Opinion of the Court and to co-operate with the Committee so that they fell within the Court's earlier ruling that the procedure must *as far as possible* conform to the procedure

[1] *I.C.J. Reports*, 1956, p. 23.

followed under the League. The Union has remained completely obdurate in face of the Court's opinions while its apartheid policy has provoked the strongest reactions in the General Assembly. The latest development is that Ethiopia and Liberia have both instituted proceeding before the International Court alleging breaches of the Mandate, and these proceedings are now pending.

Generally the functions of the United Nations in relation to a trust territory belong to the General Assembly. But a trustee agreement may designate part or all of a trust territory as 'a strategic area or areas', and when an agreement contains this provision the Security Council exercises these functions, including the approval of the agreement itself. The provision about strategic areas is believed to have been inserted in the Charter to meet the case of the Pacific islands, which the United States regards as necessary for American defence, but which the Atlantic Charter precludes her from annexing outright.

The General Assembly or the Security Council as the case may be has the assistance of a Trusteeship Council which has taken the place of the former Permanent Mandates Commission through which the Council of the League used to supervise the mandatory system. But the new body is constituted on a different plan. The Mandates Commission consisted of members chosen individually for their personal fitness for the work, and it had a majority drawn from non-mandatory states. The members of the Trusteeship Council are not individuals but states, though each state is required to designate 'one specially qualified person' to represent it; it consists of the states administering trust territories, of any of the five Great Powers which do not administer such territories, and of so many other members elected for three-year terms by the General Assembly as will ensure that the total membership is equally divided between states administering and those not administering trust territories. Its functions are to consider the annual reports which the administering authority for each trust territory within the competence of the General Assembly is bound to render; to formulate a questionnaire on the political, economic, social, and educational advancement of the inhabitants of each trust territory; and to provide for periodic visits to the trust territories at times agreed on with the administering authority.

The Mandates Commission was in general a business-like body, which recognized the difficulties as well as the obligations of colonial administrators, and the experience which it accumulated from examining the practice of states with differing colonizing methods made it a valuable repository of information available to all. The Trusteeship Council, composed as it is of representatives of governments, has shown itself more subject to political cross-currents than was the Mandates Commission, which was composed of independent experts. Like the Mandates Commission, it receives and considers petitions from the inhabitants of the territories. Unlike the Mandates Commission, however, it sends periodic visiting missions to the territories which, by showing the United Nations flag and making direct contact with the inhabitants, bring home to them the existence of the supervisory powers of the United Nations. In addition, it receives annual reports from the Administering Powers and itself sends forward a report on the territories to the General Assembly. The Assembly, where the anti-colonial movement has found the strongest expression, has sought unremittingly to accelerate the advance of the trusteeship territories to independence or self-government and has required the Administering Powers to state their programmes for achieving this purpose of the trusteeship system. Four African trusteeships have already been terminated by the territories becoming independent.

Under the mandatory system courts of law had on occasion to consider the nature and extent of the powers exercisable by the mandatory state, and some of the answers given will be equally applicable to the trusteeship system, for example on the question of sovereignty. It was held by the South African courts in *Rex* v. *Christian*[1] that the Union, as mandatory of South-West Africa, possessed sufficient internal sovereignty there to warrant a charge of high treason against an inhabitant of the mandated territory. Treason by South African law is an offence against a government which possesses *majestas* or sovereignty, and the nature of the Union's powers

[1] *S.A. Law Rep.* [1924] Appellate Division, p. 101; *Ann. Dig.*, 1923–4, p. 27.

was thus very relevant to the point at issue. But in *Ffrost* v. *Stevenson*[1] the High Court of Australia had to decide a question relating to the extent of the legislative powers of the Commonwealth in the mandated territory of New Guinea, and Latham C.J. said:

'. . . I doubt whether any light can be thrown upon the question to be decided by this Court by considering the applicability to mandated territories of a conception which is itself so uncertain and so disputable as that of sovereignty. Authorities of the highest standing differ among themselves as to whether or not the conception of sovereignty is applicable, in what sense it is applicable, and, if it is applicable, as to where sovereignty resides. The grant of mandates introduced a new principle into international law. . . . The position of a mandatory in relation to a mandated territory must be regarded as *sui generis*. . . . The mandatory, as a kind of international trustee, receives the territory subject to the provisions of the mandate which limit the exercise of the governmental powers of the mandatory. . . . A mandated territory is not a possession in the ordinary sense.'

It is believed that to introduce the concept of sovereignty into any discussion of the nature either of mandates or of trust territories is, from the point of view of international law, merely confusing. Municipal law, as in *Rex* v. *Christian*, may make it necessary to do so; international law does not. The notion that we must look for sovereignty in a mandated or a trust territory implies that sovereignty is an indestructible substance which we shall surely find

[1] *Ann. Dig.*, 1935–7, p. 98.

in any area if only we look closely enough. But government under mandate or trust is surely an alternative to, not a species of, government under sovereignty; and, just as English law has two different régimes for the holding of property, namely private ownership and trusts, so now international law has acquired two régimes for government, that is to say, sovereignty and the mandate or the trust. Like the rights of a trustee in our law, so the rights of an international trustee state have their foundation in its obligations under the Charter and under the trust agreement; they are tools given it in order to achieve the work assigned to it, and the measure of its powers, the test by which its possession of any particular power must be determined, is that the law has provided it with all the tools that are necessary for its task, but with those only.[1]

§ 4. *Leases*

Leases of territory by one state to another which closely resemble the ordinary leases of private law, for example leases of specified areas in ports for transit purposes, are not uncommon; but there are other leases, political in character, in which it is usual to regard the use of the term as no more than a diplomatic device for rendering a permanent loss of territory more palatable to the dispossessed state by avoiding any mention of annexation and holding out

[1] This view was originally suggested by the writer in an article, 'Trusts and Mandates', in *B.Y.I.L.*, 1929, p. 217, which was referred to with approval by Evatt J. in the Australian case cited in the text.

the hope of eventual recovery. In 1898 China leased
Kiao-Chau to Germany and other territories to Great
Britain, France, and Russia, the Russian lease being
transferred to Japan in 1905, and the German in
1919. But it has been justly pointed out[1] that this
interpretation of the Chinese leases is inadmissible.
Not only did China by the terms of the leases themselves retain and actually exercise more than a
nominal sovereignty over the leased territories; but
even if the lessee states intended the leases as dis-
guised cessions, this was certainly not the intention
of the lessor, China, and we are not entitled to estimate the legal character of a transaction by conjec-
turing the undisclosed intentions of one of the parties
only. Moreover, the event seems to have confirmed
the straightforward construction of these leases, for at
the Conference of Washington in 1922 the restitution
of most of the territories to China was promised. In
1930 Great Britain returned to China the leased territory of Weihaiwei.

§ 5. *Servitudes*

Many writers maintain that international law
recognizes rights over territory which correspond to
the servitudes of Roman or the easements of English
law, but the evidence they are able to adduce does
not seem to bear out their contention. The exact
point which is at issue in the controversy will be seen
if we recall the nature of a servitude in Roman law:

[1] Lauterpacht, *Private Law Sources and Analogies of International Law*,
pp. 183–90.

it is a right enjoyed by the owner of one piece of land, the *praedium dominans*, not in his personal capacity, but in his capacity as owner of the land, over land which belongs to another, the *praedium serviens*. Its essential characteristic is that it is a right *in rem*, that is to say, it is exercisable not only against a particular owner of the servient tenement but against any successor to him in title, and not only by a particular owner of the dominant tenement but also by his successors in title. It is, of course, quite common that a state should acquire rights of one kind or another over the territory of another state, the right, for example, to have an airfield or free port facilities, but ordinarily at least such rights are merely rights *in personam* like any other treaty-created right; they do not in any way resemble servitudes. The test of an international servitude can only be, on the analogy of private law, that the right should be one that will survive a change in the sovereignty of either of the two states concerned in the transaction. There is no real evidence that any such right exists in the international system.

The leading case is the award in the *North Atlantic Fisheries Arbitration* between Britain and the United States in 1910.[1] Americans enjoy certain fishing rights off the coast of Newfoundland under a treaty of 1818, and the United States argued that this treaty had created a servitude in their favour; the right was a derogation from British sovereignty over the Island, and the result of this division of the sovereignty was, it was claimed, that Britain had no

[1] Wilson, *Hague Arbitration Cases*, p. 174.

independent right to regulate the fishery. The Court rejected this contention; the right, they thought, was not a sovereign right but merely an economic one, and there was nothing in the treaty to show that the parties had intended it to be anything else. The Court did not actually say that servitudes are unknown to international law, but their language implies that that is what they thought; what they did say was that the right in this case was not a servitude. To have held that it was would have meant that the benefit would pass by operation of law, if the case should arise, to a new sovereign over the territory of the United States, and the burden of it to a new sovereign over Newfoundland. It is purely fanciful to imagine that any such remote contingency as these was present in the minds of those who made the treaty.

That then is the test; in the terminology of English real property law the right must 'run with the land', and the difficulty of arriving at a decisive conclusion of the controversy is that the occasions which allow this test to be applied so rarely occur in international life, and that even when they do the answer is more likely than not to be wholly indecisive. A case upon which most of the writers[1] who believe in the existence of international servitudes place great reliance illustrates this difficulty. It was provided in the Treaty of Paris of 1815 that the Alsatian town of Huningen was never to be fortified. This arrangement was made in the interests of the Swiss Canton of

[1] See, for example, Oppenheim, *International Law*, 8th ed. vol. i, § 207; Reid in *H.R.*, vol. xlv, p. 45.

Basle. When the treaty was made Huningen was French; in 1871 it became German; in 1919 French again. The facts are not altogether easy to ascertain, but it is said that neither France nor Germany ever fortified Huningen, and it is suggested that that proves the existence of a servitude which survived the changes of sovereignty. But, in fact, it proves nothing at all. Huningen may have been left unfortified for quite other reasons; very likely new conditions of warfare made the fortifying of it unnecessary. It does not prove that neither Germany nor France could legally have fortified it, nor that if, for example, Switzerland had been annexed by Italy, Italy would have had a right to insist on its non-fortification.[1]

No writer has satisfactorily explained how we are to distinguish a servitude from other rights that one state may have over the territory of another, for it is not suggested that all such rights are servitudes. For example, Britain had a right to keep troops on Egyptian territory, but this was clearly a merely contractual right, a right *in personam* not *in rem*. But what is it that distinguishes this right from that in the Huningen case or the *North Atlantic Fisheries case?* The only answer is that a servitude is intended to survive a change in the sovereignty. But do states ever have that intention when they make a treaty?

It seems probable that the notion of servitude has been introduced into the terminology of international law owing to the fact that the international rules

[1] See the examination of the Huningen case by Professor Kelsen in *H.R.*, vol. xlv, p. 11. Also McNair in *B.Y.I.L.*, 1925.

relating to territory were in the main originally taken from the Roman rules relating to the ownership of land. Thus the word came to be used loosely to denote merely rights held by one state over the territory of another. But if a right over territory does not have the character of being a right *in rem*, it is merely confusing to call it a servitude, for in legal analysis it does not differ from any other right created by a treaty.

§ 6. *Maritime Territory*

Internal waters and territorial sea. The sovereignty of a state extends beyond its land territory to certain areas of sea which form part of its domain either as internal waters or as territorial sea. The law governing the delimitation of these areas has been in course of formation during the past three centuries and was the principal subject of controversy at the codification conferences convened at The Hague in 1930 and at Geneva in 1958 and 1960. Many of the points of difference were resolved in the Geneva Convention of 1958 on the Territorial Sea and the Contiguous Zone, signed by some fifty states; and, although only very few of the twenty-two ratifications necessary to bring the Convention into force have so far been deposited, the text of that Convention can be regarded as representing the nearest thing that there is to an agreed statement of the modern law governing internal and territorial waters and the contiguous zone.

Internal waters. International law has from the earliest times recognized that a state is entitled, within certain limits, to treat ports, estuaries, bays, and other enclosed areas of the sea as subject to its sovereignty. Up to the end of the seventeenth century a broad view was taken of the waters which might be claimed in this way. No protest was, for example, made by any state against the so-called King's Chambers declared by James I in 1604 as the waters within which England would enforce her neutrality. These King's Chambers consisted of all the waters enclosed within imaginary straight lines drawn from the westerly tip of the Isle of Man to Anglesey and thence from extreme headland to extreme headland all the way around the English coast. At that period there still lingered much more sweeping claims to maritime sovereignty, such as those of Sweden to the Baltic, Denmark–Norway to the northern seas, Spain to the West Atlantic and Pacific, Portugal to the South Atlantic and the Indian Ocean. By the end of the eighteenth century, however, these claims had melted away and been replaced by claims to a comparatively narrow belt of territorial sea extending outwards all along the coast. Inevitably there then arose the problem whether a state was to be entitled to claim all the waters of its bays as internal waters or whether in bays, as on the open coast, it was to be limited to a belt of territorial sea; and, if bays were to be claimable as internal waters, there was the further problem of what waters could be said to fall within the concept of a 'bay'.

The Anglo-French Fisheries Convention of 1839 adopted a ten-mile rule as determining the maximum width of the bays within which exclusive fishery rights might be claimed, and the same limit appeared in other European treaties, including the North Sea Fisheries Convention of 1882. At the same time, however, quite a number of states laid claim to particular bays of greater width, whether on historic or other grounds; and, apart from the dispute between the United States and Great Britain as to fisheries in Canadian 'bays' under the Treaty of Ghent of 1818, there does not seem to have been much disposition to challenge these claims. In addition, quite a number of states, which possessed island fringes along their coasts, laid claim to the waters lying between the islands and the mainland; for example, Norway and Sweden to their fiords and Cuba to the waters within her cays. Consequently, when eventually the *North Atlantic Fisheries Arbitration*[1] took place in 1910 to settle the meaning of Canadian 'bays' in the Treaty of Ghent, state practice, though showing some tendency towards the ten-mile rule, was not uniform. Indeed, in that arbitration both the United States and Great Britain contended that no general rule of customary law had yet come into being with regard to the width of bays that might be claimed as internal waters. In 1927, in the case of the *Fagernes*,[2] the British Attorney-General again recognized that no definite limit had been established for bays; but he referred to the tendency in modern times to restrict the width of territorial bays, suggesting that a limit of the order of ten or twelve miles seemed to have

[1] Wilson, *Hague Arbitration Cases*, p. 182.
[2] [1927] P., p. 311.

most support; moreover, the Crown in that case expressly disclaimed jurisdiction at a point in the middle of the Bristol Channel where the Channel is about twenty miles wide. At the 1930 Codification Conference a ten-mile limit was proposed for bays not subject to historic claims, but owing to the breakdown of the Conference no decision was taken on the point; and when the question came before the International Court in 1954[1] the Court held that the ten-mile limit had not acquired the authority of a general rule of international law. Shortly afterwards the question was taken up by the International Law Commission, which in 1955 proposed a limit of twenty-five miles for non-historic bays but reduced it to fifteen miles in its final report.

The rule adopted in the Geneva Convention of 1958 on the Territorial Sea and Contiguous Zone[2] is that if the distance between the low-water marks of the natural entrance points of a bay does not exceed twenty-four miles, a closing line may be drawn and the waters so enclosed are to be considered as internal waters; if, however, the natural entrance points are more than twenty-four miles apart, a straight base line of twenty-four miles may be drawn inside the bay in such a way as to enclose the maximum area of water that is possible with a line of that length. The twenty-four mile limit is a novel one, and its whole authority therefore derives from the 1958 Convention, which at the same time defines with

[1] *Anglo-Norwegian Fisheries Case, I.C.J. Reports*, 1951, at p. 131.
[2] Article 7.

geometrical precision the indentations where this rule may be applied. An indentation is not to be regarded as a bay for the purpose of the rule unless its total area is at least as large as that of the semicircle whose diameter is the line drawn across its mouth. This definition is a strict one and goes a long way to obviating the risk of extravagant expansion of 'internal' waters by drawing twenty-four mile baselines across mere curvatures of the coast.

Wherever it is permitted to draw a straight line across an indentation for the purpose of claiming the waters inside it as internal waters, the line also serves as the base-line from which the belt of territorial sea is drawn at that part of the coast. The closing line of the bay becomes, as it were, the notional coast line and the territorial sea extends to seaward from the straight base-line, just as it does from the low-water mark on the open coast.

The status of waters within island fringes was the subject of the *Anglo-Norwegian Fisheries* case,[1] which was decided by the International Court in 1951. The case concerned the validity of Norwegian Decrees promulgating a series of straight base-lines along large sections of the Norwegian coast, which are either heavily indented or bestrewn with innumerable islands. These base-lines nowhere followed the shoreline, but consisted of imaginary straight lines, some as much as forty-four miles long, linking selected points either on mainland promontories or on islands or rocklets some distance out to sea; and Norway

[1] *I.C.J. Reports*, 1951, p. 116.

claimed as her internal waters all the sea areas lying inside these straight lines. The Court, by a majority, upheld the validity of these lines not only on the historic grounds claimed by Norway but also as not being contrary to international law. The Court based its finding as to the validity of the Norwegian lines under general international law essentially upon the following propositions, for which it cited no previous authority: (1) if geographically a fringe of islands forms a whole with the mainland, it may be treated as part of the mainland coast for the purpose of delimiting territorial waters; (2) the governing principle is that the belt of territorial sea must follow the 'general direction of the coast'; (3) off an ordinary coast the simplest method is for the base-line to follow the actual line of the coast, but where the coast is deeply indented or bordered by an archipelago a geometrical construction of straight lines is called for and is allowed under international law; (4) the criteria for testing the legitimacy of any particular lines are (a) whether they 'depart appreciably from the general direction of the coast' and (b) whether the sea areas lying inside them are 'sufficiently closely linked to the land domain to be subject to the régime of internal waters'.

The somewhat loose language of the judgment in the *Fisheries* case left it doubtful as to exactly how far the Court had meant to set aside the long-established principle that the territorial sea is to be measured from the low-water mark along the coast and to permit the use of straight base-lines. Whatever may have been the intention of the Court, the International Law Commission and the Geneva Conference of 1958 interpreted the judgment restrictively when incorporating the law which it laid down into the Convention on the Territorial Sea and Contiguous Zone. For Article 3 provides that 'the normal base-line for measuring the breadth of the territorial sea is the low-water line *along* the coast', while Article 7, as has already been seen, provides a specific twenty-four mile line for 'bays' and defines a 'bay' by a geometrical formula which is quite different from anything to be found in the Court's judgment. Moreover, Article 4, which introduces the principles laid down by the Court into the Convention, is in terms confined to 'localities where the coastline is deeply indented and cut into, or if there is a fringe of islands along the coast in its immediate vicinity'. It is only in those special situations that 'the method of straight base-lines joining appropriate points may be employed'; but where such a situation does exist, neither the twenty-four mile limit nor the geometrical formula applicable to bays is operative. The legality of the base-lines then depends on whether they 'depart to any appreciable extent from the general direction of the coast' and whether the 'sea areas are sufficiently closely linked to the land domain to be subject to the régime of internal waters'. Clearly, these tests are to some extent a matter of pure opinion and the basic concept of the 'general direction of the coast' is imprecise since much turns on the scale of the chart on which stretches of the coast are viewed. Nor are

these tests made any more precise by the further provision—also taken from the judgment in the *Fisheries*
case—that in determining particular base-lines 'account may be taken of economic interests peculiar
to the region concerned, the reality and the importance of which are clearly evidenced by long usage';
for this would seem to encourage recourse to a maximum use of straight lines by reference to coastal
fisheries. The only safeguard provided by the Convention is that the coastal state must clearly indicate
the straight base-lines which it claims on charts and
must give publicity to the charts.

In general, it must be said that the subjective
character of the rule applicable to heavily indented
or to island-fringed coasts, combined with the absence of any limit upon the length of the individual
straight lines, leaves some loophole for extravagant
claims to 'internal waters' on these coasts. It therefore seems particularly necessary that the rule in
Article 4 should be confined to coasts genuinely to
be regarded as 'heavily indented' or 'island-fringed',
and that in all other cases the low-water-mark rule
in Article 3 and the rule for ordinary bays in Article 7
should be strictly applied. The risk that Article 4
carries of considerable extensions of 'internal waters'
off island-fringed coasts also gives particular importance to the provision in Article 5 under which
any new enclosure of areas of territorial waters or
high sea by recourse to straight base-lines is not to
affect the right of innocent passage for vessels of other
nations. Otherwise, in a number of areas in the world,

channels inside islands, which are much used by international shipping, might cease to be subject to the right of innocent passage.[1]

The territorial sea and the contiguous zone. The doctrine of the territorial sea has traditionally been regarded as founded upon the principle laid down by the Dutch jurist Bynkershoek in his *De Dominio Maris* in 1702 that a state's sovereignty extended as far out to sea as cannon would reach; and the three-mile limit has traditionally been represented as simply the rough equivalent of the maximum range of cannon in the eighteenth century. Historically, however, the modern doctrine of a continuous belt of territorial waters appears to have been derived in the course of the eighteenth century from two sources: (1) a cannon shot rule prevalent in the Mediterranean and (2) a Scandinavian doctrine of a belt of territorial waters measured in leagues. The Mediterranean rule was earlier than Bynkershoek and did not relate to a continuous belt of territorial sea; for this rule went no further than to accord exemption from capture in time of war to merchant ships lying within cannon range of any fortified neutral port. Denmark, on the other hand, when driven to abandon her claim to all the northern seas, first reduced it to all waters within range of vision from her shores, then to four leagues, and, finally, in 1745, to one league. This league, how-

[1] This point is equally important in regard to ocean, as distinct from coastal, archipelagoes; the 1958 Convention does not, however, deal with the problem of the internal waters of ocean archipelagoes, which still remains to be solved.

ever, was not the three-mile league in use in the rest
of Europe, but the Scandinavian league of four sea-
miles. A few years later France declined to accept
Denmark's four-mile league as a neutrality limit in
the Seven Years War, countering with the suggestion
of a three-mile limit on the basis that maximum
cannon range might possibly be said to reach to that
distance. Agreement was not reached, and this accidental difference in the scale of the league used in
Scandinavian countries and in the rest of Europe was
to prove a serious obstacle to a general agreement on
the width of the territorial sea.

The three-mile limit was first applied in 1793,
when the new-born United States, caught between
France and Great Britain, was forced to define her
neutral waters, and proposed that the two belligerents should respect her neutrality up to one marine
league; and in doing so she said that the smallest
distance claimed by any state was 'the range of a
cannon ball usually stated at one sea-league'. Both
belligerents agreed, and thereby recognized the
three-mile limit as the minimum limit of neutral
waters. In fisheries the three-mile limit first appeared
in the Treaty of Ghent of 1818, defining Canada's
exclusive fisheries, then in the Anglo-French Fisheries
Convention of 1839 and in a series of later treaties
between European countries. Thus both in North
America and in Europe a one-league (whether of
three or four miles) system was prevalent. Apart
from Russia, whose claims were apt to veer between
twelve and three miles, the main dissentients were

Spain and Portugal, who had announced two-league claims in the eighteenth century. When, however, their colonies in Latin America became independent states, they did not adopt the two-league system of their mother countries but the marine league of three miles, as did the countries of the East, Persia, Siam, China, and Japan. Accordingly, by the beginning of the present century the one-league system was world-wide and had comparatively few exceptions. Further-more, although in its origins the one-league system had had associations with the cannon-shot doctrine and echoes of the doctrine were still to be found in diplomatic documents, the one-league limit had be-come an independent rule and the cannon-shot prin-ciple a mere 'historical reminiscence'.[1] On the other hand, the increase in the speed of ships and the in-vention of trawling had led to some questioning of the adequacy of a three-mile limit.

In any event, the question of the width of the terri-torial sea was complicated by additional claims to jurisdiction in 'contiguous zones', that is, zones of high sea contiguous to the territorial sea; and the concept of the contiguous zone afterwards assumed enormous importance at the 1930 Codification Con-ference and again at Geneva in 1958 and 1960. Great Britain's policy concerning contiguous zones has been erratic and unfortunate. She was herself re-sponsible for introducing them into international law in her eighteenth-century Hovering Acts, which au-thorized the seizure of smugglers on the high seas

[1] Raestad, *R.G.D.I.P.* (1912), pp. 617–23.

at varying distances, two, three, four, eight, and even, in one Act, one hundred leagues from shore. No state protested against these Acts, while the United States and a number of Latin American states, on becoming independent, adopted similar customs zones, usually of twelve miles; some European states also had customs laws authorizing seizure of smugglers outside territorial waters. In 1876, however, Great Britain completely reversed her policy. In the Customs Consolidation Act of that year she repealed the long series of Hovering Acts and took up the position that under general international law states are not entitled to exercise customs jurisdiction against foreign vessels on the high seas and that a state desiring for special reasons to do so must acquire the right by concluding a treaty with the other states concerned. The explanation of this volte-face appears to be that smuggling in the English Channel had been brought under control, while the hovering laws were proving embarrassing in contesting Spain's six-mile claim; and that it was feared that, if a definite right to a twelve-mile customs zone were recognized, it might sooner or later get converted into a twelve-mile territorial sea. The new British doctrine gained the adherence of states like Germany and Japan, but the United States and a number of other states did not abandon their view that contiguous zone jurisdiction in customs matters was an accepted customary right.

Great Britain's refusal to yield on the contiguous zone was the primary cause of her failure to secure the adoption of the three-mile limit as a general rule of international law at the 1930 Codification Conference on Territorial Waters. A minority of states were adamant for a four-mile or a six-mile limit, but a clear two-thirds—the required majority—of the Conference was in principle ready to pronounce the three-mile limit to be the accepted limit for territorial waters. A number of states, however, were not prepared to give their votes in favour of the three-mile limit unless their right to a contiguous zone up to twelve miles from shore for customs, revenue, and sanitary jurisdiction was also recognized. Great Britain, although declaring her willingness in proper cases to grant contiguous zone jurisdiction to other states over British vessels by treaty, declined to compromise, and the Conference collapsed. In retrospect, this must be considered to have been a major blunder, since a golden opportunity was lost of settling the issue of the three-mile limit on favourable terms, while the collapse of the Conference on that very issue undermined the claim of the three-mile limit to be an absolute rule. Some states went so far as to maintain that the failure of the Conference to agree upon the width of the territorial sea left every state free to fix its own limit according to its needs. But the failure of the Conference could not at a stroke wipe out all the existing state practice, under which the only universally accepted width for the territorial sea had been three miles and any larger claims had met with opposition from other states. Accordingly, if it was true that it was no longer possible to say that any claim larger than three miles was *ipso facto* contrary to international law, it was equally true that legally its enforceability depended on the extent to which it met with acceptance or opposition from other states.

In the period between 1930 and 1945 a few states formulated six-mile claims which met with protests from the United Kingdom and, in some cases, the United States. Then in 1945 the Truman proclamations concerning the continental shelf and the conservation of fisheries, which are discussed later on,[1] had a distinctly unsettling effect on state practice in regard to coastal waters. A number of Latin American states claimed exclusive rights to all the resources of the seas over their continental shelf, while further six- and even twelve-mile claims were announced by other states. Confronted with this situation, the International Law Commission did not find it possible to put forward any proposal on the width of the territorial sea. But it did formulate as a considered proposition of law the principle that 'international law does not permit an extension of the territorial sea beyond twelve miles'. It also, in another part of its report, came out strongly in favour of a right to a contiguous zone.

Many new states had come into existence since the 1930 Conference and no less than eighty-six states, over double the number of those at The Hague in 1930, voted at the Geneva Conference of 1958. The broad position at the beginning of the Conference was that some twenty-one states still claimed only three miles, seventeen states four or six miles, thir-

[1] *Infra*, pp. 213-14.

teen states between nine and twelve miles, and nine states exclusive rights in the waters of the continental shelf, while a number of others had not taken up a definite position. The three-mile states, so far from having the two-thirds majority that they had possessed in 1930, could not now muster one-third of the votes. Furthermore, fisheries assumed a far larger importance in the 1958 and 1960 Geneva Conferences than they had done in 1930, and it was fisheries, together with some purely political cross-currents, not the contiguous zone, that prevented any agreement being reached at Geneva on the width of the territorial sea. No difficulty was encountered on the coastal state's right to a contiguous zone for customs and analogous purposes. Article 24 of the 1958 Convention provides that in a zone of the high seas contiguous to its territorial sea the coastal state may exercise the control necessary to prevent and punish any infringement of its customs, fiscal, immigration, or sanitary regulations within its territory or territorial sea. The Article then declares that the contiguous zone 'may not extend beyond twelve miles from the base-line from which the territorial sea is measured'. This provision is important, not only as a limit on the width of contiguous zones, but as equally excluding all idea of a width of the territorial sea greater than twelve miles. For if a zone contiguous to the territorial sea can never extend beyond twelve miles from the base-line, it is very clear that the territorial sea cannot do so.

On the territorial sea itself there were at first

three main lines of approach: (*a*) a United States–
United Kingdom group favouring a three-mile territorial sea plus contiguous zone jurisdiction up to
twelve miles, exclusive fishery rights being confined
to territorial waters, though with provision for conservation of fisheries outside territorial waters in
another Convention; (*b*) a Canadian proposal to the
same effect but with the important difference that the
coastal state would also have exclusive jurisdiction
in fisheries within the contiguous zone, that is, up to
twelve miles from the base-line; (*c*) an Afro-Asian-
Soviet group favouring the right of a coastal state to
choose its own limit for the territorial sea up to twelve
miles from the base-line. Half-way through the Conference the United Kingdom, in an effort to break
the deadlock, offered as a compromise a six-mile
territorial sea plus the contiguous zone out to twelve
miles; this would automatically have meant that exclusive fisheries would extend to six miles from shore,
but this was not enough for Canada and some other
states. The United States two weeks later repeated
the main British proposal, with the addition of a
right for the coastal state to regulate and exploit
fisheries in the contiguous zone, subject to the preservation indefinitely of the rights of other states
which had regularly fished there during the previous
five years. The maintenance in perpetuity of existing fishing rights within a twelve-mile zone was not
acceptable to Canada, who then voted with the
Afro-Asian-Soviet group for a twelve-mile territorial
sea. Nevertheless, the United States proposal made

sufficient headway in the voting for it to be considered worthwhile to convene a second Conference in 1960 to try and resolve this issue, the only one left unsettled in the 1958 Convention. At the second Conference the United States and Canada ultimately put forward jointly a revised version of the United States proposal: a territorial sea of six miles plus a contiguous zone extending a further six miles with exclusive fishery rights in the contiguous zone for the coastal state; the 'vested interests' of other states in the contiguous zone fisheries to be preserved *but only for a period of ten years, after which they would cease.* In other words, the special importance of coastal fisheries to some states, such as Canada, Norway, and Iceland, was to be recognized by extending the exclusive rights of coastal states to twelve miles, but there was to be a ten-year moratorium in order to prevent this change in the international law of fisheries from inflicting undue hardship on foreign fishermen with 'vested interests' in the affected areas. This well-conceived compromise was supported by the United States and by many European states which have large overseas fishery interests despite the sacrifice involved, and it was confidently expected at the Conference that it would obtain a two-thirds majority at the final vote. It failed to do so by a single vote and, although it afterwards transpired that one or two states might have cast their votes differently, if they had known that their votes were necessary to save the proposal, no rule was adopted at the Conference concerning the width of the territorial sea. The compromise having failed, the United States and United Kingdom have reverted to the three-mile limit, declining, as they are entitled to do, to recognize any larger limit as valid against them without their agreement. Many other states, however, continue to claim six or twelve miles, and the question of the width of the territorial sea remains a serious potential source of future difficulties.[1]

§ 7. *The Continental Shelf*

'Continental Shelf' is a term which international law has recently borrowed from geology, while at the same time modifying its meaning. Off most of the coasts of the five continents the sea-bed shelves downwards, more or less gradually, for varying distances and then falls steeply to the ocean depths. The continental shelf thus formed is generally covered by comparatively shallow depths of sea; for the steep plunge to the ocean depths, though it occasionally occurs at greater depths, usually takes place at a depth of about 100 fathoms or 200 metres. Again, there are some seas, like the North Sea, Baltic, and Persian Gulf, which lie within the contours of the land mass of their own continents, and are indeed themselves merely submerged parts of the continents; off their coasts there is no steep descent to ocean depths, the sea-bed being covered from coast to

[1] The United Kingdom has already found it politically expedient to agree to Norway and Iceland having exclusive fisheries up to twelve miles, subject respectively to a ten-year and three-year moratorium in favour of British fishermen.

coast by comparatively shallow water. The continental shelf and other shallow areas have recently become of intense legal interest because technological progress has made it possible to extract from the subsoil of the sea-bed valuable minerals, particularly oil, by machinery installed in the open sea outside territorial waters.

Formerly, interest in the resources of the sea-bed and its subsoil was for practical purposes limited to (a) a few instances of submarine coal-mines worked by shafts driven outwards from the land through the subsoil of the sea-bed, and (b) sponge, oyster, and shell fisheries harvested by diving to the sea-bed and commonly referred to as 'sedentary fisheries'. Within the territorial sea there was no legal problem because the rights of the coastal state were recognized to embrace the sea-bed and subsoil as well as the waters of the territorial sea. It was also assumed that to extend a submarine mine shaft beyond the territorial sea was permissible, since it did not involve any interference with the use of the high seas; and for the same reason it was generally considered that the construction of a tunnel between France and Britain underneath the Channel would not be open to objection. As to 'sedentary fisheries' on the bed of the high seas, there was some difference of opinion as to how far, and by what legal method, a state could obtain an exclusive right to exploit them. There was some authority for the view that exploitation of a sedentary fishery constituted 'occupation' of the sea-bed, conferring a title to the sovereignty of the areas of sea-bed in question;[1] but another, and probably safer, view was that a prescriptive user, giving an historic title, was necessary and that it only created exclusive rights in the sedentary fisheries, not sovereignty over the sea-bed itself.[2]

The legal situation in regard to the resources of the sea-bed and subsoil under the high seas has undergone a radical change since the Second World War through a rapid development of state claims[3] to the resources of the 'continental shelf' set in motion by President Truman's proclamation in September 1945, and endorsed by the international community in 1958 in the Geneva Convention on the Continental Shelf. By the Truman proclamation the United States declared that it regarded 'the natural resources of the sea-bed and subsoil of the continental shelf beneath the high seas but contiguous to the coasts of the United States as appertaining to the United States, subject to its jurisdiction and control'; and it stated that, if the territory of another state abutted on areas contiguous to the United States, the submarine boundary between them should be agreed on equitable principles. At the same time the proclamation underlined that the 'character as high seas of the waters of the continental shelf and the right to their free and unimpeded navigation' were in no way to be affected by the United States claim. A number

---

[1] Hurst, *B.Y.I.L.*, 1923–4, p. 34.

[2] Gidel, *Droit international public de la mer*, vol. 1, pp. 500–1.

[3] See Lauterpacht, *B.Y.I.L.*, 1950, p. 376; Waldock, 36 *Grotius Society*, p. 115.

of other states followed suit with claims closely modelled on that of the United States, and amongst these were nine British-protected states in the Persian Gulf; in addition, the United Kingdom advanced claims to submarine areas off the Bahamas and certain other dependent territories with the somewhat different formula of an extension of their submarine boundaries to include the continental shelf contiguous to their coasts. Australia's claim, though modelled on the Truman proclamation, also requires special notice, for it alone specifically mentioned sedentary fisheries amongst the natural resources of the sea-bed falling within its jurisdiction under the Truman doctrine. A number of Latin-American states, as previously noted, went far beyond the Truman doctrine in claiming exclusive jurisdiction over the resources not merely of the sea-bed and subsoil but also of the high seas above the continental shelf; and Iceland soon aligned herself with these states. Moreover, Chile and some other Latin-American states, which have virtually no shallow submarine areas off their coasts, distorted the Truman doctrine even further by proclaiming their sovereignty over all the sea-bed *at whatever depth* and over all the adjacent seas *at whatever depth* to a distance of 200 miles from shore to the extent necessary to reserve, protect, and exploit all the natural resources within or below those seas.

The International Law Commission, to whom the question was referred by the General Assembly in 1951, was unwilling to give 'the authority of a legal rule to a unilateral practice resting solely on the will of the States concerned' and did not regard the already extensive state practice as sufficient to establish the existence of a customary rule. However, it found that the state practice was supported by 'considerations of general utility' providing a sufficient basis for recommending the recognition of an exclusive right in the coastal state. Once the sea-bed and subsoil had become an object of active interest to coastal states, it was impossible to consider them as *res nullius*, capable of appropriation by the first-comer; and yet it was not practical in present circumstances to entrust the exploitation of the natural resources of submarine areas to international agencies. On the other hand, the effective exploitation of those natural resources must in most cases presuppose the use of installations on the territory of the coastal state and, in general, the mere 'propinquity' or 'contiguity' of the submarine areas to the territory of the coastal state militated in favour of the latter's sovereign rights being recognized. Accordingly, the Commission prepared a draft set of rules for the adoption of the continental-shelf doctrine into international law, and this draft, subject to a few amendments, became the Geneva Convention on the Continental Shelf.[1]

The legal doctrine of the continental shelf, as adopted in the Convention, goes beyond the geological concept; for Article 1 defines it as covering not only submarine areas adjacent to the coast up to

[1] See Report on the First United Nations Conference on the Law of the Sea, Cmd. No. 584.

a depth of 200 metres but also areas 'beyond that limit to where the depth admits of the exploitation of the natural resources'. This definition is a compromise designed to meet the susceptibilities of states, like Chile, whose contiguous areas are all deeper than 200 metres, and of states, like Norway, off whose coasts a deep submarine canyon occurs with shallow areas farther out to sea. The compromise really leaves the definition with an open end which puts scarcely any bounds to the exclusive claims which coastal states may hereafter assert over the sea-bed of the oceans, and it might have been better if some maximum limit had been attached to this part of the definition. The Convention recognizes that over the continental shelf, as so defined, the coastal state possesses *ipso jure*, without any act of occupation or proclamation, '*sovereign rights for the purpose of exploring it and exploiting its natural resources*'. It deliberately refrains from granting full territorial sovereignty over the continental shelf because of a fear that this might be but a short step to sovereignty over both the waters and air space above it; and to hammer the point home it expressly declares that the coastal state's rights over the continental shelf do not affect the legal status of the superjacent waters as high seas or that of the airspace above the high seas. Indeed, the point is further underlined in the definition of the natural resources included in the coastal state's rights over the continental shelf. These comprise the mineral and non-living resources of the sea-bed and subsoil and, in addition, living organisms belonging to sedentary species which at the harvestable stage are either immobile or unable to move except in constant physical contact with the sea-bed or subsoil; but free-moving fish and crustacea, even those which have their habitat at the bottom of the sea, retain their character as high seas fisheries. Thus the Convention appears to reject completely the claims of states, like Argentina, Chile, and Iceland, to exclusive rights over the natural resources of the high seas above the continental shelf.

The Convention also contains a number of further safeguards of the rights of other states: their right to lay and maintain cables and pipe-lines on the continental shelf is preserved; exploitation by the coastal state must not result in any unjustifiable interference with navigation, fishing or conservation of living resources or with scientific research; warning must be given of installations constructed on the continental shelf and the installations themselves removed when no longer in use; installations may not be put in places where they may interfere with the use of recognized sea-lanes essential to international navigation. Furthermore, the installations are not to have the legal status of islands, nor to affect in any way the delimitation of the coastal state's territorial waters.

Disputes have occasionally arisen concerning the boundary between the territorial waters of states, either when they confront each other across narrow straits or when their coasts adjoin. Boundary disputes are no less likely to occur in regard to areas of continental shelf which are contiguous to the coasts of two or more states and to cover this possibility the Convention, in effect, provides that, unless otherwise agreed or unless special circumstances justify a different solution, the boundary is to be the median line between the two coasts; and this is defined as the line equidistant from the 'base-lines' of the respective coasts.[1]

§ 8. *Territorial Air Space*

The First World War made suddenly evident the vital importance of the legal status of the air, and the experience of that war made it certain that states would accept nothing less than full sovereignty over the air space superincumbent over their territory and territorial waters. This doctrine was adopted as the law in a Convention on Air Navigation concluded at Paris in 1919[2] and reaffirmed in the Chicago Convention of 1944. Civil aviation was in its infancy in 1919 and there was no previous practice from which could be derived a *customary* right of innocent passage for the aircraft of other states through the air space. It followed that only by virtue of a treaty could one state enjoy rights in the air space of another; and, despite the enormous development of international air traffic which has since taken place, the principle has been maintained that the right to pass through the air space of another state is not a customary right

[1] Article 6.
[2] In Great Britain effect was given to the Convention by the Air Navigation Act, 1920.

but one which depends on treaty.[1] In other words, the principle is firmly established that each state has full and exclusive sovereignty in the air space over its territory and territorial waters.

A state's territorial air space has hitherto been assumed to be the whole cone of air space extending indefinitely upwards from the surface of its territory and territorial sea. Recent developments in rocket-propulsion, however, have called in question the adequacy of this concept of territorial air space, and have underlined the need for a more precise definition of its upward extent. They have enabled man to penetrate greater and greater distances into space beyond the earth's atmosphere and have opened the way to the use of outer space for scientific purposes and telecommunications by means of rockets and artificial satellites equipped with scientific instruments and even by man-manned rockets; indeed, they have brought within contemplation the landing of man on other planets. When objects are projected into space beyond the earth's atmosphere, application of the doctrine of territorial air space becomes virtually impossible. For objects in outer space beyond the earth's field of attraction do not rotate with the earth and do not, therefore, maintain a constant relationship to particular points on the surface of our globe; and even within the earth's field of attraction rockets and orbiting satellites change their positions in relation to areas on the surface of the globe at such heights and at such high speeds as to render the

[1] See *infra*, pp. 241–3.

exercise of jurisdiction and control, which is the very core of state sovereignty, almost meaningless. Furthermore, to admit a purely notional extension of state sovereignty infinitely into outer space would be to render the flight of almost every space rocket and satellite open to objection and protest by other states and to put an almost insuperable legal obstacle in the way of man's exploration and use of outer space.

Happily, while high-altitude flights by reconnaissance aircraft and meteorological balloons have provoked protests as infringements of air space, states have so far shown no disposition to protest against the flight of rockets or the orbiting of artificial satellites in outer space. As the number of space rockets and orbiting satellites that have been launched by the United States and Soviet Union is considerable, there are now substantial grounds for assuming general acceptance of the principle that at some point territorial sovereignty in air space ends and another legal régime begins under which flight, like navigation on the high seas, is in principle free to all. The question of the legal régime to be applied in outer space is already the subject of intense study but is still decidedly speculative, and in any event we are here only concerned with determining the upper limit of territorial air space. Various criteria have been suggested for fixing that limit, among which may be mentioned: (1) the limit of the earth's atmosphere, that is, anything between 500 and 18,000 miles according to the amount of gaseous content considered to constitute the atmosphere; (2) the limit of possible flight by instrumentalities dependent on air or gas for their flight, that is, a maximum of about twenty-five miles up; (3) the point, arrived at by reference to a number of physical factors, where flight ceases to be earth-associated and becomes 'interplanetary' or 'space' flight, that is about fifty miles up.[1] Neither the United States nor the Soviet Union has committed itself to any particular limit or theory, and the most that can be said is that the limit seems more likely to be fixed by reference to the second or third form of criterion than to the first.

[1] See Jessup and Taubenfeld, *Controls for Outer Space*, ch. 7.

VI

THE JURISDICTION OF STATES

IN general, every state has exclusive jurisdiction
within its own territory, but this jurisdiction is
not absolute, because it is subject to certain limitations imposed by international law. The term 'exterritoriality' is commonly used to describe the status of
a person or thing physically present on a state's territory, but wholly or partly withdrawn from the state's
jurisdiction by a rule of international law, but for
many reasons it is an objectionable term. It introduces
a fiction, for the person or thing is in fact within, and
not outside, the territory; it implies that jurisdiction
and territory always coincide, whereas they do so only
generally; and it is misleading because we are tempted
to forget that it is only a metaphor and to deduce untrue legal consequences from it as though it were a
literal truth. At most it means nothing more than that
a person or thing has *some* immunity from the local
jurisdiction; it does not help us to determine the only
important question, namely how far this immunity
extends.[1] We shall here consider the international
aspects of the territorial jurisdiction of states and
certain real and alleged limitations upon it.

[1] In *Chung Chi Chiung* v. *The King*, [1939] A.C. at p. 175, the Privy
Council approved this criticism of the use of the term 'exterritoriality'.

§ 1. *Jurisdiction over Internal Waters*

Internal waters. A private ship in internal waters is, in principle, fully subject to the local jurisdiction, and the completeness of the coastal state's right to exercise its jurisdiction in civil matters does not appear to be questioned. There are, however, two views as to the position in criminal matters.

The British view is that the subjection of the ship to the local criminal jurisdiction is equally complete and that any derogation from it is a matter of comity in the discretion of the coastal state. At the same time, we do not regard our local jurisdiction as wholly excluding the jurisdiction of the flag state. We ourselves claim a concurrent jurisdiction over British ships in foreign waters and are equally ready to concede it with respect to foreign ships in British waters.

The other doctrine is founded on an Opinion of the French Council of State in 1806, referring to two American ships in French ports, the *Sally* and the *Newton*, on each of which one member of the crew had assaulted another. Both the American consuls and the French local authorities claimed jurisdiction, and the Council held that it belonged to the consuls, on the ground that the offences did not disturb the peace of the port. It declared that the ships were subjected to French jurisdiction in matters touching the interests of the state, in matters of police, and for offences committed, even on board, by members of the crew against strangers; but that in matters of internal discipline, including offences by one member of the crew against another, the local authorities ought not to interfere, unless either their assistance was invoked or the peace of the port compromised. This opinion effected an alteration in French practice, which had previously agreed with that still upheld by Great Britain, and although it has been followed in many continental countries it cannot be regarded as an authoritative declaration of the international law on the matter. It is, moreover, full of ambiguities. If we are asked, for example, what matters 'touch the interests of a state', we should be inclined to answer that the whole administration of the criminal law does so very closely. Further, the Opinion says nothing of the position of passengers; it does not indicate the sort of incidents which ought to be regarded as 'compromising the peace of the port', nor by whom (e.g. by a consul, by the master, by the accused, or by his victim) the assistance of the port authorities must be invoked in order to justify their interference; it does not even say whether this interference may take the form of assuming jurisdiction. The French courts indeed held, in 1859, when a ship's officer on board an American ship, the *Tempest*, had killed a seaman on the same ship, that some crimes are so serious that without regard to their further consequences, if any, their mere commission compromises the peace of the port, and therefore brings them under the local jurisdiction. Such a decision is sound sense, but scarcely an application of the Opinion of the Council of State; and it leads to the result that everything but disciplinary and minor offences among the crew will fall under the local jurisdiction.[1]

This difference of view is, however, less than it appears. According to Gidel,[2] the French system does not deny the complete jurisdiction of the state of the port over offences committed on board foreign ships; it merely declares that this jurisdiction will not be exercised in certain cases which it indicates. The English system likewise does not involve the invariable exercise of jurisdiction, but it does not declare in advance in what cases the jurisdiction will or will not be exercised. He holds therefore that the state of the port is as a matter of law within its rights in dealing with any offence against its own laws (a term which would exclude most purely disciplinary infractions) committed on board a foreign ship; that in practice this absolute territorial competence is not exercised, for reasons of general policy and expediency; and that certain states like France have, and others like Great Britain have not, announced in advance the line they will take in these matters.

A ship may have occasion to put into a foreign port when she has on board persons in custody which is legal by the law of the flag state. Can such persons claim their liberty on the ground that they have committed no offence against the law of the coastal state?

A French ship, the *El Kantara*, put into Newcastle, N.S.W., in 1922, having on board two prisoners *en route* to a French penal settlement. The prisoners

[1] Fauchille, *Traité*, vol. i, part ii, p. 1034.
[2] *Droit international public de la mer*, vol. ii, pp. 204 and 246.

escaped; the ship left without them; and they were later arrested and handed over to another French ship. Just before this latter ship sailed, an application for a *habeas corpus* rule was made to the Australian Court, but refused on the ground that there was no *prima facie* evidence to suggest that their custody was not legal by French law.[1] The decision implies that the courts of the port state may inquire into the regularity of the custody of a person on board a foreign ship, and, if necessary, release him; but that they will not interfere with a custody which appears to be regular by the law of the ship. Any other conclusion would be highly inconvenient.

Rivers. When the whole course of a river and both its banks are within the territory of a single state, that state's control over the river is as great as over any other part of its territory, unless its rights have been limited by treaty. The only rivers, therefore, which concern international law are those which flow either through, or between, more states than one. Such rivers are conveniently called 'international rivers'; and they raise the question whether each of the riparian states has in law full control of its own part of the river, or whether it is limited by the fact that the river is useful or even necessary to other states. One obviously important interest at stake is that of navigation; it may be of vital concern to an up-river state that states nearer the mouth should not cut off its access to the sea; and it may also be important to non-riparian states to have access to the upper waters

[1] See *Journal of Comparative Legislation* (1926), p. 246.

of the river. But in recent years other economic uses of rivers have become increasingly more important,[1] and it is obviously desirable that all these interests should, so far as possible, be effectively protected.

From early in the seventeenth century treaties between particular states opening particular rivers began to be common; but it was not until the Treaty of Paris in 1814 that a general declaration of freedom of navigation on all international rivers was proclaimed. The declaration was given only a limited effect, though in the course of the next forty years many rivers were opened to riparian states, but there was a tendency to exclude non-riparian states. After the Crimean War, however, the Treaty of Paris, 1856, introduced a new principle. It set up a body called the European Danube Commission, consisting of representatives both of riparian and non-riparian states, to improve the conditions of navigation on the lower Danube. The Commission was intended to be temporary, but its duration was extended and its powers enlarged by successive treaties. When it was instituted, navigation on the Danube was chaotic; the stream was obstructed by shoals, piracy and wrecking were common, and extortionate dues were charged. The Commission altered all this, and proved a most successful experiment in international co-operation. It had wide administrative powers to the

[1] Cf. H. A. Smith, *Economic Uses of International Rivers* (1931), a book which has exercised a considerable influence on legal opinion in the field.

exclusion of the sovereignty of the territorial states through which the river flows; controlled and policed navigation, fixed dues, constructed works, and tried offences against its own regulations.[1] The principle of free navigation for all states was extended by the Convention of Mannheim to the Rhine in 1868, though with some qualifications in favour of the riparian states; and in 1885 the Berlin Conference on Africa applied it to the Congo and the Niger.

The Peace Treaties of 1919 dealt with the most important rivers flowing through the ex-enemy countries, creating international commissions for some of them, and establishing on all of them equal treatment for all states.[2] The work was carried on by the League of Nations at the Barcelona Transit Conference in 1921. The two most important of the Barcelona conventions were: (1) A statute on 'navigable waterways of international concern', laying down general principles, which were intended to be applied in detail to all international rivers by

[1] After 1921 there were two Commissions for the Danube: the European Commission regulating the Danube from Braila to the Black Sea and the much larger International Commission for the upper parts of the river. In 1947 the Treaties of Peace with Roumania, Bulgaria, and Hungary again laid down that navigation should be free for all states but in the following year a conference attended by the United States, United Kingdom, and France as well as by seven Danubian states adopted, despite the objections of the three first-mentioned states, a Convention which set up a single Commission for the river confined to riparian states and largely under the control of the Soviet Union. The Convention is in operation between the Danubian states but has not been recognized by the other three Powers.

[2] Germany denounced these provisions in 1936.

separate conventions, providing for free navigation for all the contracting states, imposing the duty of maintaining the river on the riparian states, and limiting the charges that might be levied to the expenses of maintenance; a voluntary protocol was annexed, by which states might reciprocally agree to open their own national rivers or canals to other states. (2) A statute on 'freedom of transit', applying to transit of persons or goods through a state either by water or rail. Such transit was to be facilitated without distinction of nationality, and without charging dues except for certain administrative expenses.

Most river commissions, however, did not follow the Danube model; their powers were narrower. The typical functions of such a commission have been thus stated:[1] to supervise the application of the régime established for the river; to serve as a sort of standing conference of the parties; to take certain decisions, within the ambit of its powers, relating to works, dues, and technical services, such decisions binding the states affected, but being matters for the states, and not for the commission itself, to execute; sometimes to act as a court of appeal in cases of alleged breaches of the convention; to serve as an organ of liaison for the exchange of information, co-ordination of statistics, and the like; and as an organ of conciliation and sometimes of arbitration, in differences between the states.

[1] Cf. Hostie, in *Recueil des cours de l'Académie de droit international*, vol. xl, p. 438.

Navigation is only one of the uses to which the waters of a river may be put and, as the case of the Nile shows, not necessarily the most important. Other long-established uses are irrigation, water-mills, water-supply for domestic and industrial purposes, fishing and timber-floating, while in the present century the hydro-electric exploitation of rivers has become of outstanding importance. The law relating to these other uses, and indeed the customary law relating to international rivers generally, is still in course of development; for it is only in comparatively recent times that the growing industrialization of states and their increasing interdependence has focused attention upon the legal problems. As late as 1895 the United States Attorney-General Harmon expressed the opinion that, the United States being sovereign over that part of the Rio Grande which flows through its territory, it had no obligation either to share the water with Mexico or to compensate the latter for any damage in Mexico caused by diversions of the water in the United States. This absolute view of a riparian state's right to exploit a river within its territory is no longer maintained by the United States itself and it is generally accepted today that the right is subject to certain limitations resulting from the state's duty not to violate the corresponding right of other riparian states to exploit the river within their own territories. For there has now come into existence a considerable volume of treaty-practice by which riparian states have regulated their interests in particular rivers and which is not easily reconcilable with the view that a riparian state is legally free to do anything that it pleases with the water of an international river. Postwar treaties and negotiations concerning the Nile, the Jordan, the Indus, the Mekong, the Colorado River, the Columbia River, the St. Lawrence, as well as other rivers, and an arbitration between France and Spain concerning the waters of *Lake Lanoux*,[1] appear to confirm that some broad principles of international river law have now come into existence, though their precise formulation may still remain to be settled.[2] These broad principles are: (1) Where a river system drains the territories of two or more states, each state has the right to have that river system considered as a whole and to have its own interests taken into account together with those of other states; (2) each state has in principle an equal right to make the maximum use of the water within its territory, but in exercising this right must respect the corresponding rights of other states; (3) where one state's exercise of its rights conflicts with the water interests of another, the principle to be applied is that each is entitled to the equitable apportionment of the benefits of the river system in proportion to their needs and in the light of all the circumstances of the particular river system; (4) a state is in

[1] *A.J.I.L.*, 1959, p. 156.

[2] See *Legal Aspects of Hydro-Electric Development of Rivers and Lakes of Common Interest* (1952, U.N. Document E/E.C.E./136); *Principles of Law Governing the Use of International Rivers* (International Law Association, Dubrovnik Conference, 1956, and New York Conference, 1958); *Annuaire de l'Institut de droit international* (1959), vol. 48.

principle precluded from making any change in the river system which would cause substantial damage to another state's right of enjoyment without that other state's consent; (5) it is relieved from obtaining that consent, however, if it offers the other state a proportionate share of the benefits to be derived from the change or other adequate compensation for the damage to the other state's enjoyment of the water; (6) a state whose own enjoyment of the water is not substantially damaged by a development in the use of a river beneficial to another state is not entitled to oppose that development.

The application of these general principles may well involve problems of considerable difficulty in individual cases, as is shown by the detailed provisions of some of the existing treaties. Apart from an almost infinite variety in the physical, political, and economic conditions of international rivers, the exploitation of their water resources often calls for the most complex scientific studies and engineering techniques. In consequence, modern opinion considers it desirable that a state intending to undertake any new exploitation of its part of a river system should notify the other interested states of the project and, if any of them object, should seek to resolve the difference by negotiation and, if necessary, by arbitration. Furthermore, it is increasingly recognized that, for international rivers of any size, some form of joint international administration will almost certainly be needed if the resources of the river system are to be put to the fullest use for the benefit of all the riparian states. One of the most ambitious examples of such a joint authority is the International Joint Commission created by a treaty of 1909 with responsibility for all the 'boundary waters' between the United States and Canada. It consists of three Commissioners from each side, and it has jurisdiction to decide upon applications for the 'use or obstruction or diversion' of the boundary waters as defined in the treaty.

Canals. In the absence of treaty stipulations a canal, even a sea-water canal like that of Corinth, is subject to the sole control of the state in whose territory it lies; and ships of other states, although their passage may be allowed in normal times, have no right of passage through it. But three inter-oceanic canals, Suez, Panama, and Kiel, have received a special status. They are sometimes, but inaccurately, said to be 'neutralized' or 'internationalized'.

The Suez Canal lies in what is now the United Arab Republic; it was opened in 1869 under a concession which was to run for ninety-nine years and then revert to the Egyptian Government. The concession was granted to a French company in which the British Government afterwards became the largest shareholder. The international status of the Canal was established by the Convention of Constantinople, 1888, to which all the great European Powers and some others were parties, and the duration of the Convention was not limited to that of the concession. Under the Convention the Canal is to be open in war and in peace to every vessel of commerce and war, without distinction of flag. It is never to be blockaded (Art. 1); no act of war is to be committed in the Canal or within three miles of its ports of access (Art. 4); belligerent warships must pass through with the least possible delay and may not stay more than twenty-four hours at Port Said or Suez; and an interval of twenty-four hours must elapse between the sailing of two hostile ships from these ports. The defence of the Canal was committed to Turkey and Egypt (Art. 9), but this provision broke down when Turkey attacked the Canal in 1914, and under the Treaty of Lausanne Great Britain was substituted for Turkey. British participation in the defence of the canal was dealt with first by the Anglo-Egyptian Treaty of 1936, under which British troops were stationed in the Canal area, and afterwards by an Agreement of 1954, under which Egypt was only to provide facilities for British troops in certain eventualities.

The arrangements for the operation and defence of the Canal, though not its international status, underwent radical changes in 1956. First, Egypt issued a law 'nationalizing' the Suez Canal Company, which was strongly challenged as illegal by the United Kingdom and France in the Security Council, and which led eventually to the Anglo-French intervention in Egypt. The legal issues involved in these important events are too complex for discussion here, and it must suffice to state the outcome. The Canal and its administration are now vested in the Suez Canal Authority, a domestic public authority of the United Arab Republic, while Egypt made the

Anglo-French intervention the occasion for abrogating the Anglo-Egyptian Agreement of 1954. On the other hand, in a 'Declaration on the Suez Canal', registered with the United Nations in 1957 as an international instrument, Egypt solemnly reaffirmed her intention 'to respect the terms and the spirit of the Constantinople Convention of 1888 and the rights and obligations arising therefrom'; and she added that she was more particularly determined to afford and maintain free and uninterrupted navigation for all nations within the limits of and in accordance with the provisions of the Convention. The status of the Canal as an international waterway governed by the provisions of the 1888 Convention therefore remains intact.

The Panama Canal runs through a zone of Panamanian territory which is occupied and administered by the United States. It is regulated by no general international convention, but the United States, which constructed and maintains it, is under the obligations of two treaties with regard to it, the Hay-Pauncefote Treaty of 1901 with Great Britain, and the Hay-Varilla Treaty of 1903 with Panama.

By the Hay-Pauncefote Treaty she bound herself to accept certain rules, taken in the main from the Suez Canal Convention, as the basis of the so-called 'neutralization' of the Canal. Article 3 provided that

'The canal shall be free and open to the vessels of commerce and war of all nations . . . on terms of entire equality so that there shall be no discrimination against any such nation or its citizens or subjects in respect of conditions or charges of traffic or otherwise. Such conditions or charges of traffic shall be just and equitable.'

Provisions that the Canal is never to be blockaded, that no act of war is to be committed within it, though the United States may maintain military police for its protection, as to the transit of belligerent ships, and other matters follow practically the terms of the Suez Convention.

The Kiel Canal was, by the Treaty of Versailles, to be 'free and open to the vessels of commerce and war of all nations at peace with Germany on terms of entire equality'. Germany was bound to maintain it in navigable condition, and to levy only such charges as were necessary for this purpose. These provisions were held by the Permanent Court in the *Wimbledon* case[1] to convert the Canal from 'an internal and national navigable waterway, the use of which by the vessels of States other than the riparian State is left entirely to the discretion of that State' into 'an international waterway intended to provide under treaty guarantee easier access to the Baltic for the benefit of all nations of the world'. Although the Kiel Canal provisions of the Treaty were denounced by Hitler's Germany, it is generally considered that the status of an international way governed by those provisions still attaches to the canal.[2]

---

[1] (1923), Series A, No. 1.

[2] In the *Kiel Canal Collision* case (1950, *I.L.R.* 133) a German court regarded the point as doubtful.

§ 2. *Jurisdiction over the Territorial Sea*

The territorial sea is as much under the sovereignty of the coastal state as its internal waters, and when private ships are merely lying in the territorial sea their position in relation to the local jurisdiction appears to be the same as in internal waters. The coastal state's jurisdiction over ships in its territorial sea is, however, subject to certain limitations by reason of the existence of a right of innocent passage for the ships of all states through the territorial sea for the purpose either of traversing it without entering internal waters or of passing from the high seas to internal waters or vice versa. The law relating to this right of innocent passage came under the consideration of the International Court in the *Corfu Channel* case[1] and has now been codified in the Geneva Convention of 1958 on the Territorial Sea and Contiguous Zone.[2] The right of innocent passage includes stopping and anchoring in so far as these may be incidental to ordinary navigation, for example, in order to pick up a pilot, or may be rendered necessary by *force majeure* or by distress. It is a general right the exercise of which by foreign ships may be suspended only when this is essential for the protection of the security of the coastal state, and then the suspension of the right must have been duly published and must apply to all foreign ships without any discrimination. Moreover, any such suspension of the right is totally forbidden in straits, like the Strait of Gibraltar or

I.C.J. Reports, 1949, p. 4.   [2] Section III.

the Corfu Channel, which are used for international navigation between one part of the high seas and another or between the high seas and the territorial sea of a third state. In general, the coastal state must do nothing to hamper the exercise of the right and may not levy any charge on foreign ships passing through the territorial sea other than a charge for a specific service such as pilotage.

The right extends only to a passage through the territorial sea which is 'innocent', that is, innocent with respect to the coastal state; and according to the Geneva Convention this means a passage which is not prejudicial to its 'peace, good order or security' and which conforms to the provisions of the Convention and to the rules of international law. The Convention itself provides that (a) submarines must navigate on the surface and show their flag; (b) foreign ships must comply with the laws and regulations of the coastal state, particularly those relating to transport and navigation; and (c) foreign fishing vessels must observe any laws and regulations made to stop them from fishing in the territorial sea.

Clearly, the coastal state is entitled to exercise its jurisdiction over foreign private ships passing through its territorial sea to the extent necessary to enforce applicable local laws and regulations and to ensure the innocence of the passage. The question is how far it may exercise its general jurisdiction over ships in its territorial sea, and on this point the Geneva Convention now makes it clear that the coastal state's jurisdiction is much more limited than in the case of internal waters. In criminal matters the Convention lays down that the coastal state should not arrest any person or conduct any investigation on board a foreign ship passing through its territorial sea in connexion with a crime committed on board during the passage, except in four classes of case: (a) the consequences of the crime extend to the coastal state; (b) the crime disturbs the peace of the coastal state or the good order of its territorial sea; (c) the captain or the consul of the flag state requests the assistance of the coastal state; and (d) the arrest or investigation is necessary for the suppression of illicit traffic in narcotic drugs. This provision does not apply, however, where the ship is outward bound after having visited the coastal state's internal waters. On the other hand, in such a case or in any of the four classes of case where the exercise of its jurisdiction is authorized, the coastal state is placed under an obligation to pay due regard to the interests of the ship's navigation and, if so requested by the captain, to notify the consul of the flag state before taking action. Finally, the Convention expressly forbids any arrest or investigation on board in connexion with a crime committed before the ship entered the territorial sea, if the ship is merely in passage and is not bound for its internal waters. As to civil matters, the Convention similarly forbids the coastal state to stop or divert a foreign ship, which is merely in passage through the territorial sea, in order to exercise its civil jurisdiction with respect to a person on board. The coastal state is also forbidden to levy execution against, or to arrest, the ship itself, for the purpose of any civil proceedings other than proceedings in respect of liabilities connected with the ship's voyage through the territorial sea; it may do so, however, if the ship is outward bound after having visited internal waters.

The limitations on the coastal state's jurisdiction which are found in the Geneva Convention reflect the continental rather than the British doctrine on the question. For although it has been British policy as a rule not to interfere with foreign ships in passage through British territorial waters, the right to do so has been asserted. The Territorial Waters Jurisdiction Act of 1878, for example, although it does make the prosecution of a foreigner subject to the leave of a Secretary of State, gives jurisdiction to British courts over any offence whatever committed within British territorial waters. This extensive claim has been criticized in other countries and the provisions of the Geneva Convention are certainly more consonant with the principle of freedom of navigation upon which the right of innocent passage is founded.

§ 3. *Jurisdiction in Territorial Air Space*

We have seen[1] that states have sovereignty over the air space above their territories, and that other states have only such rights in it as are secured to them by convention. There are two competing interests which a satisfactory state of the law would reconcile as far as

---

[1] *Supra*, p. 218.

possible, that of the subjacent state in its own security, and that of all states in the greatest possible freedom of communications. Of the two, the interests of security have been preferred in the present law. But attempts have been made, not yet wholly successfully, to facilitate the use of the air as a medium of international communication.

In the Convention of Paris on Air Navigation of 1919 each of the parties undertook in time of peace to accord freedom of innocent passage in the air above its territory to the aircraft of the other contracting parties without distinction of nationality subject to the conditions laid down in the Convention. Aircraft must carry certificates of airworthiness and other prescribed documents; prohibited zones might be established in the interests of national security, provided that the prohibition was also applied to domestic aircraft; routes and landing-places might be prescribed; and the prohibition of the transport of persons or goods between two points in a state's territory, that is to say, the practice which in sea navigation is called *cabotage*, was authorized. But the establishment of 'international airways' was to be subject to the consent of the states flown over. Military aircraft might fly over foreign territory only by special permission. The Convention also contained comprehensive regulations dealing with registration of aircraft, certificates of airworthiness, and other technical matters, and it set up an International Commission of Air Navigation to act as a clearing-house for information on air navigation questions, to decide differences of a technical character, and having power, by a three-quarters vote of all the members, to amend some of the technical provisions of the Convention.

As the importance of civil aviation increased, a tendency arose for states to use their sovereignty over the air for securing advantages to themselves. They have, for instance, used the right of prescribing routes and security zones and their control of landing-grounds as a means of whittling away their obligation to allow innocent passage to foreign aircraft, and the omission of the Convention to regulate international airways, that is to say, regular airline services, created a very important exception to the right of innocent passage which the Convention purported to allow.

In 1944 a conference met at Chicago and attempted to reach agreement on a number of outstanding problems, the urgency of which had been immensely increased by the developments in aviation during the war. It created an International Civil Aviation Organization (I.C.A.O.) with headquarters at Montreal. This has an annual Assembly consisting of all the members, a smaller Council meeting more often, and a secretariat, and it has been accepted by the United Nations as a 'Specialised Agency'. On the technical side the Chicago Conference and I.C.A.O. have been very successful, but much less so on the economic side. Discussion centres on the so-called 'five air freedoms', namely freedom to fly across foreign territory without landing; to land for non-traffic purposes, e.g. to refuel; to put down traffic originating in the state of the air-craft; to embark traffic destined for that state, and to embark traffic destined for, or to put down traffic coming from, a third contracting state. On the question which of these freedoms should be accepted there is a cleavage of opinion between states which favour the creation of a central control authority to apportion the world's air traffic equitably between the different states and those which, like the United States, favour free competition. At present, therefore, regular airline services are made possible only by a complicated network of bilateral agreements.

§ 4. *Jurisdiction with respect to Foreign States, their Property, their Agents, and their Armed Forces*

'The principle', said Brett L.J. in the *Parlement Belge*, 'is that, as a consequence of the absolute independence of every sovereign authority and of the international comity which induces every sovereign State to respect the independence and dignity of every other sovereign State, each and every one declines to exercise by means of its courts any of its territorial jurisdiction over the person of any sovereign or ambassador of any other State, or over the public property of any State which is destined to public use, or over the property of any ambassador.' The principle is a rule of customary law rather than of mere comity, and it means that a foreign sovereign state, its public property and its official agents are in general immune from the local jurisdiction unless the foreign state consents to its exercise. If any question arises between the territorial sovereign and a foreign state it can only be taken up through the diplomatic channel or in some international forum unless the foreign state waives its immunity from the local jurisdiction.

Although the doctrine of state immunity is clear enough, its precise scope is by no means so, and we shall have to consider in turn the position of the state, the state's agents, and the state's property. It needs first to be stressed, however, that the immunity is not an immunity from observance of the law of the territorial sovereign or from legal liability; it is an immunity only from the exercise of the territorial jurisdiction. The point is illustrated by the case of *Dickinson* v. *Del Solar*.[1] The plaintiff had been injured by the car of the defendant, a secretary in the Peruvian Legation, who did not plead his diplomatic immunity, but called on his insurance company to indemnify him against the claim. The company repudiated liability, contending that the defendant himself was under no legal liability to the plaintiff, but the Court held that diplomatic agents are not immune from legal liability; they are merely exempt from being sued unless they submit to the jurisdiction. Judgment would therefore result in a legal liability for the defendant against which the company must indemnify him. Again, when a diplomat leaves his post and ceases to enjoy immunity, he may be sued in respect of purely private acts done during his tenure of the office, for he was not exempt from the law.[2] Another general point to be stressed is that the immunity is

---

[1] [1930] 1 K.B. 376; cf. *Chung Chi Chung* v. *The King, infra*, p. 268.
[2] Cf. *Musurus Bey* v. *Gadban*, [1894] 2 Q.B. 352; *Re Suarez*, [1918] 1 Ch. 176.

always that of the state itself, never that of the person whose acts it covers; accordingly a foreign state may always waive the immunity of one of its agents, regardless of his wishes.[1]

The immunity of the state. The question not infrequently arises as to whether a party in legal proceedings is or is not a sovereign state or government entitled to immunity. The British practice is for the Court to refer to the Foreign Office or Commonwealth Relations Office for information and to accept as conclusive for the purposes of immunity the declaration of the Secretary of State concerned that the party is or is not recognized by H.M. Government as sovereign.[2] The point is well illustrated by the case of the *Arantzazu Mendi*[3] which arose out of the Spanish civil war. The Republican Government had issued a writ *in rem* claiming possession of a ship which they purported to have requisitioned, but which was being held by its master to the orders of the government of General Franco. The Court was informed by the Foreign Office that Britain recognized the Franco Government as being in *de facto* administrative control of the greater part of Spain including Bilbao, which was the ship's port of registry, and not subordinate to any other government; this statement the Court interpreted to imply a recognition of that government *de facto* and the writ was set aside.

---

[1] *R.* v. *Kent* (or A.B.), [1941] 1 K.B. 454.
[2] *Duff Development Co.* v. *Kelantan Government*, [1923] A.C. 395; *Mighell* v. *Sultan of Johore*, [1894] 1 Q.B. 149.
[3] [1939] A.C. 256.

It is the central government to which the state's immunity appears to attach, though in some instances immunity has been allowed to political subdivisions. British courts have regularly accorded immunity to the rulers of 'protected' states internationally dependent on Great Britain, as have French courts to dependent states of the French Union, and United States courts to former dependencies like Hawaii and the Philippines and to the component states of the Federation. This practice is internal to the constitutional systems of the states in question, but there are also some instances where American, Australian, and French courts have declined to assume jurisdiction over the colonial dependencies of foreign states. In general, however, the practice has been to distinguish between local and central governments of foreign states and to accord immunity only to the latter. Thus, a French court has refused immunity to the city of Geneva and a United States court to the city of Rome, while United States, French, Italian, and Belgian courts have refused it to the component states of Brazil.[1] The distinction, though it may be convenient, is not wholly logical, since the government of a state comprises its local, no less than its central, organs of government.

The foreign state's constitutional law may also come into play to determine whether an agency set up by the state is to be regarded as part of the central government for the purposes of immunity. Until re-

[1] The cases are collected in Sucharitkul, *State Immunities and Trading Activities*, pp. 106–7.

cent times the organs of the central government were comparatively few and easily identifiable. Today, however, with the development of industrialized economies and the emergence of socialist states, the activities of governments have penetrated more and more into what was previously considered to be the sphere of private enterprise and in many cases agencies constituted by the state have been employed to undertake economic or social activities in the public interest. Some of these agencies, like the British Broadcasting Corporation, have been created as autonomous corporations separate from the government; others, like the Board of Trade and Ministry of Works, though separately incorporated, are an integral part of the central government. A foreign agency, which under the law of the foreign state in question is part of the central government, will be treated by our courts as entitled to immunity, even if separately incorporated.[1] This appears also to be the general practice where the function of the foreign agency is one generally recognized as a normal function of governments; the courts of some states, however, are reluctant to accept a foreign state agency as part of the central government for purposes of immunity when it engages in trade or other historically 'private' activities.

Quite apart from the question of the incorporation of government agencies, the assumption by governments of functions formerly regarded as 'private' has

[1] *Baccus S.R.L.* v. *Servicio Nacional del Trigo*, [1957] 1 Q.B. 438; *Krajina* v. *Tass Agency*, [1949] 2 A.E.R. 274.

raised a serious problem as to whether foreign states should be allowed to claim immunity in respect of all kinds of state activity and, more especially, of state trading; and considerable divergencies of view have revealed themselves in the decisions of municipal tribunals on the point. In England there is a long series of Court of Appeal decisions upholding the immunity of state agencies even in respect of trading activities. The point has most frequently arisen in regard to merchant ships engaged in commerce and in the *Parlement Belge*[1] the Court of Appeal ruled that it could not take jurisdiction in a collision action involving a ship owned by the King of the Belgians and employed partly in carrying mails and partly for trading purposes; and it afterwards did the same in the *Porto Alexandre*[2] where the ship was wholly employed in trade. In a recent case[3] it upheld the immunity of a department of the Spanish Ministry of Agriculture engaged in the import and export of grain. Jenkins L.J. took the view that the importing and exporting of a staple commodity by a department of the state in the interests of the public cannot properly be regarded as 'comparable to ordinary private trading' and must be classed as 'public purposes' invested with immunity. United States courts,

[1] (1880) 5 P.D. 197.

[2] [1920] P. 30; *Compania Mercantil Argentina* v. *U.S. Shipping Board*, [1924] 40 T.L.R. 601.

[3] *Baccus S.R.L.* v. *Servicio Nacional Del Trigo*, [1957] 1 Q.B. 438; cf. *Krajina* v. *Tass Agency*, [1949] 2 A.E.R. 274, where the Soviet News Agency was held immune in proceedings for a libel in a newspaper which it ran.

although less inclined to accept as part of the government an agency that has been separately incorporated, have also in the past generally accorded absolute immunity to government agencies whatever their functions; the immunity of foreign railway administrations has, for example, been upheld, while in the *Pesaro*[1] the Supreme Court accorded immunity to the Italian Government in respect of a merchant vessel wholly engaged in trade. Although the theory of absolute immunity has been followed in a number of other countries, some states, notably Italy, Belgium, and Egypt, have consistently refused to accord immunity in connexion with commercial activities. These states deny immunity in respect of acts *jure gestionis*, i.e. acts which, though public acts in the sense that they are performed by the state, are considered by the courts to be acts of commerce or of administration falling outside their concept of what the sovereign powers of a state comprise. They have, for example, refused to accord immunity to state-owned merchant vessels engaged in trade, to the Soviet Trade Delegation, or to state railways. These courts, in order to explain the refusal of immunity, have sometimes had recourse to a theory according to which, when a state enters into a transaction with a private individual or corporation that is not intrinsically an act of sovereignty, it impliedly agrees to waive its immunity. Unless, however, the contract contains a provision which appears to contemplate the settlement of disputes in the local tribunals, to

[1] (1926) 271 U.S. 562.

imply a waiver is really to have recourse to a fiction.

The distinction between acts *jure imperii* and acts *jure gestionis*, although superficially attractive as a means of keeping state immunity within reasonable limits, does not rest on any sound logical basis; it involves making assumptions as to what are the proper functions of government which might be justifiable assumptions according to the *laissez-faire* theories of the nineteenth century but may seem arbitrary today in a world community which contains socialist and communist as well as capitalist states. Opinions may differ widely from one state to another as to the proper functions of government and the proper limits of the economic activities of governments; and even in the United States it was said in the *Pesaro*: 'we know of no international usage which regards the maintenance and advancement of the economic welfare of a people in time of peace as any less a public purpose than the maintenance and training of a naval force'. However that may be, state practice concerning the grant or refusal of immunity with respect to state activities in spheres which historically have been regarded as spheres of private enterprise shows wide divergencies and, in the absence of a settled rule of international law, courts are free to delimit the scope of immunity in these spheres. The general trend of opinion today is moving in favour of restricting immunity at least in the sphere of state trading. Although, as we have seen, the Court of Appeal in England has uniformly granted immunity in cases of state trading, the House of Lords has not yet pronounced upon the point, and a number of the Law Lords have indicated their dislike of the doctrine of immunity being applied in this sphere.[1] Similar views have been expressed by some justices of the Supreme Court in the United States and in 1952 the State Department informed the Attorney-General that in future it intended to follow the restrictive theory of immunity in advising upon requests by foreign governments for a grant of immunity. Furthermore, so far as ships are concerned, the restrictive view seems to have been adopted both in the Geneva Convention on the Régime of the High Seas (Art. 9) and that on the Territorial Sea and Contiguous Zone (Arts. 21 and 22).[2] If the law now seems to be settling itself in the direction of withholding immunity in cases of state trading, some nice problems will remain as to what exactly constitutes trading or commercial activity on the part of sovereign states.

The immunity of state property. The immunity, as we have seen, extends to the public property of the state.[3] An action or proceeding against the property of a foreign state compels it to choose between submitting to jurisdiction or risking the loss of its interest in the property and is therefore in substance an

[1] e.g. Lords Thankerton, Macmillan, and Maugham in the *S.S. Cristina*, [1938] A.C. 485; Lords Jowitt, Porter, and Tucker in *U.S.A. and France* v. *Dollfus Mieg et Cie.*, [1952] A.C. 582; and Lord Denning in *Rahimtoola* v. *Nizam of Hyderabad*, [1958] A.C. 377.

[2] See also the Brussels Convention of 1926, which was signed but not ratified by Great Britain.

[3] The *Parlement Belge, supra*, p. 243.

impleading of the foreign state itself.[1] Accordingly the courts, said Lord Atkin in the *Cristina*,[2] 'will not by their process, whether the sovereign is a party to the proceedings or not, seize or detain property which is his, or of which he is in possession or control.' The immunity is not therefore confined to property owned by a foreign state; it extends to all cases where proceedings are taken the effect of which is to displace a foreign state from its interest in property. Precisely what kind of an interest a foreign state must show in property in order to oust the jurisdiction of the courts is a question which has much exercised judges in England in recent years, though not, it seems, to the same extent elsewhere. The *Parlement Belge*[3] and *Vavasseur* v. *Krupp*[4] are cases in which a foreign sovereign's *ownership* of the property was held to preclude the courts from taking cognizance of claims, respectively, for collision damage and for infringement of patent. In the *Cristina*, *Arantzazu Mendi*,[5] and numerous other cases the *de facto* possession of property by a foreign sovereign has sufficed to prevent the courts from entertaining any claim by the owners to recover possession or otherwise assert their title.[6] Again, it is well settled that a vessel is immune from

---

[1] Dicey, *Conflict of Laws*, 7th ed., p. 131.
[2] [1938] A.C. 485.   [3] *Supra*, p. 243.
[4] (1878) 9 Ch.D. 351.   [5] [1939] A.C. 256.
[6] It was even suggested in the *Cristina* that the courts would be barred from exercising jurisdiction in a case where possession had been obtained by a foreign sovereign in the United Kingdom itself by an unlawful use of force; but this view was rejected by the Privy Council in the recent case of *Civil Air Transport (Inc.)* v. *Central Air Transport Corporation*, [1953] A.C. 70.

suit while requisitioned or chartered by a foreign state, even although the owners may be left in possession to operate the vessel. All these examples fall within the general proposition of Lord Atkin in the *Cristina* given above, but in recent decisions the House of Lords has said that his proposition must not be understood as completely exhaustive of the categories of case in which a foreign state's interest in property may oust the court's jurisdiction. In the *Dollfus Mieg et Cie.*[1] case it admitted the claim of immunity where specific gold bars were held by the Bank of England as bailees for France and the United States jointly with the United Kingdom; and in *Rahimtoola* v. *Nizam of Hyderabad*[2] it did the same where the Nizam was claiming from the High Commissioner of Pakistàn money received by the latter and transferred by him into a bank account opened on the instructions of his government. In these cases, the House of Lords has insisted that the true principle is that immunity must be accorded if the proceedings in substance implead the foreign sovereign, and that the operation of the principle in our courts must not be allowed to depend on peculiarities of our own property law.

When a plea of immunity with respect to property is upheld, the court is wholly debarred from considering whether the foreign state's claim to an interest in the property is in truth well-founded. There is in consequence a risk of grave injustice to the other parties to the suit, and one which in *Juan Ysmael & Co.* v. *The Republic of Indonesia*[3] the Privy Council was

[1] [1952] A.C. 582.   [2] [1958] A.C. 377.   [3] [1955] A.C. 72.

not prepared to contemplate, when the foreign sovereign was professing to have acquired a ship under
a purchase agreement which it knew to be un-
authorized. The Privy Council there held that the
bare assertion of an interest by a foreign sovereign is
not enough to oust the court's jurisdiction; the sovereign must go so far as to 'produce evidence to satisfy
the court that its claim is not merely illusory nor
founded on a title manifestly defective'. There is,
moreover, a definite exception to the general rule of
immunity in the case of trust funds, for long-standing
Chancery decisions[1] establish that a foreign sovereign
cannot prevent the trustees of a fund from administering the trust by showing a beneficial interest, however clear, in the fund.

The immunity of state agents. Foreign heads of state,
whether monarchs or presidents, embody in their
persons the sovereignty of their states and, when they
visit or pass through the territory of another country,
they are wholly exempt from the local jurisdiction,
both civil and criminal. Curiously enough, in England the principle of immunity was settled a good
deal earlier in the case of ambassadors than in that of
the sovereigns whom they were sent to represent.
Perhaps the reason was that the exemption of heads
of state was taken for granted; at any rate it was not
until 1844 that the question came before the courts
in *Duke of Brunswick* v. *King of Hanover*,[2] and the immunity was recognized. The immunity, being that of

[1] See *Larivière* v. *Morgan* (1875), L.R. 7 H.L. 423.
[2] (1844) 6 Beavan 1.

the state itself, no longer attaches to the monarch or president if he ceases to occupy that position, and it seems that afterwards he might be liable to proceedings in respect of purely private acts done while he was head of state.[1]

Formerly, apart from heads of state, the law of immunity only knew two other categories of state agents—diplomats and consuls. The greatly increased intercourse among states and improved communications have, however, led to the rapid growth of what the International Law Commission has referred to as *ad hoc* diplomacy. Prime Ministers, Foreign Ministers, Ministers of Commerce, &c., visit each other for direct personal negotiations; itinerant envoys are sent out on special missions to several countries in succession; technical missions are sent to other countries for special purposes. These *ad hoc* missions now play an important enough role in modern diplomacy to have attracted the attention of the International Law Commission. Practice in regard to them has not perhaps fully crystallized and it must suffice to say here that in its preliminary report the Commission appears to have considered that *ad hoc* missions of this kind should be entitled, on a short-term basis, to privileges and immunities similar to those accorded to diplomats.[2]

In Great Britain the immunities granted to foreign diplomats rest partly on the Common law and partly on the Diplomatic Privileges Act, 1708, and in some

---

[1] See Sucharitkul, op. cit., pp. 32–34.
[2] *Report of the International Law Commission*, 1960, Ch. III.

respects they go beyond what international law requires. Indeed, it has not always been easy to state
precisely what are the requirements of international
law in the matter because practice has varied in detail
as to the extent of the immunities and also because it
has sometimes been uncertain whether a particular
immunity which it is usual to allow is a matter of law
or of courtesy. A greater measure of certainty has,
however, now been given to the law by the Vienna
Convention on Diplomatic Relations drawn up in
April 1961 by a United Nations Conference of
eighty-one states on the basis of a text prepared by the
International Law Commission. The Convention,
which needs twenty-two ratifications to bring it into
force, is not yet law; but, as in the case of the Geneva
Conventions of 1958 on the law of the sea, the mere
fact that it has been signed by such a large number of
the states of the world gives it a certain persuasive
authority in any dispute as to the applicable rule of
customary law. On the other hand, the Convention
does not profess to be exhaustive and expressly provides that the rules of customary law shall continue
to govern questions not regulated by the Convention
itself.

The person of a diplomatic agent is inviolable and
he is immune from any form of arrest or detention
and from all criminal proceedings. It is his duty to
respect the criminal law and police regulations of the
country but, if he breaks them, the only action that
may normally be taken against him is a diplomatic
complaint to his government or, in an extreme case,

a demand for his withdrawal as a *persona non grata*. But in exceptional cases, although nothing is said of this in the Convention, the principle of inviolability does not, according to the International Law Commission, preclude measures being taken against a diplomat either in self-defence or to prevent him from committing crimes.

A diplomat is also in general exempt from civil proceedings, even from being required to give evidence in a court of law. In Great Britain the terms of the Act of 1708 are very sweeping; all writs whereby the person of an ambassador may be arrested or his goods seized are null and void, and any person presuming to sue forth such a writ and all officers executing it 'shall be deemed violators of the laws of nations and disturbers of the publick repose'. British courts have interpreted the Act as giving a diplomat virtually complete immunity from civil proceedings,[1] extending it even to cases where he is sued in respect of private business ventures in which he has engaged.[2] Full immunity from civil jurisdiction was considered by a Government Committee in 1951 to be a requirement of international law,[3] and that was probably the general view. However, three definite exceptions to it have now been recognized in the Vienna Convention:[4] (a) real actions relating to private immovable property unless held on behalf of the sending

[1] Cf. *The Amazone* (1940), p. 40.
[2] See, for example, *Re Republic of Bolivia Exploration Syndicate Ltd.*, [1914] 1 Ch. 139.
[3] Report on Diplomatic Immunity (Cmd. 8460).
[4] Article 31.

state for the purposes of the mission; (*b*) actions relating to succession to property in which the diplomat is involved as a private person; and (*c*) actions relating to any professional or commercial activity exercised by the diplomat outside his official functions. Moreover, it expressly contemplates that in these three cases the other party to the proceedings may obtain execution against the diplomat, subject to the inviolability of his person and residence not being infringed. In view of the existing English case law, legislation may be found necessary in order that these exceptions may be made applicable in our courts. Parliament, however, has in recent years shown a strong desire to keep down the number of cases of exemption from jurisdiction so that on this point the Vienna Convention is likely to commend itself to the legislature.

That a diplomat has some immunity from taxation has always been recognized, but systems of taxation show almost infinite variations, and practice has varied as to the extent of the immunity. A greater measure of uniformity should, however, result from the Vienna Convention, Article 34 of which states that in principle a diplomat is exempt from all dues and taxes, whether personal or real, national, regional, or municipal, and then lists exhaustively the categories of tax which are excepted from this principle. These exceptions include indirect taxes, such as 'purchase tax', which are normally incorporated in the price of goods or services, taxes on purely private immovable property, on private income or investments arising in the receiving state to which the diplomat is accredited, and estate or other inheritance duties. The Convention specifically exempts from any customs duties articles imported for the personal use of a diplomat or for members of his family who form part of his household. The International Law Commission considered this exemption to have been previously regarded as a matter of comity rather than of law; but it thought that the practice had become so general that it ought now to be accepted as law, and this recommendation was followed by the Vienna Conference.

The premises of a diplomatic mission are inviolable and may not be entered by agents of the receiving state except with the consent of the head of the mission. The premises, the property, and other effects of the mission and its means of transport are immune from any search, requisition, attachment or execution, and the premises are exempt from all forms of taxation, except such as represent payment for specific services.[1] Similarly, the official correspondence of the mission is inviolable, the diplomatic bag may not be opened, and the mission has the right to send messages in code and cipher.[2] On the other hand, the diplomatic bag may only contain diplomatic documents or articles intended for official use and, in case of suspected abuse, the receiving state

[1] The exemption does not apply where the law of the receiving state makes a tax payable by a person contracting with the sending state or the head of the mission.

[2] However, it may only install and use its own wireless with the consent of the receiving state.

may take the matter up with the head of mission or his state. The foregoing immunities in respect of the mission premises and communications, which are dealt with in some detail in the Convention, are of course essentially immunities attached to the property and communications of the state itself. The Convention, however, expressly provides that the private residence, papers, and correspondence of a diplomat shall enjoy the same inviolability as in the case of the mission itself; and this is equally true of his property except in the cases mentioned above, where he is not immune from civil jurisdiction.

The inviolability of diplomatic premises does not mean that they are to be considered as altogether outside the application of the law of the receiving state—a foreign enclave within its territory. Diplomatic missions, it is true, normally perform certain kinds of legal act for subjects of their home state, such as registration of deaths, births and marriages, legalization of signatures, issue of passports, &c. But the premises are not extra-territorial, and the head of mission cannot himself assume general powers of jurisdiction, even with respect to his own nationals; in 1896 when Sun Yat Sen, then a political refugee from China, had been induced to enter the Chinese Legation in London and was detained there in order to be sent to China, the British Government refused to accept the minister's contention that the Legation was Chinese territory, and peremptorily demanded his release, which was granted. Similarly, a crime committed in a foreign embassy is a crime committed

in the United Kingdom and the offender, if not protected by diplomatic immunity, is liable to prosecution in our courts.[1] Nor—the question of political
asylum apart[2]—may diplomatic premises be used as
an asylum for fugitives from justice. If a suspected
criminal takes refuge in diplomatic premises, the
proper course of the head of mission is either to surrender him or to consent to his arrest by the local
police on the premises. The immunity is granted only
for the purposes of the mission and the premises must
not be used in any manner incompatible with the
functions of the mission as laid down in the Vienna
Convention, in general international law or in particular treaties in force between the states concerned.

The immunities of a diplomat extend to members
of his family who form part of his household; they
also extend to the administrative and technical staff
of the mission, with the exceptions that they are only
exempt from civil proceedings with respect to acts
performed in the course of their duties and that the
exemption from customs duties only applies to
articles imported at the time of their first installation
in their posts. Under the Vienna Convention service
staff of the mission enjoy immunity in respect of acts
performed in the course of their duties and tax
exemption in respect of their wages as members of the
mission staff. Private servants also have tax exemption
in respect of their wages but otherwise only have such

[1] See *R.* v. *Kent* (or A.B.), [1941] 1 K.B. 454.
[2] Certain Latin-American states recognize as between themselves
a right to grant diplomatic asylum to political offenders.

privileges and immunities as may be accorded to them by the receiving state. In England domestic servants are expressly protected from civil proceedings by the Act of 1708, unless they engage in trade, but they are probably not exempt from criminal jurisdiction.[1]

The practice is for each head of mission to submit to the Foreign Office the names of those persons for whom any form of diplomatic status is claimed and, if accepted, they are included in a published list to which the courts will refer; in case of doubt the statement of the Foreign Office will be treated by the courts as conclusive of the matter.[2] Although acceptance by the Foreign Office normally leads automatically to the grant of the appropriate privileges and immunities, this is not so if, as not infrequently happens with administrative, technical, and domestic staff, the person concerned is a national of the United Kingdom.[3] Personal immunities are not granted to local nationals, only immunity in respect of their official acts on behalf of the foreign state; and this has been adopted as the general rule in the Vienna Convention.[4]

The immunities of an individual entitled to any form of diplomatic immunities normally cease either when he leaves the country or after the expiry of a reasonable period allowed to him in which to do so.[5]

---

[1] The 1951 Government Committee considered the liability of domestic servants to criminal jurisdiction to be an open question, and recommended that it should be left to the courts to decide.

[2] *Engelke* v. *Mussman*, [1928] A.C. 433.

[3] *Macartney* v. *Garbutt* (1890), 24 Q.B.D. 368.

[4] Article 38. [5] *Musurus Bey* v. *Gadban*, [1894] 2 Q.B. 352.

The Vienna Convention, having regard to difficulties experienced in the Second World War, lays down expressly that diplomats have the right to leave, and enjoy their personal immunities until allowed to do so, even in case of an armed conflict.[1] After their privileged status has finally ceased, diplomats remain immune in respect of acts performed in the exercise of their functions as a member of the mission, for those acts being attributable to the state itself remain protected;[2] on the other hand, as previously pointed out, they become liable to proceedings in respect of purely private acts, e.g. private investments or matrimonial irregularities, done during the tenure of their diplomatic posts.[3]

In the past third states have not infrequently accorded certain facilities to diplomats in passage through their territories to and from their posts; but it was generally considered that this was a matter only of comity and that third states were neither under an obligation to allow passage to foreign diplomats nor, if they did so, to accord them any special privileges or immunities. The Vienna Convention, while refraining from saying that there is any obligation on a third state to allow passage, does lay down as a new rule that, if a foreign diplomat is in its territory on the way to or returning from his post, a third state must accord him inviolability and such other immunities as are required to ensure his transit; and the same is provided for a member of his family form-

[1] Articles 39 and 44.
[2] Vienna Convention, Article 39.   [3] *Supra*, p. 244.

ing part of his household, while the third state is 'not to hinder the passage' of administrative, technical or service staff. It is also laid down that third states are bound to accord to diplomatic correspondence and communications and diplomatic couriers in transit over their territory the same freedom, protection, and inviolability as must be accorded to them by the state to which the diplomatic mission in question is accredited. These provisions mark an important innovation in the law of diplomatic relations.

Consuls are not diplomatic agents; they perform various services for a state or its subjects in another state, without, however, representing the former in the full sense. They may be nationals of either state, and generally they are made subject to the authority of the diplomatic representative of the state for which they act. They watch over commercial interests of the state for which they act; collect information for it; help its nationals with advice, administer their property if they die abroad, and register their births, deaths, and marriages; they authenticate documents for legal purposes, take depositions from witnesses, visa passports, and the like. They also have important functions concerned with shipping, sending home, for instance, shipwrecked or destitute persons, and settling disputes between master and crew.

Consular immunities have been much less well defined than those of diplomats and, according to a former Foreign Office legal adviser,[1] nowhere were they at a lower ebb than in the United Kingdom.

[1] Sir E. Beckett, *B.Y.I.L.*, 1944, p. 35.

Even so, two rules had, he thought, become established in customary law: the first was the inviolability of consular archives and correspondence, and the second the immunity of consular officers from either criminal or civil proceedings in respect of acts performed in their official capacity. Furthermore, during the past fifty years there has come into existence a large network of bilateral consular conventions setting out in considerable detail the privileges and immunities which the contracting parties were prepared to concede to each other's consuls; and these conventions show that there was more common ground in regard to consular status than had formerly been supposed. The International Law Commission, in preparing a Convention on Consular Intercourse and Immunities, has drawn largely upon the principles contained in these conventions without attempting to determine to what extent each one has already been accepted in customary law. It has also taken account of a tendency in recent times to assimilate, as far as is called for by their different functions, the status of career consuls to that of diplomats. The Commission's draft convention[1] admittedly contains a number of elements of 'progressive development' of the law which go beyond existing practice in regard to immunities of consuls, and it remains to be seen how far it will commend itself to governments. The Commission's text recognizes the inviolability of the consulate and of the consular archives, correspondence and communications, and the exemption

[1] *Report of the International Law Commission*, 1961, Ch. II.

of the consulate from taxation[1] on much the same
lines as in the case of diplomatic missions. It also
grants to career officials[2] exemption from taxation
and customs duties on the same lines as for diplomats,
but their exemption from the local jurisdiction is considerably more limited. Consuls are to be immune
only in respect of acts performed in the exercise of
consular functions, and they are expressly declared
to be bound to submit to the jurisdiction in criminal
proceedings.[3] These must, however, be conducted so
as to interfere as little as possible with the exercise of
their functions and for the same reason, except in the
case of a grave crime, career consuls may not be
arrested or detained pending trial and may not be
committed to prison save in execution of a judicial
decision of final effect. A further point is that consuls
are expressly stated to be liable to give evidence in
matters not connected with the exercise of their functions, though the Convention, going beyond the
existing practice, would not permit any sanction to
be applied to them should they decline to give evidence.[4] In other matters, such as the termination of
immunities and the obligations of third states, the
Convention largely follows the terms of the Vienna
Convention. Finally, it may be said that, if the Commission's draft Convention becomes law, not the
least important of its provisions will be those in

[1] Articles 30, 31, 32, and 35.
[2] Articles 48 and 49; the immunities of honorary consuls, i.e. non-
career officials, and of local nationals serving in foreign consulates.
[3] Article 43.   [4] Article 44.

Article 36, which guarantee the right of communication between a consulate and nationals of its home state within the district which it serves.

Immunity of armed forces. These, if not state agents in the ordinary sense, are state instrumentalities which may be found passing through or sojourning in another state's territory with the latter's consent, and delicate problems of their immunity from jurisdiction may arise. As to their transport and equipment, there can be no doubt; it is state property and, as such, immune from process. The leading case on the whole subject is the *Schooner Exchange*[1] in 1812, in which Chief Justice Marshall laid down that a foreign ship which enters a port with the express or implied consent of the local state is immune from jurisdiction, and a few years later our own Lord Stowell refused to allow a salvage lien to be enforced against a Netherlands warship.[2]

Warships and other public ships pose a special problem in that they are more than mere property; they form a closely integrated unit with their crews and constitute in the military sphere a state agency not very unlike an embassy or legation in the diplomatic. At any rate, not only can no process be instituted against the ship, but she is inviolable, and the local authorities may not enter her for any purpose without the consent of the commanding officer. This does not mean that a public ship, any more than an embassy, is immune from the local law and in that

[1] 1 Cranch 116.
[2] *The Prins Frederik* (1820), 2 Dods. 451.

sense extraterritorial; on the contrary she is bound to observe it in any matter which has effects external to the ship. For example, while she is entitled to apply her own law in matters of discipline, she must observe the local port and health regulations. If she breaks the local law she may be ordered to leave, but otherwise the only redress is through diplomatic action. That a warship is not outside the local law clearly appears in the decision of the Privy Council in *Chung Chi Chiung* v. *The King*,[1] where a British subject, member of the crew of a Chinese public ship, had murdered the captain on board the ship while in the territorial waters of Hong Kong. Having tried to commit suicide he was taken to a hospital in the Colony and, the Chinese Government's consent having been obtained, was subsequently tried and convicted in a Hong Kong court. On appeal, it was argued that the court had had no jurisdiction, and if a public ship really is extraterritorial and must therefore be considered foreign territory, the argument would have been sound. The Privy Council, however, took the view that a public ship merely has certain immunities and that, except to the extent that it is impeded by these immunities, the local law is applicable so that, the bar of the immunities having been removed, the local court was entitled to exercise its jurisdiction.

The laws and discipline of the sending state may be enforced on board a foreign public ship by court martial or otherwise, without infringing the sovereignty of the territorial state, and members of the

[1] (1939) A.C. 160.

crew are wholly exempt from the local jurisdiction so long as they remain on board. If they go ashore on official business, there is authority[1] for the view that they are in principle exempt from the local jurisdiction; and that, while they may be put under restraint should they commit offences ashore, they must be handed over to be dealt with under the laws of the sending state, if the commanding officer so requests. On the other hand, if they go ashore merely on leave, they are not exempt and may be arrested and tried before the local courts for breaches of the local law;[2] but if they regain their ship without having been arrested, the local authorities cannot insist upon their surrender, only that they should be dealt with under the law of the sending state.[3]

The above principles would appear to apply *mutatis mutandis* to military aircraft and to land forces passing through or visiting another state's territory as organized units, though opinion has been more divided on the question of land forces.[4] The view has sometimes been expressed in the United States that visiting foreign armed forces are wholly exempt from the local jurisdiction;[5] the general opinion, however, is that under general international law the exemption is

[1] Institute of International Law, 1928; *Ministère Public* v. *Triandafilou, Ann. Dig.*, 1919–42, Case No. 86.

[2] Where the offence is a minor one, it is usual as a matter of comity to hand the offender over to the commanding officer for disciplinary action.

[3] *Orfandis* v. *Ministère Public, Ann. Dig.*, 1943–5, Case No. 38.

[4] See generally Barton, *B.Y.I.L.*, 1949, p. 380, and 1950, p. 186.

[5] See King, *A.J.I.L.*, 1942, p. 557.

limited to matters connected with the discharge of the official business of the force. As in the case of ships, the sending state is fully entitled to exercise its disciplinary jurisdiction with respect to the members of its own forces: 'it is obvious', said Jordan C.J. in an Australian case,[1] 'that discipline could not be maintained if, when a member of the force had been confined to barracks, a local court would entertain an action by him against his superior for false imprisonment'. But whenever, outside the performance of official duties, a breach of the local law is committed, the local courts in principle have jurisdiction which they are entitled to insist upon exercising, although, if the breach of the local law, as is usually the case, is also an offence against discipline, the military authorities have a concurrent jurisdiction. The position in regard to military camps is less well defined. On the analogy of warships and embassies the local authorities would not be entitled to enter the camp to make an arrest or take evidence without the consent of the commandant; on the other hand, the local law would apply within the camp and an offence committed there would be cognizable in the local courts if the accused could be brought before them and the necessary evidence obtained; even so, it would be a question whether the consent of the sending state was necessary if the accused was a member of the foreign force. How far these principles are in fact admitted as the customary law on the matter is by no means clear, despite the now prevalent practice

[1] *Wright* v. *Cantrell, Ann. Dig.*, 1943–5, Case No. 37.

of associated states stationing contingents of their armed forces in each other's territories. The jurisdictional questions which arise are attended by so much risk of friction when foreign troops are stationed in a state's territory for any length of time that it has become the invariable practice to regulate them by treaty, either bilateral, such as the United States–Japan Administrative Agreement,[1] or multilateral, such as the N.A.T.O. Status of Forces Agreement.[2] These treaties, which also deal with such matters as tax and customs exemptions, recognize the dual systems of the disciplinary jurisdiction of the sending state and the territorial jurisdiction of the local state, and, where these are concurrent, regulate the priorities in regard to their application and their inter-relation with each other; they also provide for mutual assistance in effecting arrests. In general, these treaties give priority to the disciplinary jurisdiction where the offence is committed by a member of the visiting force against the sending state itself or its property or against another member of the force, but otherwise to the territorial jurisdiction; again, while they recognize the right of the military authorities to police their own camps, they also reserve the right of the local police to enter for the purpose of arresting an offender against the local law.

Waiver of immunity. The immunity, we have previously said, is in all cases that of the foreign state

[1] *State Department Bulletin*, 1953, p. 595.

[2] *A.J.I.L.*, 1954, Supplement, p. 83; and cf. Visiting Forces Act, 1952.

itself, which may waive its immunity, if it wishes, and consent to the court's jurisdiction being exercised either with respect to its own interests or those of its agents or armed forces. The question being that of the submission of a foreign sovereign to jurisdiction, the rules are strict. The Vienna Convention[1] lays down, with reference to diplomatic immunity, that 'waiver must always be express' and the rule can hardly be less strict in the case of proceedings directly involving the state itself. Under the existing practice, where a diplomat or state has appeared in the proceedings and has unequivocally put in a defence to the claim on the merits, waiver of immunity has been inferred; the courts have considered themselves entitled to assume that the diplomat or those representing the state in the proceedings had the necessary authority from the foreign government to submit to jurisdiction.[2] This practice has always involved the risk of a later objection from the government that it knew nothing of the matter and never authorized the waiver of its immunity, in which case the proceedings must be discontinued.[3] It seems reasonable to assume that in the case of a subordinate member of a diplomatic mission a waiver by the head of mission would be binding on his government, since the representation of his government in such a matter is within his

[1] Article 32; the text of the International Law Commission had contemplated that in civil proceedings waiver might be express *or implied*.

[2] *Taylor* v. *Best* (1854), 14 C.B. 487.

[3] See *Re Republic of Bolivia Exploration Syndicate* (1914), 1 Ch. 139; and *R.* v. *Madan*, [1961] 2 Q.B. 1.

diplomatic functions.[1] But the Court of Appeal has recently held that where the head of a foreign state trading agency, unaware of its privileged status, took steps without the knowledge of his home government to defend a case in which the agency was involved, this did not debar the government from afterwards invoking its immunity.[2] The court can scarcely be blamed for failing to insist upon evidence of waiver when a foreign trading organization does not indicate its connexion with its government. But the moment the court sees itself confronted with a foreign state or a privileged state agent it now seems clear—and the Vienna Convention indicates it—that its proper course is to call for express evidence of the waiver of immunity. When a foreign state or state agency has itself instituted proceedings, or a foreign diplomat has started an action on his own behalf, it has usually been regarded as an implied waiver of immunity for the purpose of the proceedings.[3] Certainly, it amounts to a submission to jurisdiction and it is well settled that the submission entitles the other party to make a counter-claim, or to ask for any other form of relief, which arises out of the same transaction as that which is the subject of the claim;[4] it does not, however, entitle him to set up another claim in respect of another matter not directly connected with the claim of the Government or diplomat, as the case may

---

[1] See *Price* v. *Griffin*, *B.Y.I.L.*, 1949, p. 433.
[2] *Baccus S.R.L.* v. *Servicio Nacional del Trigo*, [1957] 1 Q.B. 438.
[3] *Republic of Costa Rica* v. *Erlanger* (1876), 3 Ch.D. 62.
[4] *The Newbattle* (1885), 10 Ch.D. 33.

be.[1] There appears to be some tendency in United States courts to widen the scope of the submission to cover counter-claims not directly connected with the case submitted to the court by the government or diplomat.[2] But this view was not followed in the Vienna Convention, which simply provides that the institution of proceedings shall preclude a diplomat 'from invoking immunity in respect of any counter-claim directly connected with the principal claim'.

The more restrictive provision of the Vienna Convention is an application of the general principle that waiver must be express, which finds another important application in the rule—also adopted in the Convention—that waiver of immunity from jurisdiction does not imply at the same time a waiver of immunity from the execution of the judgment. A separate and express waiver of this immunity is necessary before a judgment obtained against the state or diplomat can be enforced by execution.[3] In other respects, however, a submission to jurisdiction does cover the whole course of the proceedings, including all appeals up to the highest court, so that a foreign sovereign who wins in the first court cannot then withdraw from the proceedings content with his victory.[4]

Finally, there is one point in which British practice is stricter than that of other countries, in a way

---

[1] *South-African Republic* v. *La Compagnie Franco-Belge du Chemin de Fer du Nord*, [1898] 1 Ch. 191.

[2] See R. B. Looper, *I.C.L.Q.*, 1956, p. 276.

[3] *Duff Development Co.* v. *Kelantan Government*, [1924] A.C. 797.

[4] *Sultan of Johore* v. *Abubakar etc.*, [1952] A.C. 318.

that seems most undesirable. British courts have held that a waiver of immunity, in order to be effective, must be one made 'in face of the court', that is, with respect to the actual proceedings in which the question of immunity is raised;[1] and this means that a state cannot bind itself beforehand by contract to submit disputes arising out of the contract to adjudication in British courts. Thus, in the recent case of *Kahan* v. *Federation of Pakistan*,[2] the government entered into a contract for the purchase of military equipment which provided that its interpretation should be governed by English law and stated that the government agreed 'to submit, for the purposes of the agreement, to the jurisdiction of the English courts'; yet, when disputes arose and the government objected to jurisdiction, the Court of Appeal felt constrained by the above-mentioned rule to hold that the waiver of immunity in the contract was ineffective. The Court of Appeal considered itself bound by a previous decision of its own and by that of the House of Lords in *Duff Development Co.* v. *Kelantan*;[3] but in a recent article[4] Dr. E. J. Cohn has urged that the Court was under some misapprehension as to the basis of the previous decisions and that it is not too late for the courts to change the rule. He also points out that, if the rule is not changed, the result is likely to be that parties contracting with foreign governments

---

[1] Cf. *Mighell* v. *Sultan of Johore*, [1894] 1 Q.B. 149; and *Duff Development Co.* v. *Kelantan Government*, [1924] A.C. 797.

[2] [1951] 2 Q.B. 1003.

[3] [1924] A.C. 797.

[4] *B.Y.I.L.*, 1958, p. 260.

will make their contracts subject to the jurisdiction of courts other than those of the United Kingdom.

§ 5. *Limitation upon a State's Treatment of Aliens*

No state is legally bound to admit aliens into its territory, but if it does so it must observe a certain standard of decent treatment towards them, and their own state may demand reparation for an injury caused to them by a failure to observe this standard. The legal basis of such a demand, in the words of the Permanent Court, is that

'in taking up the case of one of its nationals, by resorting to diplomatic action or international judicial proceedings on his behalf, a state is in reality asserting its own right, the right to ensure in the person of its nationals respect for the rules of international law. This right is necessarily limited to the intervention on behalf of its own nationals because, in the absence of a special agreement, it is the bond of nationality between the state and the individual which alone confers upon the state the right of diplomatic protection, and it is as a part of the function of diplomatic protection that the right to take up a claim and to ensure respect for the rules of international law must be envisaged.'[1]

There is a certain artificiality in this way of looking at the question. No doubt a state has in general an interest in seeing that its nationals are fairly treated in a foreign country, but it is an exaggeration to say that whenever a national is injured in a foreign state, his state as a whole is necessarily injured too. In

[1] *Panevezys-Saldutiskis Railway Case,* Series A/B 76, p. 16.

practice, as we shall see, the theory is not consistently adhered to; for instance, the logic of the theory would require that damages should be measured by reference to the injury suffered by the state, which is obviously not the same as that suffered by the individual, but in fact the law allows them to be assessed on the loss to the individual, as though it were the injury to him which was the cause of action. The procedure, too, is far from satisfactory from the individual's point of view. He has no remedy of his own, and the state to which he belongs may be unwilling to take up his case for reasons which have nothing to do with its merits; and even if it is willing to do so, there may be interminable delays before, if ever, the defendant state can be induced to let the matter go to arbitration. Delay, besides being unjust to the claimant, creates difficulties in securing satisfactory evidence, and also often leads to the original claim being exaggerated beyond all recognition. It has been suggested that a solution might be found by allowing individuals access in their own right to some form of international tribunal for the purpose, and if proper safeguards against merely frivolous or vexatious claims could be devised, that is a possible reform which deserves to be considered. For the time being, however, the prospect of states accepting such a change is not very great.

These claims are a fertile source of controversy among states, and much of the time of the legal department of every foreign office is devoted to them. They are also particularly suitable for judicial settlement, and there already exists a great volume of case law upon them. But in the absence of a regular procedure for dealing with them the rules by which they ought to be determined have been obscured, both by the tendency of the stronger powers to press the claims of their nationals without much regard to legal justification, and by that of the weaker powers to try to avoid responsibilities for corrupt or incompetent administration by exaggerated emphasis on the rights supposed to be inherent in their independent status.

In general a person who voluntarily enters the territory of a state not his own must accept the institutions of that state as he finds them. He is not entitled to demand equality of treatment in all respects with the citizens of the state; for example, he is almost always debarred from the political rights of a citizen; he is commonly not allowed to engage in the coasting trade, or to fish in territorial waters; he is sometimes not allowed to hold land. These and many other discriminations against him are not forbidden by international law. On the other hand, if a state has a low standard of justice towards its own nationals, an alien's position is in a sense a privileged one, for the standard of treatment to which international law entitles him is an objective one, and he need not, even though nationals must, submit to unjust treatment. This statement of the law is denied by certain Latin-American states, which hold that if a state grants equality of treatment to nationals and non-nationals it fulfils its international obligation; but such a view would make each state the judge of the standard required by international law, and would virtually deprive aliens of the protection of their own state altogether. 'Facts with respect to equality of treatment of aliens and nationals may be important in determining the merits of a complaint of mistreatment of an alien. But such equality is not the ultimate test of the propriety of the acts of the authorities in the light of international law. That test is, broadly speaking, whether aliens are treated in accordance with ordinary standards of civilization.'[1] As Hall[2] points out, international law itself is a product of the special civilization of modern Europe, and reflects the essential facts of that civilization so far as they are fit subjects for international rules; and among those facts is the existence in most states of a municipal law, consonant with modern European ideas, and so administered that foreigners may obtain criminal and civil justice from it. A state professing to be subject to international law is bound to furnish itself with such a system. The rule therefore that an alien must accept the institutions of a foreign state is qualified by the requirement that those institutions must conform to the standard set by international law; and if an alien suffers injury in person or property through the failure of a state to conform to that standard, his own state may prefer a claim to reparation on his behalf.

This international standard cannot be made a matter of precise rules. It is the standard of the 'reasonable state', reasonable, that is to say, according to the

[1] Opinions of U.S.-Mexican Claims Commission, *Roberts* case, at p. 105. [2] *International Law*, 8th ed., pp. 59–60.

notions that are accepted in our modern civilization. It was thus described by the U.S.-Mexican Claims Commission:[1]

'the propriety of governmental acts should be put to the test of international standards, and . . . the treatment of an alien, in order to constitute an international delinquency, should amount to an outrage, to bad faith, to wilful neglect of duty, or to an insufficiency of governmental action so far short of international standards that every reasonable and impartial man would readily recognize its insufficiency. Whether the insufficiency proceeds from deficient execution of an intelligent law or from the fact that the laws of the country do not empower the authorities to measure up to international standards is immaterial.'

The standard therefore is not an exacting one, nor does it require a uniform degree of governmental efficiency irrespective of circumstances; for example, measures of police protection which would be reasonable in a capital city cannot fairly be demanded in a sparsely populated territory, and a security which is normal in times of tranquillity cannot be expected in a time of temporary disorder such as may occasionally occur even in a well-ordered state. But the standard being an international one, a state cannot relieve itself of responsibility by any provision of its own national law. Thus the central government of a federal or other composite state may be *constitutionally* unable to secure that justice is rendered to an alien by the authorities of a member state or of a colony,

[1] Opinions of Commissioners, *Neers* case, at p. 73.

but if the central government is the only government which has relations with other states its *international* responsibility is not affected by the domestic limitation of its own powers.

It is ordinarily a condition of an international claim for the redress of an injury suffered by an alien that the alien himself should first have exhausted any remedies available to him under the local law. A state is not required to guarantee that the person or property of an alien will not be injured, and the mere fact that such an injury has been suffered does not give his own state a right to demand reparation on his behalf. If a state in which an alien is injured puts at his disposal apparently effective and sufficient legal remedies for obtaining redress, international law requires that he should have had recourse to and exhausted these remedies before his own state becomes entitled to intervene on his behalf.[1] The principle of this rule is that a state is entitled to have a full and proper opportunity of doing justice in its own way before international justice is demanded of it by another state. The local remedies which must be exhausted include administrative remedies of a legal nature but not extra-legal remedies or remedies as of grace.[2] They have also been held in the *Ambatielos Award*[3] to include purely procedural rights, such as the right to call a witness, if the exercise of the procedural right was essential to the success of the case. The Tribunal

---

[1] See *Resolution of the Institute of International Law* (1956), vol. 46, p. 364.
[2] *Finnish Vessels Arbitration* (1934), 3 *R.I.A.A.*, p. 1479.
[3] 1956 *International Law Reports*, p. 306.

in that arbitration summed up the rule by saying that 'it is the whole system of legal protection, as provided by municipal law, which must have been put to the test'. Although, therefore, the local remedies rule is applied with a certain strictness, it does not mean that it is necessary for the individual to exhaust remedies which, though theoretically available, would be ineffective or insufficient to redress the injury of which he complains; for example, if the case or statute law binding upon the local courts was such as must compel them to reject his claim, or if, his claim having been lost in a lower court, it was useless to appeal because the critical point was one of fact and the higher court had no power to alter findings of fact.[1] If the local tribunals are notoriously corrupt or notoriously discriminate against foreigners, the individual is not required 'to exhaust justice when there is no justice to exhaust'.[2] Again, if the wrong has been committed by the legislature itself or by some high official, it not infrequently happens that the local law provides no remedy and in that case there are no local remedies to exhaust.[3] In general, therefore, the prior exhaustion of local remedies is a condition of presenting an international claim unless it can be shown that either there were no local remedies to exhaust or that it was obviously futile to have recourse to those that were available.[4]

---

[1] *Finnish Vessels Arbitration, supra*, p. 281.
[2] *Robert E. Brown Case* (1923), *R.I.A.A.*, vol. 6, p. 120.
[3] See *Interhandel Case, I.C.J. Reports*, 1959, p. 27.
[4] See generally Judge A. Bagge in *B.Y.I.L.*, 1958.

Another condition of presenting an international claim is that there should be a bond of nationality between the claimant state and the person injured.[1] So much is the bond of nationality a condition of an international claim that it must not only exist at the date of the original injury but must also continue until the date of the judgment or award. Thus, if the beneficial interest in the claim has meanwhile passed, by death or by assignment, from the person originally injured to a person of a different nationality, the right to bring an international claim will lapse.[2] In principle, international law leaves it to each state to settle by its own laws the rules determining the persons whom it considers to be its own nationals. The International Court, however, has laid down in the *Nottebohm* case[3] that the provisions of a state's municipal laws are not necessarily conclusive to establish its right to exercise diplomatic protection under international law, if the bond of nationality between the person injured and the claimant state is not a real and effective one. In the particular circumstances of that case the Court declined on this ground to treat a naturalization decree, effective to confer Liechtenstein nationality under Liechtenstein law, as sufficient to establish Liechtenstein's right to bring an international claim on behalf of the individual concerned. On the other hand, international law does admit a few, very special, cases in which a right to

---

[1] *Panevezys-Saldutiskis Railway Case*, Series A/B No. 76, p. 16.

[2] *The Stevenson Claim* (1903), 9 *R.I.A.A.*, p. 494.

[3] *I.C.J. Reports*, 1955, p. 23.

exercise diplomatic protection of non-nationals is recognized on the basis that the persons concerned are to be assimilated to nationals, for example, inhabitants of a protected state or aliens serving on the merchant ships or in the armed forces of the claimant state.[1]

A state may incur responsibility by the act or omission of any of its organs, legislative, executive, or judicial, but these cases require separate consideration. As an example of legislative action towards an alien in violation of international law may be cited the Costa Rican law, already referred to,[2] nullifying contracts made by the *de facto* government of Tinoco. In recent years difficult questions have been raised by legislation in certain states expropriating private property without compensation. There is no doubt that such a measure directed against the property of aliens as such would violate international law, but if it is applied for some public purpose without discriminating either avowedly or in fact between nationals and aliens the matter is less clear. The precedents are indecisive; but it is submitted that Sir John Fischer Williams[3] is right in concluding that there is not, nor is it desirable that there should be, any absolute rule forbidding the taking of an alien's property by a state without compensation. The sanctity of private property may be in general a sound maxim of legislative

---

[1] *Reparation for Injuries Case, I.C.J. Reports,* 1949, p. 202.

[2] *Supra,* pp. 144–5.

[3] 'International Law and the Property of Aliens', *B.Y.I.L.,* 1928, p. 1; cf. A. P. Fachiri, *B.Y.I.L.,* 1929, p. 32.

policy, but it is difficult in these days to hold that it
may in no circumstances be required to yield to some
higher public interest. 'Whatever may be our views
as to the relative merits of socialist and individualist
doctrines, it is impossible to assert that modern
civilization requires all states to accept unreservedly
the theories of one side in the great economic conflict.'

In certain circumstances the wrongful act of an
official may involve his state in responsibility to the
state of an injured alien. In the first place the official
must have acted within the scope of his office; otherwise his act would be like that of a private individual.
Secondly, a state has a higher responsibility for the
acts of superior officials than for those of subordinates.
For the former it is responsible, provided only that
the local remedies, if any, have been exhausted without redress being secured. Thus in *The Sidra*[1] the
Anglo-American Claims Tribunal awarded damages
to Great Britain in respect of injury to a British merchant vessel to which the negligent navigation of an
American government vessel in Baltimore harbour
had contributed; and in the *Zafiro*[2] the same tribunal awarded compensation for British property
looted by the Chinese crew of an American supply
ship at Manila, on the ground that in the circumstances the American officers were at fault in letting
the crew get out of hand; there would have been no
liability for the action of the crew as such. For the
actions of subordinate employees of the state, such as

[1] *Nielsen's Report*, p. 452.   [2] *Nielsen's Report*, p. 578.

unofficered soldiers, members of a crew, policemen, and the like, some further act or omission is necessary to fix the state with responsibility, that is to say, something more than a mere failure to redress the wrong. There must be either a 'denial of justice' in the sense defined below, or something which indicates the complicity of the state in, or its condonation of, the original wrongful act, such as an omission to take disciplinary action against the wrongdoer.

The term 'denial of justice'[1] is sometimes loosely used to denote *any* international delinquency towards an alien for which a state is liable to make reparation. In this sense it is an unnecessary and confusing term. Its more proper sense is an injury involving the responsibility of the state committed by a court of justice, and on the question what acts of this kind do involve the state in responsibility there are two views. Most Latin-American states insist on a very narrow interpretation, and contend in effect that if the courts give a decision of any kind there can be no denial of justice and consequently no responsibility of the state for their conduct. Nothing but the denial to foreigners of access to the courts can be properly regarded as a denial of justice. This view, which involves the virtual rejection of the principle of an international standard applicable to the action of courts of law towards foreigners, cannot be accepted. There are many possible ways in which a court may fall below the standard fairly to be demanded of a civilized state without

[1] See Fitzmaurice, 'Meaning of the Term Denial of Justice', *B.Y.I.L.*, 1932, p. 93.

literally closing its doors. Such acts cannot be exhaustively enumerated, but corruption, threats, unwarrantable delay, flagrant abuse of judicial procedure, a judgment dictated by the executive, or so manifestly unjust that no court which was both competent and honest could have given it, are instances. Possibly it is convenient also to include in the term certain acts or omissions of organs of government other than courts, but closely connected with the administration of justice, such as execution without trial, inexcusable failure to bring a wrongdoer to trial, long imprisonment before trial, grossly inadequate punishment, or failure to enforce a judgment duly given. But no merely erroneous or even unjust judgment of a court will constitute a denial of justice, except in one case, namely where a court, having occasion to apply some rule of international law, gives an incorrect interpretation of that law, or where it applies, as it may be bound by its municipal law to do, a rule of domestic law which is itself contrary to international law.

It will be observed that even on the wider interpretation of the term 'denial of justice' which is here adopted, the misconduct must be extremely gross. The justification of this strictness is that the independence of courts is an accepted canon of decent government, and the law therefore does not lightly hold a state responsible for their faults. It follows that an allegation of a denial of justice is a serious step which states, as mentioned above, are reluctant to take when a claim can be based on other grounds.

The desire of certain states to limit their international responsibility as strictly as possible in the matter of the treatment of foreigners has already been referred to; it appears clearly in the decisive importance which they try to attach to the absence of discrimination between foreigners and nationals, and in the narrow sense which they give to a denial of justice. But besides contending for a restricted interpretation of their legal obligations, some states have attempted to exclude their responsibility altogether by a term in the contract which they make with the alien whereby the latter purports to waive the protection of his own state. Such a term is known as a 'Calvo Clause'. It takes different forms, but the following is a typical illustration:

'The contractor and [his employees] shall be considered as Mexicans in all matters within the Republic of Mexico concerning . . . the fulfilment of this contract. They shall not claim, nor shall they have, with regard to the interests and the business connected with this contract, any other rights or means to enforce the same than those granted by the laws of the Republic to Mexicans. . . . They are consequently deprived of any rights as aliens, and under no conditions shall the intervention of foreign diplomatic agents be permitted.'[1]

The validity of a Calvo clause has often been considered by international tribunals and their decisions are not uniform. The objection to it is that the individual who enters into the contract cannot waive a right which belongs not to himself but to his government;

---

[1] *North American Dredging Co. of Texas* v. *Mexico*. Opinions of U.S.-Mexican Claims Commission, p. 21.

and if the clause is so framed as to make him purport to do this, to that extent at any rate it should be held to be a nullity. 'Such government', as the Commission said in the case from which the clause above is taken, 'frequently has a larger interest in maintaining the principles of international law than in recovering damage for one of its citizens in a particular case, and manifestly such citizen cannot by contract tie in this respect the hands of his government.'

It is apparent from the preceding discussion that a state incurs no responsibility for an injury suffered by an alien unless some fault either of commission or omission can be attributed to itself. It follows that it is not responsible for an injury which results from the act of a private individual. Such an act, however, may be an occasion out of which state responsibility may indirectly arise, but only if it is accompanied by circumstances which can be regarded as in some way, by complicity before or condonation after the event, making the state itself a party to the injurious act of the individual. It is therefore necessary in such a case to ask, firstly, whether the state ought to have prevented the injurious act, and secondly, whether it has taken the remedial steps which the law requires of it. Thus where the injury in question would not have occurred if the state through its officers had been reasonably diligent, responsibility will be incurred. The standard of diligence naturally varies with circumstances. For example, the fact that the individual was one of a mob of rioters or of a body of insurgents might, according to circumstances, indicate either that special precautions ought to have been taken, or that the authorities were faced with a situation so difficult that they could not reasonably be expected to do more than they did.[1]

The application of this principle to *political* crimes was authoritatively defined by a Committee of Jurists appointed by the Council of the League after the murder of the Italian General Tellini on Greek territory in 1923, in the following terms:

'The responsibility of a State is only involved by the commission in its territory of a political crime against the persons of foreigners if the State has neglected to take all reasonable measures for the prevention of the crime and the pursuit, arrest, and bringing to justice of the criminal. The recognized public character of a foreigner and the circumstances in which he is present in its territory, entail upon the State a corresponding duty of special vigilance on his behalf.'

If there has been no failure of diligence on the part of the state in its preventive measures, it may still incur responsibility through the injurious act of a private individual, but only in the event of a denial of justice in the sense already discussed. A state is not required to *guarantee* the effectiveness of its remedial machinery, and therefore the mere failure of the injured person to secure adequate redress through the courts, if it falls short of a denial of justice, is not enough to fix the state with liability.

[1] Compare the case *Youmans* v. *Mexico*, U.S.–Mexican Claims Commission Reports, p. 150, with that of the *Home Missionary Society*, before the Anglo-American Claims Tribunal, *Nielsen's Report*, p. 421.

It has been stated that the theory underlying the law of state responsibility for injuries to foreigners is that the claimant state seeks redress, not directly for an injury to one of its nationals, but for an injury suffered by itself *through* its national. If this principle were consistently applied, we might expect that the measure of damages would be determined by assessing the injury suffered by the state, and so arriving at a figure which would bear no necessary relation to the extent of the loss suffered by the injured individual. This, however, is not the law; for though in practice tribunals exercise a rather wide discretion in fixing the amount of reparation due, they base it primarily on an estimate of the loss caused to the injured individual, or, if he has lost his life, on the loss caused by his death to his dependants.[1]

§ 6. *Limits upon a State's Treatment of its own Nationals*[2]

Under customary law no rule was clearer than that a state's treatment of its own nationals is a matter exclusively within the domestic jurisdiction of that state, i.e. is not controlled or regulated by international law. It is true that on a number of occasions the Great Powers intervened in the Turkish Empire to prevent large-scale atrocities, and that there was some support among writers for a right of collective humanitarian intervention, but that was all so far as

[1] For a discussion of some of the difficulties of applying this principle see Brierly, 'The Theory of Implied State Complicity in International Claims', in *B.Y.I.L.*, 1928.

[2] See generally Lauterpacht, *International Law and Human Rights* (1950).

customary law was concerned. Otherwise, almost the only restrictions placed upon a state's treatment of its own nationals before the League period were to be found in a handful of treaty provisions for religious protection.[1] The first major advance came with the insertion in the peace treaties after the First World War of clauses for the protection of minorities; for the execution of these clauses was placed under the guarantee of the League, and in some cases the clauses even included a right to bring petitions before a special tribunal.[2] But, of course, these treaty clauses only covered the case of the minorities in question and did nothing to create general obligations to respect fundamental human rights. One development of a more general kind, however, was the conclusion of a number of labour conventions under the International Labour Organization.

The appalling atrocities of the Nazis against the Jews and against other races during the Second World War led to a strong movement for the international protection of fundamental human rights, and the Charter contains numerous references to them. The more important of them are (a) Article 1, which states one of the purposes of the United Nations to be to achieve co-operation in promoting and encouraging respect for human rights and fundamental freedoms for all without distinction as to

[1] e.g. Augsburg (1555), Osnabrück (1648), Utrecht (1737), and the Congress of Vienna (1815).

[2] e.g. The Upper Silesian Tribunal; see *Steiner & Gross* v. *The Polish State, Ann. Dig.* (1927–8), Case No. 88.

race, sex, language, or religion; (*b*) Article 55, which
repeats that purpose in the form of an *obligation* upon
the United Nations Organization; and (*c*) Article 56,
by which individual members pledge themselves to
take 'joint and separate action' in co-operation with
the Organization to the same ends. The Charter does
not, however, define what exactly are the fundamental human rights and freedoms of which it
speaks, nor does it make any mention of machinery
to secure their observance. On the contrary, it states
as a general principle in Article 2 (7) that nothing
in the Charter is to 'authorize the United Nations to
intervene in matters which are essentially within the
domestic jurisdiction of any State'. This provision
at once raises the query as to how far, if at all, the
Organization is entitled to look into allegations of
breaches of human rights by individual members as
distinct from trying to encourage respect for human
rights generally among members; and some even
argue that the Charter clauses only contain a pious
injunction to co-operate in promoting respect for
human rights and do not impose any legal obligation
on members with regard to their own nationals. The
latter argument seems in any event to go too far,
since a pledge to co-operate in promoting at least
implies a negative obligation not so to act as to
undermine human rights; for this reason South
Africa's racial segregation policies appear to be out
of harmony with her obligations under the Charter.
But the absence of any definition of human rights
and freedoms in the Charter did, of course, greatly

weaken the legal content of the Charter clauses, and so an attempt was made to fill them out by drawing up in 1948 the 'Universal Declaration of Human Rights and Fundamental Freedoms'. This document, which defines in some detail fundamental rights, such as the rights to life and liberty of the person, to a fair trial in criminal proceedings, &c., and fundamental freedoms such as freedom of expression, religion, association, &c., is a declaration adopted by resolution, not a treaty; and it was not intended to be a legal instrument binding on members. Nevertheless, it has gained considerable authority as a general guide to the content of fundamental rights and freedoms as understood by members of the United Nations, and it is important as providing a connecting link between different concepts of human rights in different parts of the world. Subsequently, efforts have been made to arrive at *covenants* further defining the rights and freedoms and providing machinery for dealing with complaints of violation of the covenants. However, over-elaboration and doctrinaire approaches to controversial issues deprived these efforts of any chance of success, and the United Nations has had to be content with completing a few special conventions, such as those on 'genocide' and the political rights of women, which contain no machinery for their application.

How far, then, is the United Nations entitled to concern itself with complaints of violations of human rights? Relying on its general power to discuss any matters within the scope of the Charter, the Assembly has asserted the right to discuss such complaints and to make recommendations in regard to them; it has, for example, debated such matters as the Soviet refusal to allow the Russian wives of foreigners to leave with their husbands, the oppression of the religious leaders in Hungary, Bulgaria, and Roumania, the treatment of persons of Indian race in South Africa, South Africa's segregation measures. This interference in the internal jurisdiction of member states with respect to their own nationals has been defended[1] on the basis that mere discussion and recommendation do not amount to 'intervention' within the meaning of Article 2 (7); according to this doctrine there would only be intervention if the United Nations went further and made recommendations in regard to human rights, with the implication of possible enforcement action if they were not complied with. Although this line of argument presents certain difficulties, the practice of the United Nations makes it clear that the Organization holds itself entitled to 'consider', 'discuss', and 'recommend' with regard to breaches of human rights; on the other hand, it cannot address dictatorial injunctions to the offending state unless the breaches are of such a kind as to endanger peace. Politically, the human rights activities of the United Nations have had a certain importance and the Universal Declaration and other instruments have made a certain contribution to 'promoting' the cause of human rights; but the United Nations has not so far proved an effective

[1] See Lauterpacht, op. cit., ch. 10.

instrument for remedying flagrant violations of elementary rights and freedoms.

Progress in the enforcement of human rights is perhaps more likely to be made through regional organizations, and a promising beginning has been made by the Council of Europe with the European Convention for the Protection of Human Rights and Fundamental Freedoms, which came into force in 1953. This Convention in the first instance restricted the rights to be protected to a limited number of elemental rights and freedoms, to which others are gradually being added by new Protocols; and it established machinery for their enforcement which consists of a Commission and a Court of Human Rights, backed by the Committee of Ministers. Members are not, however, all obliged to accept the Court's jurisdiction, but, as with the International Court, may do so either by a general declaration or *ad hoc* for the particular case. The system of guarantees is twofold, one compulsory and the other optional. Under the compulsory system every state, party to the Convention, has the right unilaterally to bring before the Commission alleged breaches of the Convention; if the Commission considers the case *prima facie* admissible, it is referred for examination to a sub-commission, which hears the parties and has power, if necessary, to carry out investigations in the territory concerned. If the sub-commission fails to obtain a friendly settlement, the Commission draws up a report to the Committee of Ministers, giving its findings as to whether the facts disclose a breach. At this point the question arises whether the case is to be referred to the Court and, assuming that the parties have both accepted the Court's jurisdiction, either the Commission or one of the parties may bring it before the Court at any time within three months after the filing of the Commission's report with the ministers. In that event, the Court takes up the investigation of the case and its decision is final and binding on the states concerned. If the case does not go to the Court, the Committee of Ministers themselves give the final decision by a two-thirds vote, and their decision also is binding on the parties. In either event the responsibility of securing compliance with the decision rests with the Committee of Ministers.

The other system is the grant to individuals or groups of individuals of a right themselves to address a petition to the Commission without the intervention of any state on their behalf; this system is, however, optional for each state, and it says much for the Council of Europe that no less than ten of the fourteen[1] contracting parties have accepted the obligation to meet the complaints of their own nationals before the Commission. Naturally, it is a precondition of this right of petition that the individuals should have exhausted the domestic remedies available in their own country; and the Commission also has the power and duty to reject *in limine* all petitions which are incompatible with the Convention, manifestly ill-founded, or an abuse of the right of petition. Petitions from individuals which are

[1] France has not ratified the Convention.

accepted by the Commission as *prima facie* admissible—and these are a very small proportion—are handled in the same way as applications from states. Individuals, however, have no right of access to the Court, so that these petitions may only be brought before the Court by the Commission itself or by a state.

Three cases have been brought by states, two by Greece with respect to matters in Cyprus and one by Austria against Italy with respect to a matter in the Alto Adige. In all of them, therefore, the applicant state was specially interested, and it is frequently urged that state action is likely to prove an inadequate form of guarantee and that the right of individual petition is an essential part of an international system for the protection of human rights. The right of individual petition is open to considerable abuse, and one of the Commission's essential functions is to sift the large numbers of petitions sent to it and retain only those which appear to have some semblance of a basis.[1] In some six years it has handled over one thousand applications, retaining only a very small proportion for close examination. The Court has only been in operation for about two years, and up to date two cases have been referred to it, and it has delivered one important judgment[2] concerning the detention of persons without trial in the Irish Republic. The European Convention has passed out of the stage of experiment, and is now established as a fully

[1] For the handling of these petitions, see Waldock, *B.Y.I.L.*, 1959, p. 362.
[2] The *Lawless* case, *A.J.I.L.*, 1962, p. 171.

working system. It has shown that, at least among peoples of similar cultures and traditions, the international protection of human rights need not be dismissed as altogether visionary.

§ 7. *The Limits upon a State's Criminal Jurisdiction*[1]

International practice on this matter is not uniform. It is agreed that a state is competent to deal with any offence committed within its territory, without regard to the nationality of the offender. It is agreed also that a state may assume jurisdiction over offences committed by its own nationals abroad, though not all states do so. It is not agreed whether a state may in any circumstances punish a foreigner for an act committed outside its territory, and therefore at a time when he was not subject to that state's criminal law.

Three different practices exist on the matter. One group of states, which includes Great Britain and the United States, takes its stand on the principle of the territoriality of criminal jurisdiction; we do not admit that a state may punish an alien for a breach of its criminal law, if the act was committed outside its territory and therefore in a place at which that law was not in force. This was the difficulty in bringing the Irishman, 'Lord Haw-Haw', to trial for subversive broadcasts made from Germany during the Second World War, a difficulty which the courts surmounted by finding a kind of constructive allegiance to the Crown in his use of a British passport.[2] Another group, which includes France, Germany, and perhaps

[1] Cf. W. E. Beckett, ibid., 1925, p. 44, and 1927, p. 108.
[2] *Joyce* v. *Director of Public Prosecutions*, [1946] A.C. 347.

a majority of states, also accepts the principle of territoriality, but admits certain exceptions, generally for acts directed against the security of the state or its financial credit. The third group, which includes Turkey, Italy, and some others, rejects the territorial principle, and seems to base its law on the theory that crime, wherever committed, is a social evil which all civilized states are interested in suppressing; in practice these states avoid the anarchy of jurisdictions to which this so-called 'universal' theory of crime might lead by certain concessions to the territorial principle, and apply their criminal law only to the acts of foreigners committed abroad when these are prejudicial to the state or to one of their own nationals.

Great Britain and the United States, however, though they deny the legitimacy of exceptions to the territorial basis of criminal jurisdiction over non-nationals, admit that in certain circumstances a crime may be committed *within* the territory of a state and therefore be justiciable by its criminal courts, even though the actor may be physically outside the territory. An obvious illustration would be that of a man who fires a gun across a frontier and kills another man in a neighbouring state; in such a case the jurisdiction of the country from which the gun is fired has been called 'subjective', and that of the country in which the shot takes effect 'objective territorial jurisdiction'. The existence of this objective territorial jurisdiction has been recognized frequently by English and American courts, e.g. in *Rex* v. *Godfrey*,[1] an English

[1] [1932] 1 K.B. 24.

court ordered the extradition to Switzerland for trial there of a man who, being himself in England, was alleged to have procured his partner, who was in Switzerland, to obtain goods there by false pretences; and in *Ford* v. *United States*[1] in 1927 the Supreme Court upheld the conviction for conspiracy against the United States liquor laws of certain British subjects whose ship was at the time on the high seas. Such cases appear to justify the dictum of Judge Moore in the *Lotus* case, mentioned below, that

'It appears to be now universally admitted that when a crime is committed in the territorial jurisdiction of one state as the direct result of the act of a person at the time corporeally present in another state, international law, by reason of the principle of constructive presence of the offender at the place where his act took effect, does not forbid the prosecution of the offender by the former state, should he come within its territorial jurisdiction.'

It is clear that the recognition of an objective territorial jurisdiction by states which do not in terms admit any exception to the territorial basis of criminal jurisdiction, much reduces the gulf between their view and that of the second group of states just mentioned, at any rate if we may assume that these states would not claim to define acts directed against their security in an arbitrary way so as to include, for example, criticism of their governments published in a foreign press. But the objective territorial theory does not meet at all the views of states which claim a universal competence for their criminal courts, and

[1] 273 U.S. 593.

even if this claim is limited in practice to a claim to try offences against nationals, it rests on a false view of the nature of the right of protecting nationals which international law recognizes; states have a right of diplomatic protection, a right to demand reparation for injuries done to their nationals abroad, but not a right to throw the shield of their own criminal law round them at a time when they have left its shelter.

The Permanent Court considered the law on this matter in the *Lotus* case,[1] which arose out of a collision outside Turkish territorial waters, between the French steamer *Lotus* and the Turkish collier *Boz-Kourt*, in which the *Boz-Kourt* was sunk with loss of life. The *Lotus* proceeded to Constantinople, where the officers in charge of both ships were tried and convicted of manslaughter. The Turkish court appears to have acted under an article of the Turkish Penal Code, giving jurisdiction, with certain limiting conditions, to Turkish courts to try any foreigner who commits an offence abroad to the prejudice of Turkey or of a Turkish subject. The French Government denied the validity of this article in international law. Six judges refrained from expressing an opinion on the international validity of the article, but held that no rule of international law forbade the Turkish court to assume jurisdiction in the specific facts of this case, since the effects of the offence had been produced on the Turkish vessel, although the actor himself was on board the French vessel. Judge Moore agreed with the result at which the majority had arrived, but

[1] Publications of the Permanent Court, Series A, Judgment No. 10.

held that the article was 'contrary to well-settled principles of international law'. It meant, he said, that

'the citizen of one country, when he visits another country, takes with him for his protection the law of his own country, and subjects those with whom he comes into contact to the operation of that law. In this way an inhabitant of a great commercial city, in which foreigners congregate, may in the course of an hour unconsciously fall under the operation of a number of foreign criminal codes. . . . No one disputes the right of a state to subject its citizens abroad to the operations of its own penal laws, if it sees fit to do so. . . . But the case is fundamentally different where a country claims either that its penal laws apply to other countries and to what takes place wholly within such countries, or, if it does not claim this, that it may punish foreigners for alleged violation, even in their own country, of laws to which they were not subject.'

The five remaining judges dissented from the judgment of the Court.

It will be observed that the majority of the Court, by assimilating the Turkish vessel to Turkish territory, brought the case under the principle of the 'objective territorial jurisdiction'. That principle, as stated above, is accepted generally, but its application to the collision of two ships at sea was described by Lord Finlay in his dissenting judgment as a new and startling application of a metaphor, and he added: 'The jurisdiction over crimes committed on a ship at sea is not of a territorial nature at all. It depends upon the law which for convenience and by common consent is applied to the case of chattels of such a very special nature as ships.' . . . Lord Finlay's concern at the implications of the decision of the majority was shared by maritime organizations, who feared that masters might be exposed to double prosecutions—in the foreign port and by the authorities of the flag state—and that ships would be held up by proceedings in foreign courts. The rule laid down by the Court in the *Lotus* case has, in fact, been set aside by the Brussels Convention of 1952[1] and by the Geneva Convention of 1958 on the Régime of the High Seas.[2] Under these Conventions, when a collision takes place on the high seas, penal and disciplinary jurisdiction with respect to the master of any vessel involved belongs exclusively to the flag state of his vessel, with the single exception that if the master is a national of another state, the right of that state to discipline or prosecute its national is reserved.

§ 8. *Jurisdiction on the High Seas*

At the dawn of international law most maritime states claimed sovereignty over certain seas; Venice claimed the Adriatic, England the North Sea, the Channel, and large areas of the Atlantic, Sweden the Baltic, and Denmark–Norway all the northern seas. Indeed the modern theory that the open sea is free

[1] International Convention for the Unification of Certain Rules relating to Penal Jurisdiction in matters of Collision or other Incidents of Navigation (H.M. Stationery Office, Cmd. No. 8954).
[2] Article 11.

and common to all would have been unsuited to
the times. The state which claimed the seas often
rendered a service to all by policing them against
piracy; and in return it claimed proprietary rights
over them. It might require ceremonial honours to
be paid to its flag; it might reserve the fisheries for
itself, or make foreigners take out a licence; it might
levy tolls on the ships of other nations; sometimes it
even prohibited navigation to them altogether.

The reaction came in the sixteenth century. Under
Bulls of Pope Alexander VI of 1493 Spain and
Portugal claimed to divide the New World between
themselves; Spain claimed the whole Pacific and the
Gulf of Mexico; Portugal the Indian Ocean and most
of the Atlantic, and both excluded foreigners from
these vast areas. In 1609 Grotius published his *Mare
Liberum* in justification of Dutch resistance to the
Portuguese claims, maintaining that the sea could
not be made the property of any state. In England
John Selden replied to him with the *Mare Clausum*,
published in 1635, maintaining the English claims.
As yet there was no general hostility to the existence
of sovereignty over the sea; what the nations wanted,
and what they eventually succeeded in establishing,
was freedom of navigation, which was quite consistent with the existence of sovereignty. Gradually,
the more extreme claims were dropped and by the
beginning of the nineteenth century the principle of
the freedom of the high seas had been established.
'Upon the ocean, in time of peace', said a great
United States judge in 1826, 'all possess an entire

equality. It is the common highway of all, appropriated to the use of all, and no one can vindicate to himself a superior or exclusive prerogative there.'

So far as concerns use, the freedom of the high seas meant that each and every state was recognized in law to have an equal right to navigate upon and to exploit the high seas right up to the edge of the territorial sea; and they possessed this right not jointly but severally, each one having the same unrestricted right of use and enjoyment. It also meant that no preference or priority was recognized in favour of the nearest coastal state or of the states of the particular region. Thus, while adjacent states tended to play the major part in the exploitation of fisheries, yet in several areas high-seas fisheries were exploited by more distant states and important multi-national fisheries established, for example, off Iceland and Newfoundland and in the North Sea. Similarly, whaling and sealing have been carried on by the nationals of states remote from the whaling and sealing grounds. In this way a number of states had built up something like vested interests in the resources of particular areas.

So far as concerns jurisdiction, the freeing of the high seas from the exclusive sovereignty of individual states did not leave them subject to no jurisdiction. The right of jurisdiction, like the rights of navigation and exploitation, became vested in each and every state. It was not, however, a condominium with all states exercising concurrent jurisdiction over all vessels and persons on the high seas; the jurisdiction of each state was limited to its own vessels and nationals. This cardinal rule of the law of the sea was established by decisions of English[1] and American[2] courts early in the nineteenth century in connexion with British arrests of foreign vessels engaged in the slave trade. Even a treaty for the abolition of the slave trade was held not to justify the arrest of a vessel of the other party, unless the treaty specifically conferred that right upon the contracting states. Cases of piracy,[3] where the protection of the national flag is forfeited, were recognized to be an exception to the general rule; and in one other case, 'hot pursuit', the arrest was permitted on the high seas of a foreign vessel, which, having been detected in a breach of the law of the coastal state, was chased in hot pursuit on to the high seas. Otherwise, and apart from the controversial question of the 'contiguous zone', the only right admitted with respect to foreign vessels in peacetime was a right to approach them for the purpose of verifying their identity. The general rule, in the words used by the Permanent Court in the *Lotus* case,[4] was:

'Vessels on the high seas are subject to no authority except that of the State whose flag they fly. In virtue of the principle of the freedom of the seas, that is to say, the absence of any territorial sovereignty upon the high seas, no State may exercise any kind of jurisdiction over foreign vessels upon them.'

[1] *Le Louis* (1817), 2 Dodson 210.
[2] *The Antelope* (1825), 10 Wheaton 66.
[3] *The Magellan Pirates* (1853), 1 Spinks 81.
[4] (1928) Series A/10, p. 25.

The twin principles, that on the high seas each state severally has free use of the natural resources and exclusive jurisdiction over its own vessels, necessarily led to the result that conservation of the natural resources of the high seas could only be achieved by agreement between the interested states. The point was high-lighted in the *Behring Sea Fur Seal Arbitrations* of 1892 and 1902, the first of which concerned United States arrests of Canadian sealers on the high seas, who were taking large numbers of pregnant female seals and in this way endangering the Alaskan seal stocks, while the second concerned Russian arrests of United States sealers who were similarly endangering Russian seal stocks. In both these cases the Tribunal rejected the idea that a coastal state has a right to apply conservation to foreign vessels in areas of the high seas adjacent to its coasts for the purpose of safeguarding valuable natural resources against selfish and wasteful exploitation and confirmed that, in the absence of a treaty, a coastal state could only apply conservation measures to vessels of its own flag. These decisions were only made tolerable by the subsequent conclusion of conservation treaties between the interested states, and they primarily served to underline the inadequacy of the existing law for preventing the exhaustion of high seas resources through excessive or wasteful exploitation. In fisheries and whaling also the development of new techniques was raising the problem of conservation and a number of regional agreements, like the North Sea Fisheries Convention of 1882, were concluded. Treaties, however, are only binding on the contracting parties, and the fish or whale stocks always remained exposed to aggressive exploitation by the vessels of states outside the treaty.

The Geneva Convention of 1958 on the Régime of the High Seas codifies the basic principles of the freedom of the seas which have been discussed above. Although the former law has in the main been re-affirmed, it has been amended or clarified on some points; moreover, it has been supplemented by an entirely new general Convention on Fishing and the Conservation of the Living Resources of the High Seas, which derives much of its inspiration from President Truman's proclamation in 1945 concerning the conservation of fisheries to which reference has already been made. In addition, the High Seas Convention has to be read in conjunction with the Continental Shelf Convention and with the Convention on the Territorial Sea and Contiguous Zone, both of which confer on coastal states substantial rights of jurisdiction over adjacent areas of the high seas.

The High Seas Convention declares that, *inter alia*, the freedom of the high seas comprises: (1) freedom of navigation, (2) freedom of fishing, (3) freedom to lay submarine cables and pipelines, and (4) freedom to fly over the high seas; and it adds that these freedoms and any others recognized by the general principles of international law must be exercised with reasonable regard to the interests of other states in the exercise of their freedoms. This seems to indicate that under the Convention a selfish disregard for the interests of other states would now be considered 'an abuse of rights'. Furthermore, the freedoms of the high seas are expressly recognized to attach to all states whether or not they have a seaboard, and Article 3 for the first time lays down as a general principle that landlocked states should have 'free access to the sea' and that intervening states have a duty to enter into agreements with them under which, on the basis of reciprocity, they are to be given free transit through their territory to the sea. If Article 3 still leaves a good deal to the mutual agreement of the states concerned, the recognition of the right of access to the sea is none the less important.

The Convention recognizes the right of every state to sail ships under its own flag and to determine the conditions for the grant of its nationality to ships, for the registration of ships in its territory and for the right to fly its flag. It declares that ships shall have the nationality of the state whose flag thay are entitled to fly, but at the same time provides that a 'genuine link' must exist between the state and the ship and that in particular the state must effectively exercise its jurisdiction and control over ships of its flag in administrative, technical, and social matters. This provision was intended to put some check upon the placing of ships under 'flags of convenience', that is, the placing of ships under the flags of states like Panama, Honduras, and Liberia, whose laws impose the minimum of conditions for obtaining their flag and the minimum of control on ships under their flag. The Convention also prohibits changes of flag during a voyage and the sailing of a ship under two or more flags, using them according to the convenience of the particular voyage.

The Convention then re-states the fundamental rule, that, apart from treaty and the exceptional cases recognized in the Convention, ships on the high seas are subject to the exclusive jurisdiction of one state only and that the state whose flag they are entitled to fly. As mentioned earlier,[1] it negatives the decision of the Permanent Court in the *Lotus* case and expressly lays down that no penal or disciplinary proceedings may be instituted in respect of an incident upon the high seas except before the appropriate authorities either of the flag state or of the state whose national is the object of the proceedings. The exceptions to the exclusive jurisdiction of the flag state recognized in the Convention are (1) piracy, (2) the slave trade, and (3) hot pursuit, in addition to the right of approach to foreign vessels for purposes of verification. The Convention contains comprehensive provisions concerning 'piracy' and 'hot pursuit' which constitute the first attempts to formulate authoritative statements of the law on these matters.

Under an ancient rule of maritime law, pirates are offenders against the law of nations, *hostes humani generis*, who may be arrested on the high seas by the warships of any state and brought into port for trial together with their ship. The right to arrest foreign vessels on the high seas on allegations of piracy is,

[1] *Supra*, p. 304.

however, necessarily limited to acts which are piracy *jure gentium* and hitherto there has been some confusion as to exactly what does constitute piracy in international law. Part of the confusion arose from the fact that the municipal laws of some states punish under the name of piracy acts which do not constitute piracy *jure gentium*. French law, for example, treats any armed vessel navigating with irregular papers in peace-time as piratical, while under an Act of 1824 any British subject engaging in the slave trade is guilty of piracy; but neither of these cases is piracy *jure gentium*. Confusion also existed in regard to the belligerent acts of ships operated by unrecognized insurgents, a confusion which manifested itself in the recent incident of the seizing of the *Santa Maria* by the Portuguese rebel leader Captain Galvao. When insurgent leaders have not been recognized as a government, either *de jure* or *de facto*, rebel warships and seamen do not, in the eyes of outside states any more than of their own government, have any lawful authority behind them, if they take action against merchant ships and cargoes in purported exercise of belligerent rights. Although it has long been the practice of outside states not to treat insurgents as pirates provided that they do not interfere with foreign vessels, that has not always been the case when they have operated against foreign vessels. Both Great Britain in the *Huascar* incident in 1877 and the United States in the *Ambrose Light* in 1885 asserted the right to treat unrecognized insurgents as pirates. Moreover, in 1934 the Privy Council in its opinion *In re*

Piracy Jure Gentium[1] certainly appeared to endorse the view that any ship not commissioned by a lawful authority which engages in acts of war is a pirate and, in addition, to consider that any rising on the high seas by the crew or passengers of a ship against the captain or officers for the purpose of seizing the ship and converting her to their own use is in law an act of piracy, which was the very case of Captain Galvao. On these points, however, the Privy Council's opinion reflected views that were already out of date and have now been definitely rejected in the Geneva Convention of 1958. Piracy is there defined as 'any illegal acts of violence, detention or any act of depredation, committed *for private ends* by the crew or the passengers of a private ship or aircraft, and directed on the high seas[2] against another ship or aircraft, or against persons or property on board such ship or aircraft'. This excludes from piracy *jure gentium* both acts solely inspired by political motives and acts committed on board a ship or aircraft by the crew or passengers and directed against the ship or aircraft itself or persons or property on board. Naturally, the exclusion of these acts from being considered criminal acts of piracy under international law does not in any way relieve the persons concerned of any criminal liability which may attach to them

[1] The case concerned a frustrated attempt at armed robbery on the high seas by Chinese pirates and the Privy Council's main finding that a completed robbery is not a necessary element in piracy is clearly correct; [1934] A.C. 586.

[2] The Convention also makes it piracy to do these acts 'in a place outside the jurisdiction of any State'.

in respect of these acts under the law of the flag state or of the state whose nationals they may be.

Hot pursuit of a foreign ship on to the high seas and her arrest there are permitted under the Convention when a coastal state has good reason to believe that the ship has broken its laws, subject to the following conditions: (1) the pursuit is begun when the foreign ship or one of its boats is still within the internal waters, the territorial sea, or the contiguous zone of the pursuing state; (2) a reasonable visual or auditory signal to stop has been given; (3) the pursuit is not interrupted; (4) the foreign ship has not succeeded in reaching the territorial sea of its own or of a third state; and (5) the pursuit is carried out by a warship or military aircraft or other government ship or aircraft specially so authorized. These provisions are in accord with the law of hot pursuit, as it was previously understood; but the extension of the doctrine to a pursuit begun in the contiguous zone is an innovation and it is to be emphasized that this extension only applies when the law that has been broken by the foreign ship is a customs, fiscal, immigration, or sanitary regulation for the protection of which the contiguous zone was established.

The Geneva Convention of 1958 on fishing and conservation is based on the concept in the Truman fisheries proclamation of conservation zones established by agreement between interested states, but also takes account of the bias in favour of coastal states which manifested itself at a technical conference convened at Rome in 1955 by F.A.O. The Con-

vention places an obligation on all states themselves
to adopt or to co-operate with others in adopting
conservation measures, when these are necessary, and
then draws up the following detailed system for conservation of the resources of the high seas:

(1) Any state with an established national fishery
in an area not exploited by others is required unilaterally to introduce conservation measures, when
these are necessary.

(2) If two or more states have established fisheries
in the same area, they have the right to call upon
each other to conclude a conservation régime for the
area and, if agreement is not reached, either or any
of them may invoke the procedure for settlement of
disputes specified in the Convention.

(3) A state which is a newcomer to an established
fishery is liable, unless it objects, to have any existing
conservation régime enforced against its nationals
equally with those of States to which the régime
already applies; if it does object, the procedure for
settlement of disputes applies, but meanwhile the
existing conservation régime remains in force.

(4) A coastal state is recognized to have a special
interest in the maintenance of the living resources in
any area of the high seas adjacent to its territorial sea
and accordingly it has the right:

  (a) to participate in a conservation régime whether
      or not it has an established fishery in the area;
  (b) to introduce a conservation régime unilaterally
      when negotiations with other interested states

have not led to agreement within a reasonable time, but this will only be binding on other states, if it is justified by the scientific evidence and it does not discriminate against foreigners.

In case of disagreement the procedure for settlement of disputes is to apply.

(5) Again, even a non-coastal state may call for conservation measures in an area where it has no fishery of its own, if abusive exploitation of that area may affect fisheries elsewhere, for example, in the case of migratory species, and if there is disagreement the procedure for settlement of disputes is to apply.

Finally, self-defence, according to the view of some authorities, may justify the exercise of authority by a state on the high seas. For example, in 1873 the Spaniards captured on the high seas an American vessel, the *Virginius*, which was on its way to assist insurgents in Cuba. Some of those on board were British subjects, and they were summarily executed on their arrival in Cuba. The British Government protested against the executions, which could not be justified on the ground of self-defence, but they were disposed to accept the capture of the ship and the detention of those on board as justified. This view, although consistent with the principle which allows a right of self-defence in the event of an immediate and overwhelming necessity, is not accepted by everyone.

TREATIES

CONTRACTUAL engagements between states are called by various names—treaties, conventions, pacts, acts, declarations, protocols. None of these terms has an absolutely fixed meaning; but a treaty suggests the most formal kind of agreement; a convention or a pact generally, but not always, an agreement less formal or less important; an act generally means an agreement resulting from a formal conference and summing up its results; a declaration is generally used of a law-declaring or law-making agreement, e.g. the Declarations of Paris and of London, but such agreements are equally often called conventions, e.g. the Hague Conventions; 'protocol' is a word with many meanings in diplomacy, denoting the minutes of the proceedings at an international conference, an agreement of a less formal kind, or often a supplementary or explanatory addendum to another treaty, e.g. the Geneva Protocol of 1924, so called because intended to amend the Covenant.

§ 1. *Formation of Treaties*

International law has no technical rules for the forms of treaties. In most respects the general principles applicable to private contracts apply; there must be consent and capacity on both sides, and the object must be legal; though naturally, rules peculiar to a special system of municipal law, such as the Common Law rules about consideration, have no application. But there is one startling difference. Duress does not invalidate consent, as it does in the private law of contract. A dictated treaty is as valid legally as one freely entered into on both sides.

Historically the explanation of this state of the law is easily understood; it is that so long as international law was not strong enough to forbid the settlement of disputes by force, it would have been idle for it to refuse to recognize an agreement induced by force. Clearly there is here a grave defect in the law. On the other hand, it is important not to mistake the direction in which it is desirable that the law should move in this matter. A dictated treaty obviously violates the first principle of any civilized law of contracts, which is freedom of consent on both sides, and, so long as we regard it as a contract, we are naturally tempted to look forward to a time when the law will be strong enough to deny its validity. But if we look more closely at some of the consequences of such a development we may begin to suspect that there may be some fallacy in the premisses from which we have started. For instance, if after the defeat in war of an aggressor state the victors dictate a treaty imposing an indemnity for the damage caused by the aggression and containing terms designed to prevent its repetition, such a treaty, as the law stands, will be binding; but do we really believe that it *ought not* to be binding, and that if international law were a more satisfactory system than it is, it would not be so? The matter is even more clear if we look forward to a time when, we may hope, the law will have been provided with a workable system of sanctions against aggression; surely then we shall not say that if, under pressure of sanctions, an aggressor state has been forced to accept certain onerous obligations, those obligations ought not to be upheld by the law.

The truth is that it is only in outward form that a dictated treaty is a contract; really it belongs to a different category of legal transactions, for the essence of it is that the state or states imposing the treaty are claiming the right to *legislate* for the state coerced. The true anomaly in the present law is not that it should be legal to coerce a state into accepting obligations which it does not like, but that it should be legal for a state which has been victorious in a war to do the coercing; and the change to which we ought to look forward is not the elimination of the use of coercion from the transaction, but the establishment of international machinery to ensure that when coercion is used it shall be in a proper case and by due process of law, and not, as at present it may be, arbitrarily. The problem of treaties imposed by force is therefore in its essence not a problem of treaty law, but a particular aspect of that much wider problem which pervades the whole system, that of subordinating the use of force to law.

Ordinarily there are two stages in the making of a treaty, its signature by 'plenipotentiaries' of the contracting states, and its ratification by or on behalf of the heads of those states. There are good reasons why this second stage should be necessary before a treaty, at any rate an important treaty, becomes actually binding. In some states, for example, constitutional law vests the treaty-making power in some organ which cannot delegate it to plenipotentiaries, and yet cannot itself carry on negotiations with other states; for example, in the United States the power is vested in the President, but subject to the advice and consent of the Senate. But, apart from such cases, the interests with which a treaty deals are often so complicated and important that it is reasonable that an opportunity for considering the treaty as a whole should be reserved. A democratic state must consult public opinion, and this can hardly take shape while the negotiations, which must be largely confidential, are going on. These being the reasons that render ratification necessary, it is clearly impossible, as is done by some writers, to specify the circumstances in which a refusal to ratify is justified and those in which it is not. There is no legal nor even a moral duty on a state to ratify a treaty signed by its own plenipotentiaries; it can only be said that refusal is a serious step which ought not to be taken lightly.[1]

Ratification is not, however, a legal requisite in all

---

[1] But this is only the modern law. Formerly a plenipotentiary was what the name implies, an agent having 'full powers' to bind his principal by his acts. Ratification was then merely the formal confirmation of an obligation which the agent had already created for his principal, and it could not honourably, or perhaps even legally, be withheld. It is probably a relic of this former state of things which leads to the doubts still sometimes expressed on the matter. The question is examined in J. Mervyn Jones's *Full Powers and Ratification*.

cases. There are many agreements of minor importance in which it would be an unreasonable formality, and ordinarily the treaty itself shows, either expressly or by implication, whether it is to become binding on signature or not until it has been ratified. Whether, if no indication of intention can be obtained in this way, we are to presume that ratification is intended to be necessary, or that the treaty is to be binding without it, is not certain. Most modern writers have taken the former view, but this has been doubted.[1] It is pointed out that when states think it necessary to reserve a treaty for ratification, their practice is to insert an express reservation of the right to ratify in the 'full powers' of their plenipotentiaries, and that this practice would be unnecessary if there existed a rule making ratification necessary unless it is expressly or impliedly dispensed with. In any case the doctrine accepted by most text-writers does not, it seems, represent the ordinary practice of diplomacy.

Signature followed by ratification, or signature alone when ratification is dispensed with, is the procedure by which a state has traditionally indicated its willingness to be bound by a treaty, but the only essential requirement is that this willingness should be unequivocally shown, and recent practice, especially in multilateral conventions drafted under the auspices of the United Nations, has tended towards

[1] See Fitzmaurice, in *B.T.I.L.*, 1934, 'Do Treaties Need Ratification?' The Permanent Court, however, has referred to 'the rule that conventions, save in certain exceptional cases, are binding only by virtue of ratification' as one of 'the ordinary rules of international law'. (Series A, No. 23, at p. 20.)

the use of less formal procedures. Many such conventions contain a common form clause providing that they shall become binding on 'acceptance', the effect of which is to leave it to the prospective parties to choose the particular form in which they will indicate their readiness to be bound.

States which have not taken part in the negotiation of a treaty are sometimes invited by the negotiating states to become parties by 'acceding' to the treaty. Naturally all the negotiating states must consent to this invitation for no state can be brought into treaty relations with another except by its own consent. But many multilateral conventions today depend for their value on securing as many parties as possible and a clause opening them to accession is therefore very common. Here again it is a common modern practice to allow an acceding state to choose its own method of indicating its acceptance, for example, by signature alone, or by signature subject to ratification, or by some other procedure.

In accepting a treaty a state sometimes attaches a 'reservation', that is to say, it makes the acceptance conditional on some new term which limits or varies the application of the treaty to itself. Such a qualified acceptance is really a proposal for a treaty different from that agreed on, and if the reservation is persisted in and is not accepted by the other states concerned it amounts to a rejection. But it is sometimes difficult to determine what states are 'concerned' for this purpose. When a treaty has only two parties, the matter is simple; if the other party does not accept the tendered reservation the treaty will fall. But when there are numerous parties the matter becomes more complicated, for some of these may be willing to accept the reservation and others may not. One possible view, which is favoured by the Latin American states, is that in that event the convention will come into force, in the form in which it was negotiated, between the states that accept it without any reservation, and it will come into force, as modified by the reservation, between the reserving state and those willing to accept the reservation; it will not come into force between the reserving state and those that do not accept the reservation. But there are strong objections to this solution. In many conventions, especially those of a law-making character, the integrity and uniform application of the provisions is often a consideration of the first importance, whereas this system has the effect of splitting up what was intended to be a multilateral convention into a number of bilateral conventions with terms differing from one another. To allow a state to become a party while maintaining a reservation over the objection of any party to the convention may well have the effect of destroying for that state whatever advantage it may have expected from the convention. Another solution has been applied by the International Court without, however, laying it down as a general rule of law; it held that in the case before it a state making a reservation to which some but not all the parties objected would become a party if its reservation should be 'compatible with the object and purpose of the convention', but not otherwise.[1] It is difficult to see how such a system could fail to lead to confusion and uncertainty. As the Court itself admits, there is no objective test of 'compatibility', and as each of the parties must decide that question for itself there would be no certain means of deciding whether the reserving state had or had not become a party to the convention. Probably the rule formerly followed by the Secretariat of the United Nations, though it does not avoid all the difficulties, is the best practical solution; this is that before a convention has entered into force a reservation can be admitted only with the consent of all the states which accept the convention before its entry into force, and after the entry into force only with the consent of all the states which have accepted the convention before the reservation is tendered.[2]

Article 102 of the Charter of the United Nations requires that 'every treaty and every international agreement entered into by any member of the United Nations after the present Charter comes into force shall as soon as possible be registered with the Secretariat and published by it'. A somewhat similar article in the Covenant of the League of Nations had left in some doubt the effect that a failure to register would have on a treaty. The Charter now makes it clear that the effect is not to take away the validity of the treaty for all purposes, but that it may not be invoked 'before

[1] Advisory Opinion on Reservations to the Convention on Genocide, *I.C.J. Reports*, 1951.

[2] See the International Law Commission's Report to the General Assembly for 1951 in the Official Records, Supplement No. 9. This solution was not, however, accepted by the Assembly.

any organ of the United Nations'. As one of these organs is the International Court of Justice the effect of non-registration may be very important.

There are no technical rules in international law for the interpretation of treaties; its object can only be to give effect to the intention of the parties as fully and fairly as possible. But lawyers who are trained in the methods of interpretation applied by an English court should bear in mind that English draftsmanship tends to be more detailed than continental, and it receives, and perhaps demands, a more literal interpretation.[1] Similarly, diplomatic documents, including treaties, do not as a rule invite the very strict methods of interpretation that an English court applies, for example, to an Act of Parliament. In particular the method of *historical* interpretation, which allows the history of the negotiations, the *travaux préparatoires* as they are called, to be examined for the purpose of ascertaining the intention of the parties, as well as the actual terms of the treaty in which they have attempted to express this intention, is admissible in international law; though the Permanent Court has pointed out that this method should be resorted to only when the terms of the treaty itself are not clear, and only when all the parties before the Court have taken part in the preparatory work.[2]

The general rule is that treaties create rights and duties only for the parties to them; *pacta tertiis nec*

[1] Cf. Westlake, *International Law*, Part I, p. 282.
[2] e.g. Series A, Judgment no. 9, p. 16, and no. 23, p. 41.

nocere nec prodesse possunt. But the Permanent Court has held that if it is shown that the parties intended to confer a right to enforce the treaty on a state not a party to it, there is nothing in international law to prevent effect being given to this intention. It is not, they say,[1] to be lightly presumed that this was the intention; but in each case it must be ascertained 'whether the states which have stipulated in favour of a third state meant to create an actual right which the latter has accepted as such'. But this view is not free from difficulties, some of which were pointed out by dissenting judges on the Court. Does it mean that the parties cannot modify or abrogate the right which they have conferred by their treaty on a third state? It would be going rather far to hold that the parties to a treaty cannot alter its terms if they are all agreed in wishing to do so; but if they are free to take away what they have given, what the third state has received can hardly be called an 'actual right'. Perhaps, however, the carefully guarded language of the Court removes this difficulty. The parties can tie their own hands if they wish to do so, but the question is one of intention and such an intention must be very clear.

International law has also begun to recognize that some treaties have an objective, legislative character, for example where they create international situations or entities binding upon all states, whether contracting parties or not. Examples of the first category are (*a*) the Aaland Islands Convention of 1856, which

---

[1] *Free Zones of Upper Savoy and the District of Gex*, Series A/B, No. 46, at p. 147.

neutralized those islands in the Baltic and which was held by a Commission of Jurists established by the League Council to be objectively valid as against third states; and (*b*) the Suez Canal Convention of 1888 and the clauses of the Versailles Treaty concerning the Kiel Canal, both of which converted the Canals into international waterways. Examples of the second are instruments, like the Charter of the United Nations, creating international organizations. Another case is where a treaty effects a change in the sovereignty of territory as, for example, a treaty of cession. In all these cases, the treaty has objective effects and does not merely affect the contracting parties.[1]

§ 2. *Discharge of Treaties*

Of the methods by which a treaty may be discharged,[2] some, such as mutual consent, performance of the obligations under it, or the expiration of a time-limit need no special discussion. But there are more difficult cases. From the time of Grotius[3] many writers have propounded the view that the breach of *any* term of a treaty by one party will release the other from all obligations of the treaty, but this doctrine, applied to any of the more important treaties, would lead to results so startling that it has never been adopted in international practice, and ought equally to be rejected by legal theory. There is an absence of decisive

[1] See generally Lord McNair, *Papers on International Law in Honour of Dr. T. Perassi*, p. 23.

[2] On this question see McNair, 'La Terminaison et la dissolution des traités', in *Hague Recueil*, 1928, vol. xxii, p. 463.

[3] *De jure belli*, ii. 15. 15.

authority on the matter, but common sense seems to impose a distinction between terms which are material to a main object of the treaty and those which are not[1] and between breaches which are serious in themselves and those which are trivial. There can be no right to rescind on account of the breach of a stipulation which is itself unimportant, nor on account of a trivial breach even of an important stipulation. No doubt such distinctions may not always be easy to apply, but the difficulty is one for which every national law of contract has to seek, and generally finds, a solution.

The outbreak of war is another event which may bring a treaty to an end, but the modern view is that it does not necessarily do so. 'The effect of war upon the existing treaties of belligerents', said Mr. Justice Cardozo in *Techt* v. *Hughes*,[2] 'is one of the unsettled problems of the law. The older writers sometimes said that treaties ended *ipso facto* when war came. The writers of our own time reject these sweeping statements. International law today does not preserve treaties or annul them regardless of the effects produced. It deals with such problems pragmatically, preserving or annulling as the necessities of war exact. It establishes standards, but it does not fetter itself with rules.' He went on to say that in his opinion the standard is that 'provisions compatible with a state of hostilities, unless expressly terminated, will be enforced, and those incompatible rejected'.

One reason for the uncertainty of the law on this

---

[1] The treatment of this question by Hall, *International Law*, 8th ed., p. 408, is useful.   [2] (1920) 229 N.Y. 222.

subject is that belligerents do not as a rule leave the fate of their pre-war treaties to depend on the operation of legal principles; in order to avoid uncertainty they usually specify, in the treaty ending a war, which of their pre-war treaties are to be revived and which are to lapse. It is only if this has not been done that it is left to courts to determine their fate, and to establish sound principles of law on the matter.

Sir Cecil Hurst[1] has suggested a rather different approach to the question, that the fate of a treaty depends on the intention of the parties. In some cases their intention is clear; for instance, a treaty which regulates the conduct of war, as many of the Hague Conventions did, is clearly intended to retain its force if war breaks out. But more often the minds of the parties have not been addressed to the possibility that they may some day be at war with one another, and they cannot be said to have had any real intention as to what should happen to their treaty in that unforeseen event. Such a difficulty as this, however, is in no way peculiar to the interpretation of treaties, and law often does not hesitate to attribute an intention to parties who have never thought of the situation with which in the event the law has to deal. In such a case the so-called intention is a 'presumed' intention, it is what the law thinks it reasonable to suppose that the parties *would* have intended if the situation had been present to their minds.

Probably we shall arrive at much the same result whether we apply the objective test suggested by

[1] 'The Effect of War on Treaties', *B.Y.I.L.*, 1921–2, p. 37.

Mr. Justice Cardozo or the subjective test of Sir Cecil Hurst. In either case we must not assume that all treaties can be neatly classified into the three categories of those which are abrogated, those which are only suspended, and those which are not affected, by the outbreak of a war. We have rather to examine the particular treaty with which we are concerned in the light both of its subject-matter and of all the relevant surrounding circumstances. Certain presumptions will no doubt emerge. Treaties dealing with political matters or with commercial relations may be assumed to have been made with reference to the relations existing between the parties at the time, and generally we shall find that the provisions of such treaties are incompatible with a state of war, or, if we prefer to put it in the other way, that the parties must have intended that war should abrogate them. On the other hand, a multilateral treaty, such as a postal convention, though its operation will obviously have to be suspended between the belligerents while the war lasts, will by the same reasoning generally revive and recover its force when the war is over.

One of the most difficult and practically important questions of the law of treaties relates to the termination of treaties which contain, at any rate in their expressed terms, no provision for that purpose. Such treaties raise two questions which require discussion: firstly, whether one party may in any circumstances give notice to terminate the treaty without the consent of the other, and secondly, whether it is liable to be terminated by the operation of any rule of law.

The answer to the first of these questions is probably that we must inquire into the intention of the parties. There is certainly no general right of denunciation of a treaty of indefinite duration; there are many such treaties in which the obvious intention of the parties is to establish a permanent state of things, for example, the Pact of Paris; but there are some which, from the nature of the subject-matter or the circumstances in which they were concluded, we may fairly presume were intended to be susceptible of denunciation even though they contain no express term to that effect. A *modus vivendi* is an obvious illustration; treaties of alliance and of commerce are probably in the same case, though in practice such treaties ordinarily have a fixed period of duration. On the other hand, the probability is that a treaty providing for exterritoriality or for neutralization would be intended to be permanent.

The second question brings us to the great problem of the obligatory force of treaties in general.

It is a truism to say that no international interest is more vital than the observance of good faith between states, and the 'sanctity' of treaties is a necessary corollary. On the other hand, the circumstances in which a treaty was made may change, and its obligations may become so onerous as to thwart the development to which a state feels itself entitled; and when this happens, it is likely, human nature being what it is, that a state which feels itself strong enough will disregard them, whether it has a legal justification for doing so or not. This is particularly likely to

happen when a treaty has been imposed on a state
after defeat in a war; and while it may be expedient
in the present state of international relations to uphold the principle which declares such a treaty to be
as binding in law as one voluntarily entered into on
both sides, it argues a lack of candour to support that
practice by appealing to moral considerations, as we
do when we speak of the 'sanctity' of all treaties without distinction. It may be, therefore, that if international law insists too rigidly on the binding force
of treaties, it will merely defeat its own purpose by
encouraging their violation.

Every system of law has to steer a course between
the two dangers of impairing the obligations of good
faith by interfering with contractual engagements,
and of enforcing oppressive or obsolete contracts. In
our national law we have long ceased to regard absolute freedom of contract as either possible or socially
desirable; our courts will not enforce contracts which
have been induced by fraud or duress, or whose object
is contrary to public policy, and legislative interference with contracts becomes more and more active as
social relations become more complicated. No such
process has yet been possible in international law; no
doctrine of international public policy exists as yet to
restrict the freedom of states to insert in their treaties
such provisions as they think fit. One or two illustrations will show how dangerous is the problem which
this state of the law creates.

By the Treaty of Paris, 1856, the Black Sea was
declared to be neutralized, and Russia, which had

just been defeated in the Crimean War, agreed not to
maintain a fleet on it. In 1870 she took advantage
of the Franco-German War to repudiate this obligation. Great Britain protested against this action, and
eventually the powers that had been parties to the
Treaty of Paris agreed, in the Treaty of London,
1871, to release Russia from the restriction; and they
solemnly united in this declaration: 'It is an essential
principle of the law of nations that no power can free
itself from the engagements of a treaty, nor modify
its terms, except with the assent of the contracting
parties by means of a friendly understanding.' No
doubt it was impressive that the chief powers of
Europe should unite in maintaining the sanctity of
treaties, even while they condoned the breach of one
by Russia, but it was also very futile; in effect they
were burying their heads in the sand, and refusing
to admit that a real problem existed. Again, by the
Treaty of Berlin, 1878, Bosnia and Herzegovina,
provinces of Turkey, were to be 'occupied and
administered' by Austria–Hungary; and Bulgaria was
to be an autonomous principality under the suzerainty
of the Sultan. In 1908 the Prince of Bulgaria took
advantage of the Young Turk Revolution to declare
Bulgaria independent; at the same time Austria took
advantage of Russia's weakness after the Russo-Japa-
nese War to annex Bosnia and Herzegovina. Sir E.
Grey protested against these violations of the Treaty
of Berlin, and demanded a conference to consider
whether its revision was necessary; but in the end the
violations had again to be condoned. Once again, in

April 1935, the Council of the League reaffirmed the declaration of 1871, and solemnly condemned Germany's repudiation of the military articles of the Treaty of Versailles. On each of these occasions a state may or may not have had some moral claim to have the obligations of a treaty revised, but it also had good reason to believe that it was unlikely to be able to secure that revision by action within the law.

J. S. Mill, writing of the Russian action in 1870, uttered a warning which international law has yet to take to heart:

'If a lawless act has been committed in the present instance, it does not entitle those who imposed the conditions to consider the lawlessness only, and to dismiss the more important consideration whether, even if it was wrong to throw off the obligation, it would not be still more wrong to persist in enforcing it. If, though not fit to be perpetual, it has been imposed in perpetuity, the question when it becomes right to throw it off is but a question of time. No time being fixed, Russia fixed her own time, and naturally chose the most convenient.'[1]

Mill also suggested two rules for adoption by the nations: 'they should abstain from imposing conditions which, on any just and reasonable view of human affairs, cannot be expected to be kept. And they should conclude their treaties, as commercial treaties are usually concluded, only for a term of years.'

These are counsels of perfection which states at

---

[1] Quoted from the *Fortnightly Review* by Moore, *Digest of International Law*, vol. v, p. 339.

present are not always willing to follow. In the meantime the problem of the attitude of international law to oppressive or obsolete treaty obligations remains, and an attempt has been made by many writers to solve it by the doctrine known as the *clausula rebus sic stantibus*. In every treaty, it is said, there is implied a clause which provides that the treaty is to be binding only 'so long as things stand as they are'; the expressed terms may be absolute, but a treaty is never more than conditional, and when a 'vital change of circumstances' has occurred, the condition of the treaty's validity has failed, and it ceases to be binding.

Such a doctrine, if it is to be accepted into the law, clearly needs careful definition. Otherwise it is capable of being used, and it often has been used, merely to excuse the breach of a treaty obligation that a state finds it inconvenient to fulfil. For example, German controversialists appealed to it to justify the violation of Belgian neutrality in 1914, in breach of the guarantee contained in the Treaty of London, 1831.

There seems to be no recorded case in which its application has been admitted by both parties to a controversy, or in which it has been applied by an international tribunal. But in the case of the *Free Zones of Upper Savoy and the District of Gex*[1] the Permanent Court had to consider an argument by France that the provisions made after the Napoleonic Wars for the withdrawal of the French customs lines some distance behind the Franco-Swiss boundary should be held to have lapsed owing to a change of circum-

[1] Series A/B, No. 46, at p. 155.

stances. The change alleged was that whereas in 1815 the withdrawal of the customs line had made Geneva, then practically a free trade area, together with the 'Free Zones', an economic unit, the institution of Swiss federal customs in 1849 had destroyed this unit. The Court said that to establish this position it would be necessary to show that it was *in consideration* of the absence of customs duties at Geneva in 1815 that the Zones were created, and this France failed to prove.

Despite the caution of the language of the Court it seems to define clearly the scope of the doctrine. Not every important change of circumstances will put an end to the obligations of a treaty. The *clausula* is not a principle enabling the law to relieve from obligations merely because new and unforeseen circumstances have made them unexpectedly burdensome to the party bound, or because some consideration of equity suggests that it would be fair and reasonable to give such relief. It bears no analogy to such a principle as that of *laesio enormis* in the Roman law. What puts an end to the treaty is the disappearance of the foundation upon which it rests; or if we prefer to put the matter subjectively, the treaty is ended because we can infer from its terms that the parties, though they have not said expressly what was to happen in the event which has occurred, would, if they had foreseen it, have said that the treaty ought to lapse. In short, the *clausula* is a rule of construction which secures that a reasonable effect shall be given to the treaty rather than the unreasonable one which would result from a literal adherence to its expressed terms only.

On this view the similarity between the doctrine of *rebus sic stantibus* and that of the 'implied term' in the English law of the frustration of contract is very close. Neither a treaty in international nor a contract in English law is dissolved merely by a change of circumstances; they are only dissolved if a term can fairly be read into them providing that in the event which has happened they *are* to be dissolved. Both doctrines attempt not to defeat but to fulfil the intention, or as the English cases call it the 'presumed intention', of the parties.

It is easy to confuse, but it is important to distinguish, the doctrine of *rebus sic stantibus* and the doctrine which, as we have seen,[1] makes a treaty in certain cases terminable by unilateral denunciation. The same facts may make it necessary to consider both these possibilities, but the similarity between them is only superficial. In 1926 a difference arose between Belgium and China out of the denunciation by the latter of a treaty of 1865,[2] and China in the first instance alleged that she was entitled to denounce the treaty under an article contained in the treaty itself. Belgium disputed this interpretation. Then at a later stage of the discussions China changed her ground, claiming that the point at issue was not one of the technical interpretation of this article, but whether or not the principle of *rebus sic stantibus* applied to the case. In the subsequent application of Belgium to the Permanent Court, which unfortunately never reached the stage of judgment, the Belgian memorial

[1] *Supra*, p. 331.   [2] See *A.J.I.L.*, 1927, p. 289.

stated the question to be whether the unilateral denunciation by China could be considered legally
valid *either under the terms of the treaty, or in virtue of the
general principles of the law of nations,* and under the
latter head it presented arguments dealing with *rebus
sic stantibus.* The case illustrates the essential difference between the two modes of terminating a treaty.
In one the treaty is terminated by the act of one party
because the terms of the treaty, express or implied,
give that party the right to terminate it by giving
notice; in the other it is not the act of one of the parties
that puts an end to the treaty, but the operation of a
principle of law, although naturally the question can
only be raised if one of the parties gives notice that
it claims that the principle applies to the case in
hand.

As defined by the Permanent Court the doctrine of
rebus sic stantibus is clearly a reasonable doctrine which
it is right that international law should recognize.
But as so defined it is a doctrine of limited scope which
has little to do with the problem of obsolete or oppressive treaties, for which it is too often supposed to
be the solution. We may well hold that the obligation of a treaty comes to an end if an event happens
which the parties *intended,* or which we are justified in
presuming they would have intended, should put an
end to it; the more difficult problem concerns an
obligation which the parties did *not* intend to be ended,
but which it would be oppressive to enforce, and which
will probably in fact be violated, in the events which
have happened. It is because so many writers have

sought to find in *rebus sic stantibus* a solution for this latter problem that the doctrine has become one of the most controversial in international law. But it is a mistake to think that by some ingenious manipulation of existing legal doctrines we can always find a solution for the problems of a changing international world. That is not so; for many of these problems— and oppressive treaties are one of them—the only remedy is that states should be willing to take measures to bring the legal situation into accord with new needs, and if states are not reasonable enough to do that, we must not expect the existing law to relieve them of the consequences. Law is bound to uphold the principle that treaties are to be observed; it cannot be made an instrument for revising them, and if political motives sometimes lead to a treaty being treated as 'a scrap of paper' we must not invent a pseudo-legal principle to justify such action. The remedy has to be sought elsewhere, in political, not in juridical action.

The problem of oppressive or obsolete treaty obligations is in fact only one aspect, and not the most important aspect, of a much wider problem of international relations, for the danger to international order comes more often from oppressive *conditions*, and especially frontier conditions, than from the obligations of a still executory treaty. Whether these conditions were or were not originally created by a treaty, and whether they have or have not been brought into existence by some change of circumstances, are from a practical point of view irrelevant considerations. But this problem of 'peaceful change' belongs to international relations rather than to international law.[1]

Law by its very nature is a conservative force. This bias, too, ought to be stronger in international than it is in municipal law, for whereas the latter has to adjust the ever-shifting demands and interests of millions of people jostling one another in close and continuous relations, the states with which international law is concerned are few in number, and their needs are more stable and so do not constantly call for fresh adjustments. This is not to say that in international law no problem of change exists, but only that we should see that problem in its proper focus. So much was said and written in the years between the two world wars about the need for new methods of peaceful international change that there is a real danger of getting the problem out of focus. Almost before the ink was dry on the settlement of 1919 an agitation was started for its revision. People tried to prove, or more often asserted without proving, that the treaties had been a monument of injustice, and that unless they could be quickly altered the world would be headed for a new war. They had very little thought to spare for the sheer complication of the issues on which the treaty-makers had had to take decisions, and they did not ask whether, if their decisions had been different, as great or greater grievances would not have been created for states other than those which appeared to them to have been hardly

[1] The passages which follow are largely taken from Brierly, *The Outlook for International Law*, ch. viii.

treated. We were offered clichés about the essential
'dynamism' of international relations, or about the
danger of allowing a division of states into 'haves'
and 'have-nots' to continue, until one might almost
have supposed that the mere fact that a state was dissatisfied was enough to create a bias in favour of
changing the law to its advantage. It is important
therefore that we should try to get a clear picture in
our minds of the real nature and extent of the contribution that we expect a procedure of peaceful
change to make to the international order. It is misleading to refer, as is often done, to the problem of
peaceful change as a problem of the 'revision of treaties'. The revision of treaties is only one aspect of it,
and that a minor one. The grievance which a state
desires to have removed may indeed be a burden that
some treaty imposes on it. Thus when Turkey demanded at Montreux in 1933 that the régime which
the Treaty of Lausanne had established for the Bos-
porus and the Dardanelles should be amended, she
was asking for the revision of a treaty which was still
in force and still creating obligations which she regarded as burdensome. But this is not the most common case. As a rule when a state puts forward a
grievance against the existing order it does not ask
to be relieved from some continuing, or as lawyers
would call it some still 'executory', obligation of a
treaty which is still in force; it asks that some established condition of things—and an existing frontier is
the commonest and the most difficult case—should be
altered to its advantage. That condition of things may

have originally come into existence by virtue of a treaty, or it may have arisen in some other way; the problem is exactly the same in either case. Even if it did arise out of a treaty, it is a misuse of terms to say that when it is altered the treaty is 'revised', just as it would be absurd in municipal law to describe a conveyance of property as a 'revision' of some earlier conveyance under which the grantor had acquired it. The treaty, like the conveyance, is merely a link in the chain of events which has brought about the situation or condition of things which is now being revised. Most treaties do not create permanent obligations, and the revision of treaties in the proper sense of the phrase only exceptionally creates a difficult problem; hence if peaceful change is identified with it, it is made to appear a less difficult problem than it really is.

The object of a procedure of peaceful change would presumably be to facilitate the making of changes when changes are just, and not merely when they are politically expedient. No doubt expediency will continue to be a factor in international relations even if the maintenance of order becomes more firmly assured than it has been, and changes will be made, as we know they often are inside the state, not because they are just, but because they are demanded by those who have the power to make their demands prevail. Nevertheless the only legitimate object of such procedure would be to ensure, so far as we can, that when a demand for some change is put forward by a state, the justice and not merely the expediency of acceding to it shall be fairly considered, and that the change shall be made if it is decided that it is just, but not otherwise.

Now it can be agreed without any reservation at all that to remove injustices from the international order is a worthy aim for its own sake. Not only that, but the existence of injustices is an irritant which may make the peace more difficult to maintain than it need be, and their removal therefore is yet another way in which 'good laws' can be used to sustain 'good arms'. But in the practical working out of this admirable ideal we shall find that certain factors present themselves which it is easy to overlook while the question is merely being considered in the abstract.

One such factor is that in many, perhaps in most, of those differences between states which arise out of the dissatisfaction of one of the parties with things as they are there is no single solution which can be called 'just' in contradistinction to other possible alternative solutions, and even more rarely any which both the parties concerned are likely to consider just. Nearly always the business of settlement is one of balancing one against other interests which are not merely diverse but actually incommensurate. The same question, for example, often involves political, strategic, economic, and even sentimental or historical interests, and all these interests may deserve to be weighed in the account because all of them may be reasonable interests in themselves; yet in an imperfect world they cannot all be satisfied by any conceivable solution because they conflict with one another. The Polish–German frontier, which was the occasion for the Second World War, is an illustration of this difficulty. We may call it 'unjust' that East Prussia should have been cut off from the rest of Germany by 'the Polish Corridor', but would the settlement have been more 'just' if it had adopted the only alternative solution of barring Polish access to the sea and leaving in Germany a considerable population which was non-German in race and sympathy? Some of the perfectly legitimate interests of one side or the other or of both had inevitably to be disregarded in any possible settlement of that intolerably complicated question, and the settlement adopted in 1919 was the result of a meticulously careful attempt to lay down an arrangement as nearly just as the circumstances allowed. The settlement left grievances behind it, and because it satisfied neither party both of them regarded it as 'unjust'; whereas in fact it was precisely the kind of settlement that a procedure of peaceful change in working order, and having for its object the promotion of just settlements, would probably have arrived at. It was not because it was unjust that it led eventually to trouble, but because the justice which it tried to establish had not been provided with a backing of power. It had been assumed apparently, as many of the arguments for peaceful change still assume, that justice would be self-maintaining.

There is another important fact which is too often overlooked. It concerns the relation of peaceful change to the general problem of order. Peaceful change has been too often recommended to us as if it were an alternative to power in the organization of security, a sort of 'soft option'; for why, it is argued or implied, should states want to fight if they can get their just grievances redressed by a peaceful procedure? Of course the answer is that whereas peaceful change would give them what it is just that they should have, war, if it succeeds, will give them what they want, and it is a dangerous self-deception to suppose that these two things coincide. On the contrary, a procedure of peaceful change will itself depend absolutely for its working on a prior assurance of a stable order, and like all other proposals for the better development of international law, it leads us back to the fundamental question of security.

VIII

INTERNATIONAL DISPUTES AND THE MAINTENANCE OF INTERNATIONAL ORDER

§ 1. *Amicable Methods of Settlement*

DISCUSSION of the problem of settling international disputes has been confused by the unfortunate practice of using the word 'arbitration' as though it meant nothing more than the peaceful settlement of a dispute. Actually arbitration is a definite legal process, and only one among several methods of peaceful settlement; it is not the only alternative to war. The loose usage of the word is more than a mere matter of terminology; it leads to loose thinking about the problem, for controversy passes unconsciously from one meaning of the word to the other, and gives a false impression of simplicity to what is really a most complicated question of international relations.

The problem of effecting the peaceful settlement of a dispute either between two individuals or between two states admits of two alternative methods of approach; we may either induce the disputing parties to accept terms of settlement which are dictated to them by some third party, or we may persuade them to come together and agree on terms of settlement for themselves. In the international field the former of these methods takes the form either of arbitration or of judicial settlement, the latter either of good offices, or mediation, or conciliation.

§ 2. *Arbitration and Judicial Settlement*

These two procedures are closely allied; indeed the former is only a species of the latter, for an arbitrator is a judge, although he differs from the judge of a standing court of justice in being chosen by the parties, and in the fact that his judicial functions end when he has decided the particular case for which he was appointed.[1] The distinction is important, because a standing court is able to build up a judicial tradition and so to develop the law from case to case; it is, therefore, not only a means of settling disputes, but to some extent a means of preventing them from arising. But so far as the parties are concerned, they are as likely to get a satisfactory decision from a court of arbitration as from a court of justice, and there may even be special circumstances which make the former a preferable tribunal; for example, some special technical skill in the members of the court may be more important than a profound knowledge of law. Arbitrators and judges are alike bound to decide according to rules of law; neither possess a discretionary power to disregard the law and to decide according to their own ideas of what is fair and just. No doubt the parties, if they choose, may confer such a power

[1] Cf. the provisions of Art. 37 of Hague Convention I of 1907: 'International arbitration has for its object the settlement of disputes between States by Judges of their own choice and on the basis of respect for law. Recourse to arbitration implies an engagement to submit in good faith to the award.'

on an arbitrator, or they may agree on special rules which he is to apply to the exclusion of the ordinary rules of law, but they may also confer a special power of this kind on a judge, as is expressly provided in Article 38 of the Statute of the International Court of Justice. It should be added, however, that this purely judicial character of an arbitrator's function is not always recognized; the continental view of it has been less strict than our own, and arbitrators have sometimes claimed and exercised a discretionary power to give what they regard as a just, rather than a strictly legal, decision. In practice also, courts of arbitration have not always in the past given the reasons on which their decisions were based, so that it is impossible to be sure what view they may have taken of their function.

Arbitration was a fairly frequent method of settling international disputes in medieval times, but with the rise of the modern state system it fell into disuse until its revival in the nineteenth century, largely through the example of Great Britain and the United States in submitting the *Alabama Claims* to arbitration in 1871. Many different ways of constituting the court have been used; sometimes the head of some foreign state has been appointed, and the award is given in his name, though he is not expected to act personally; sometimes the arbitrators have consisted of representatives of the disputing states, with or without the addition of other members. In the present century a very large number of standing arbitration treaties have been entered into, the earliest being one between

Great Britain and France in 1903, which provided that 'differences of a legal nature or relating to the interpretation of treaties' were to be referred to the Hague Permanent Court of Arbitration, provided 'they do not affect the vital interests, the independence, or the honour of the two states, and do not concern the interests of third parties'. In each case a special agreement had to be concluded defining the matter in dispute and the scope of the arbitrator's power, and when the United States has made such a treaty, the Senate has insisted on treating the special agreement as a treaty, thus refusing to give a general consent to arbitrate differences, and making its own special consent a necessary condition of each proposed reference.

It is clear that the 'vital interests' clause in these treaties seriously weakened their practical force, for in effect it left the parties free to refuse to arbitrate whenever they thought fit. But this clause only gave a rather crude expression to the fact, not always sufficiently realized by its advocates, that arbitration is not, and cannot be made, a suitable method for settling disputes of every kind. On the whole, however, such value as the treaties had lay rather in expressing the general sentiment of most states in favour of peaceful settlement than in any practical influence on events, for it is improbable that any dispute has ever been arbitrated in virtue of one of these treaties which would not have been arbitrated in any event. A more useful side of the modern movement for encouraging resort to arbitration and judicial settlement is to be found in the institution of convenient machinery for the purpose, which, without interfering with the freedom of states to agree on any other method, is always available if they care to use it.

The Permanent Court of Arbitration was created by the Hague Convention for the Pacific Settlement of International Disputes, made in 1899, and revised in 1907. Each state signatory to the Convention appoints four members, and when two states refer a dispute to the Court, each, unless they agree otherwise, selects two arbitrators from the members, of whom only one may be a national, and the four arbitrators then choose an umpire. The machinery has proved simple and useful, and several important cases have been heard by the Court, including the *North Atlantic Fisheries* case between Great Britain and the United States in 1910. But the name 'Permanent Court' is a misnomer. There is a *permanent panel of arbitrators*, but the Court itself has to be constituted anew for each case.

An arbitral award is final unless the parties have otherwise agreed. But arbitrators have only such powers as the parties have conferred upon them in the *compromis*, the document by which they refer the dispute to the court, and if the court should depart from the *compromis*, for example, by purporting to decide some question which was not submitted to it, or by not applying the rules of decision agreed to by the parties, it follows that the award is a nullity without binding force. It is, in fact, not an award at all. Unfortunately if, after the award has been given, one of the parties should allege that it is null and void on this ground, for *excès de pouvoir* as it is commonly expressed, international law does not yet provide any means of determining whether the allegation is or is not well founded. Occasionally the departure from the terms of the *compromis* has been so evident that the parties have agreed to regard the award as null,[1] and sometimes they have agreed to refer the question of nullity itself to a further arbitration.[2] But in default of such an agreement there is a deadlock; there is a gap in the law, or rather in the machinery for applying the law. Fortunately it is not easy for a state to reject an award on the ground of nullity, and so long as arbitration remains a voluntary procedure states count the cost of a possibly adverse decision before they submit to it. Instances of the repudiation of awards on grounds of nullity have therefore not been very common. A remedy might be provided by conferring on the International Court of Justice an appellate jurisdiction in such cases, but though this has often been suggested it has not yet been done. Therefore, it is only when the states concerned agree, or have accepted the compulsory jurisdiction of the International Court, that the validity of an arbitral award can be submitted to the decision of that Court.[3]

The Permanent Court of International Justice was created by a treaty, generally called the 'Statute' of

[1] e.g. the award in the *Maine Boundary* dispute in 1831.

[2] e.g. in the *Orinoco Steamship Co.* case between the United States and Venezuela (Scott's *Hague Court Reports*, p. 226).

[3] e.g. the case of the *Arbitral Award Made by the King of Spain* (*I.C.J. Reports* 1960, p. 192).

the Court, in 1921. Under the Charter of the United Nations it is now replaced by the International Court of Justice, but the Statute of the new Court, which forms part of the Charter, is identical with that of the old, except for a few and not very important changes. The judges are appointed by the following procedure: Each of the national groups of members of the Permanent Court of Arbitration nominates not more than four persons, who must be qualified in their own country for the highest judicial office or be jurisconsults of recognized capacity in international law, and not more than two of whom may be fellow nationals of their nominators, as candidates for appointment as judges. The object is to reduce the likelihood of political influence by giving the power of nominating candidates to persons who would be independent of their governments, but it is probable that this object has not been achieved, and indeed there is no very strong reason why the nominations should not be governmental. From the list of candidates so made up the Security Council and the General Assembly each separately choose fifteen judges. Any person who is chosen by a majority vote in both bodies is elected, except that, if two persons of the same nationality are chosen, only the elder becomes a member of the Court. There are detailed provisions to meet the event of the Council and the Assembly being unable to agree on the full number of judges; and in the event of a deadlock between the two bodies, in the last resort vacant places are to be filled by the judges already elected. This double election was intended to secure that each of the Great Powers, who in 1921 formed a majority in the Council of the League, should be assured of a judge on the Court, but as the Great Powers have no majority in the Security Council it no longer ensures that result. Nevertheless the smaller Powers have not so far shown any wish to deprive a Great Power of its judge. Five judges are elected every three years; they serve for nine years and are re-eligible; they can be dismissed only if in the unanimous opinion of the other members of the Court they have ceased to fulfil the required conditions. For a sitting of the Court the quorum of judges is nine; but a smaller Court may sit to hear certain classes of cases, such as those in which the parties desire a speedy decision by summary procedure. A judge of the same nationality as one of the parties retains the right to sit, but if a party has no judge of its nationality on the Court, it may nominate one for the particular case. This provision for *ad hoc* 'national' judges can only be defended if it is necessary, as perhaps it is, for political reasons. It is a concession to the vicious theory that in some sense a judge ought to 'represent' the parties, and it places the 'national' judge himself in a difficult position.

The law that the Court is to apply is, as previously stated, laid down as follows: (1) international conventions, (2) international custom as evidence of a general practice accepted as law, (3) the general principles of law recognized by civilized nations, (4) judicial decisions and teachings of publicists as subsidiary means for the determination of the law.

If, but only if, the parties agree, the Court may decide *ex aequo et bono*.[1] Other points of interest in the Statute are, that cases must be heard in public unless the Court decides otherwise or the parties demand a private hearing; that reasons for the decision are to be stated, and dissenting judgments may be given; that the official languages are French and English, but the Court may authorize other languages; that decisions are only binding between the parties and for the particular case. This last provision merely means that the binding authority which Anglo-American law attaches to precedents does not apply to the decisions of the Court; it does not mean that the decisions may not be quoted as precedents, or that the Court will not strongly incline to follow them, for no court can be indifferent to its own previous decisions.

The Court is open to all the states which are parties to its Statute, and to others on conditions laid down by the Security Council. Its jurisdiction covers 'all cases which the parties refer to it and all matters specially provided for in treaties and conventions in force', and 'in the event of a dispute as to whether the Court has jurisdiction, the matter shall be settled by the decision of the Court'. In principle, therefore, the jurisdiction arises only when the parties have agreed to submit a dispute to it; but the Court also possesses a quasi-compulsory jurisdiction in two ways: (i) a large number of treaties have provided in general terms for submission to the Court of disputes arising

[1] *Infra*, pp. 371-3.

under them; and (ii) Article 36 of the Statute contains an 'optional clause', whereby members may declare 'that they recognize as compulsory *ipso facto* and without special agreement in relation to any other state accepting the same obligation, the jurisdiction of the Court in all legal disputes concerning (*a*) the interpretation of a treaty, (*b*) any question of international law, (*c*) the existence of any fact which, if established, would constitute a breach of an international obligation, (*d*) the nature or extent of the reparation to be made for the breach of an international obligation'. But even under the treaties and the clause the basis of the Court's jurisdiction is voluntary; under them states merely accept it in anticipation of their being involved in a dispute.

The 'Optional Clause' has been accepted by a fair number of states, about one-third of the international community being at present subject to it, but many of them have attached reservations to their acceptances. Moreover, the limiting effect of reservations is multiplied by the fact that acceptance of the Optional Clause is on a reciprocal basis, each state only accepting compulsory jurisdiction *vis à vis* another state to the extent that the obligations undertaken in their respective declarations mutually correspond. This means that for the Court to have compulsory jurisdiction over any given dispute both states, plaintiff and defendant, must have made declarations which comprise that dispute within its scope.[1] It also means that a defendant state, even when its own

[1] *Anglo-Iranian Oil Co. Case, I.C.J. Reports*, 1952, p. 93.

declaration comprises the dispute within its scope, is always entitled to invoke a reservation in its opponent's declaration for the purpose of seeking to exclude the Court's jurisdiction in the case. In other words, as the *Norwegian Loans* case[1] shows, a reservation may have a boomerang effect on the state which makes it, defeating its own attempt to bring another state before the Court.

Prior to the Second World War the reservations made to acceptances of the Optional Clause were neither very numerous nor far-reaching. Some states —and the United Kingdom was one—in limiting their acceptances to future matters of dispute used a double form of limitation susceptible of extensive interpretation: 'disputes *arising after* the ratification of the present declaration *with regard to situations or facts subsequent* to the said declaration'. But the Court has kept the reservation within reasonable bounds by holding that a dispute is not to be considered as arising out of facts antecedent to the declaration, unless those facts were the actual source—the real cause —of the dispute.[2] Another quite common reservation—also contained in the United Kingdom's declaration—was of 'disputes with regard to questions which by international law fall within domestic jurisdiction'. This reservation has almost no practical effect as a limit upon the Court's jurisdiction; for all that it does is to deny to the Court the right to examine into matters which international law itself

[1] *I.C.J. Reports*, 1957, p. 24.
[2] *Rights of Passage Case, I.C.J. Reports*, 1960, p. 34.

leaves within the exclusive jurisdiction of states and in regard to which therefore a state is not under any international obligations to other states as to the way in which it may act.[1] For example, general international law in principle leaves to each state complete discretion to determine for itself the persons whom it will regard as endowed with its nationality or the conditions under which it will allow the entry into its territory of persons who are not its nationals. Accordingly, if a case should be brought before the Court which relates solely to the way in which the defendant state has in a given instance exercised its discretion in either of these matters, the Court will be bound to hold that the defendant state is under no obligation in international law to answer to the plaintiff state for the way in which it has exercised its discretion and, secondly, that the Court itself has no competence to examine into the subject-matter of the plaintiff's claim. The position will, however, be different if the defendant state should have entered into a treaty obligation towards the plaintiff state which limits the exercise of the discretion vested in it under general international law. Then the matters in question cease to be matters of domestic jurisdiction to the extent that through the treaty they have become the subject of international obligations, and the Court is to that extent competent to examine into them. It is in any event clear that, notwithstanding a reservation of matters of domestic jurisdiction, the

[1] See generally, *Nationality Decrees in Tunis and Morocco Advisory Opinion*, [1923] Series B, No. 4; and Waldock, *B.Y.I.L.*, 1954, p. 96.

Court must always go into the substance of the case
at least to the point of ascertaining whether the case
prima facie discloses any arguable ground on which
the defendant state might possibly be found to be
under an international obligation to the plaintiff
state in regard to the matters in issue. Indeed, the
question of 'domestic jurisdiction' is so closely related
to the 'merits' of the case that up to the present the
Court has never pronounced in favour of a plea of
'domestic jurisdiction' in preliminary proceedings.
It has always either rejected the plea as ill-founded
or, more usually, deferred the decision on its jurisdiction until after making a full examination of the
case on the merits. In the latter event it makes little
difference to the result whether the Court treats the
plea of 'domestic jurisdiction' as an objection to its
jurisdiction or simply as a good defence to the plaintiff state's claim on the merits. Thus a reservation of
matters of domestic jurisdiction in the United Kingdom form can only suffice to stop the Court from
examining the merits in the rare instance when it is
manifest on a summary view of the case that it does
not contain any possible basis for holding the defendant state to be under some form of international
obligation towards the plaintiff state.

Since the Second World War there has been a
noticeable decline in the quality of acceptances of
compulsory jurisdiction under the Optional Clause.
In the first place, there has been some tendency to
resort to subjective forms of reservation designed to
enable a state to determine for itself whether any

given case falls within the scope of its acceptance of the Court's jurisdiction. Thus, the United States accepted the Optional Clause with a reservation of 'disputes with regard to matters which are essentially within the domestic jurisdiction of the United States *as determined by the United States*'. This reservation, in a variety of forms, was imitated by seven other states, while the United Kingdom adopted a similar device in its declarations of 1955 and 1957 in connexion with questions affecting 'national security'. This form of reservation is open to the objection that its apparent intention is to reserve to the defendant state the power to decide whether the Court has jurisdiction, whereas Article 36 (6) expressly places the power to decide any dispute as to its jurisdiction in the hands of the Court itself. The Court itself has in two cases[1] refrained from pronouncing upon the legality of this form of reservation when it had the opportunity to do so; but a number of individual judges and writers have condemned them as contrary to the Statute. France and India have abandoned it in face of this criticism, as has the United Kingdom for events occurring after 26 November 1958; and it was hoped that the United States itself would do likewise, but this has not yet happened. Nevertheless, judicial criticism of this form of reservation appears to have checked its growth.

In the second place states have shown an increasing tendency not to enter into long-term commitments

Norwegian Loans Case, I.C.J. Reports, 1957, p. 24; *Interhandel Case,* ibid., p. 105, and 1959, p. 6.

but to leave themselves free to vary their acceptances or to cancel them altogether at short notice. Thus, of the thirty-nine acceptances in force in 1960 no less than twelve are immediately terminable by simple notice to the Secretary-General, three upon six months' notice and two more on twelve months' notice. This tendency began innocently enough through states accepting compulsory jurisdiction for terms of five or ten years with a proviso that the acceptance should afterwards continue in force until notice of termination was given. But the use of acceptances terminable upon notice has now become more deliberate and there have already been instances of the right to terminate being employed to prevent particular impending cases from being brought before the Court. The tactic adopted has been to cancel the existing declaration and to reissue it with a new reservation excluding the particular class of case from the acceptance of jurisdiction. In addition two states, Portugal and the United Kingdom, have expressly reserved to themselves the right to vary the terms of their acceptances at any time by a simple notice to the Secretary-General, and this form of reservation has been upheld by the Court.[1] The only check that the Court has found it possible to impose on the evasion of its jurisdiction under the Optional Clause by resort to notices to terminate or vary declarations has been the rule in the *Nottebohm* case.[2] The Court there held that, if an Application

---

[1] *Rights of Passage Case, I.C.J. Reports*, 1957, p. 125.
[2] *I.C.J. Reports*, 1953, p. 111.

has been regularly filed, in a particular case at a time when the declarations of the plaintiff and defendant states were both current and both included that case within their terms, the subsequent termination of one of the declarations does not deprive the Court of jurisdiction to adjudicate. In other words, a notice to terminate or to vary a declaration is effective to avoid jurisdiction in a particular case only if given before the plaintiff state files an Application; if given afterwards, by however short a space of time, it will be ineffective to deprive the Court of jurisdiction over a case of which it had already been validly seized.

Clearly, the new practices described in the preceding paragraph constitute a serious weakening of the Optional Clause system of compulsory jurisdiction, since they enable states to contract in and out almost at will. If it is right and salutary to criticize these practices, it must at the same time be recognized that they are but a reflection of the prevailing tensions and lack of mutual confidence in international affairs. Until a greater feeling of confidence and solidarity between states can be established, it is idle to look for any spectacular advance in the compulsory judicial settlement of international disputes.

Besides its contentious jurisdiction over disputes referred to it by states, the Court under Article 96 of the Charter may be requested by the General Assembly or the Security Council 'to give an advisory opinion on any legal question'. Other organs of the United Nations and Specialized Agencies may also request advisory opinions on 'legal questions arising within the scope of their activities', if authorized to do so by the General Assembly, and a considerable number of United Nations organs and Specialized Agencies have in fact been so authorized. It should, however, be noted that the Secretary-General has not been empowered to seek advisory opinions from the Court and that under the Charter individual member states have no such right and cannot therefore individually challenge the legality of any action of the United Nations before the Court. Under the League the advisory jurisdiction proved unexpectedly important, for the Council, a political body, was often glad to avoid making a decision itself by referring a legal issue to the Court; it is also the fact that all the advisory opinions given by the Permanent Court were requested by the Council and none by the Assembly. The United Nations has been generally less disposed to ask for advisory opinions and has tended to do so only after it has exhausted all the possibilities of political pressure within the United Nations. Moreover, the position as between the Assembly and the Council has been the reverse of that under the League, and reflects the shift under the United Nations of political initiative from the Council to the Assembly; for all the advisory opinions which have been sought by the United Nations have been requested by the General Assembly and none by the Security Council. The Specialized Agencies also have been slow to use their power to obtain advisory opinions, and in only one case has one of these Agencies requested enlightenment from the Court as to the correct interpretation of its constitution.

Article 65 of the Statute does not bind the Court to give an advisory opinion whenever requested to do so, for the language is merely permissive; and although the Court has said that 'a reply to a request for an opinion should not in principle be refused', it has also insisted on its right to refuse an opinion in circumstances when to give one would be to compromise the Court's judicial character. In 1923 it refused to give an opinion in the *Eastern Carelia* case[1] when the League Council, at the instance of Finland, requested an opinion on Russia's obligations under the Treaty of Dorpat and the Soviet Government, denying the Court's competence to investigate the dispute, declined to take any part in the proceedings. In that case the Permanent Court appeared to express the view that, whenever the subject-matter of a request for an advisory opinion relates directly to the substance of an existing dispute between two states one of which has not consented to the Court's investigation of the dispute, the general rule of international law that jurisdiction depends on consent must be respected and that the Court ought therefore to refrain from giving an opinion. But the Court also emphasized that to give an opinion in that particular case would necessarily have involved arriving at a decision upon certain facts which were in controversy and that to do this without the participation of both parties would be to depart from 'the essential rules

[1] Series B, No. 5.

guiding their activity as a Court'. In the *Interpretation of Peace Treaties* case[1] the present Court, while professing merely to 'distinguish' the *Eastern Carelia* case, appears to have receded to some extent from the Permanent Court's position concerning the consent of the parties to the dispute. For it said that the situation in advisory proceedings is different from that in contentious cases even where the request for an opinion relates to a legal question actually pending between states; that the opinion is only of an advisory character without binding force; and that no state can prevent the giving of an advisory opinion which the United Nations considers to be desirable in order to obtain enlightenment as to the course of action it should take. In the *Peace Treaties* case the dispute between the parties really involved two disputes, (1) a dispute as to the violation of the human rights clauses of the treaties by Roumania, Bulgaria, and Hungary, and (2) a dispute as to the application of the arbitral machinery provided in the treaties for settling that dispute. The Court appears to have considered that, if it had been asked for an opinion relating to the first dispute, the refusal of the three states to participate would have made it impossible to give one, because the first dispute was the main point and real 'merits' of the contention between the parties; but that, despite the non-appearance of the three states, there was no impropriety in giving an opinion relating to the second dispute concerning application of the arbitral procedure of the Peace Treaties. Exactly how

[1] *I.C.J. Reports*, 1950, p. 65.

far the Court may have moved away from the position of the Permanent Court on the need for the consent of the parties in advisory proceedings relating to an existing dispute is not clear, and the point is an important one. For advisory opinions, though not legally binding, are *judicial* opinions and it is evident that to give advisory opinions on the merits of existing disputes between states without their consent would be to introduce by the back door a qualified form of compulsory jurisdiction.

In the *Eastern Carelia* case the Court clearly felt that its character as a judicial tribunal requires it to hear both sides of a case: *audi alteram partem*. It has also adopted the same standpoint in advisory proceedings where in substance it is being asked to act as an arbiter between individuals and an international organization. Thus when U.N.E.S.C.O. appealed to the Court, by means of the advisory procedure, from judgments of the I.L.O. Administrative Tribunal given against U.N.E.S.C.O. and in favour of four dismissed officials, the Court, while entertaining the request for an opinion, was insistent that both sides must have an opportunity to submit their views.[1] 'The judicial character of the Court', it said, 'requires that both sides directly affected by these proceedings should be in a position to submit their views and their arguments to the Court'; and since its Statute did not permit it to hear oral argument on behalf of the individual officials, it confined the proceedings to written pleadings. Indeed, it has been the consistent

[1] *The Administrative Tribunal of the I.L.O., I.C.J. Reports*, 1956, p. 77.

policy of the Court to treat its advisory jurisdiction as a judicial function, and it has assimilated in most respects the procedure in advisory cases to that used in its contentious jurisdiction.

§ 3. *The Limits of Arbitration and Judicial Settlement*

It has been a common assumption among international lawyers that not all disputes between states are 'justiciable', that is to say, susceptible of decision by the application, in an arbitral or judicial process, of rules of law. This is a mere truism in one sense, because it is obvious that, so long as states are not compelled to submit to legal process, no dispute is 'justiciable' unless the parties have made it so by undertaking an obligation to treat it as such. But the distinction between 'justiciable' and 'non-justiciable' disputes usually implies more than this; it implies the belief that international disputes are of two distinct kinds, one of which, the justiciable or legal, is inherently susceptible of being decided on the basis of law, while the other, the non-justiciable or political, is not.

International lawyers, at any rate until recently, have generally agreed that this distinction exists, but they have not been agreed on its content. One view commonly held has been that a justiciable dispute is one for which a rule of law applicable to the dispute exists. This implies that for other disputes, the non-justiciable, no applicable rules exist in the law, and accordingly that a court of law called upon to deal with such a dispute would find itself unable to pronounce a decision. It has already been shown[1] that this difficulty is imaginary. It is a corollary of the extreme positivist view of the nature of international law, according to which, since nothing is law except the rules that states have consented to, the number of legal rules is necessarily finite. It overlooks the dynamic element, which the international like every other system of law reveals as soon as it ceases to be a merely academic study and begins to be applied to factual situations by the accepted processes of judicial reasoning.

International law then is never formally or intrinsically incapable of giving a decision, on the basis of law, as to the rights of the parties to any dispute, and if that is so,[2] we must look for the difference between justiciable and non-justiciable disputes elsewhere. Probably today most writers would regard it as depending upon the attitude of the parties: if, whatever the subject-matter of the dispute may be, what the parties seek is their legal rights, the dispute is justiciable: if, on the other hand, one of them at least is not content to demand its legal rights, but demands the satisfaction of some interest of its own even though this may require a change in the existing legal situation, the dispute is non-justiciable. It is certain that many disputes, probably most of the serious disputes, of states are of this kind, and this is an important fact

[1] *Supra*, p. 68.
[2] Julius Stone has suggested that there may be cases in which by pronouncing a court would be going beyond the limits of judicial legislation and really acting as a legislature, and that then it ought to refuse to adjudicate; see *B.Y.I.L.*, 1959, p. 124.

in the relations of states, of which, whether we like it or not, we must take account. But it does not supply what the controversy on the subject has assumed to exist, an objective test whereby we may classify disputes into two kinds; it does not enable us to predict, merely from a knowledge of the subject-matter of a dispute, that it will be justiciable or that it will be non-justiciable; it merely reminds us of an already known fact, namely that states do sometimes regard a decision on the basis of law as a satisfactory method of disposing of their disputes, and that sometimes, for whatever reason, good or bad, they or at least one of the states concerned does not.

No lawyer is likely to doubt the desirability of a much greater readiness on the part of states than they at present show to accept the settlement of their disputes on the basis of law. The present unlimited freedom of states to reject that method of settlement is entirely indefensible; it makes possible the grossest injustices, and it is a standing danger to the peace of the world by encouraging the habit of states to regard themselves each as a law unto itself. On the other hand, the problem is not a simple one, and it is not likely to meet a quick solution, such as was aimed at in the General Act of Geneva of 1928, by the acceptance of existing law as a universally applicable basis for the settlement of all disputes. A declaration of their legal rights when states are quarrelling about something other than their rights is not in any true sense a 'settlement' of their dispute: it may occasionally facilitate a settlement by subsequent agreement, but it may also have exactly the opposite effect by making a compromise seem unnecessary to the party that is satisfied with the declaration. It is tempting to appeal to the analogy of the individual and his relation to the courts of the state, but this is in many respects misleading. International law at its present stage of development gives a far less effective protection to the reasonable interests of states than does the law of a constitutional state to those of individuals, both because the substance of the law is defective relatively to the interests which it ought to be able to protect, and because the circumstances in which it has to be administered are more difficult. Thus of many anti-social acts which affect the perfectly reasonable interests of another state, international law, if appealed to, could only say that they are matters exclusively within the domestic jurisdiction of the state whose conduct is in question, and therefore that no legal right of the injured state has been violated. A national court, again, is normally supplied with a body of well-established doctrine; its judges share the traditions and sentiments of those to whom they administer justice; and a regular system of appeals exists to correct their mistakes; but none of these safeguards exists in the international system.

These differences are not likely to be overlooked, but there are also certain limitations on the potentialities of judicial procedure in general which it is well to bear in mind. One is that a dispute does not necessarily receive its quietus because a court of law may have pronounced upon it. There are historical instances in which the decisions of courts have had exactly the reverse effect, and have been contributory causes of the outbreak of war. This is true of *Hampden's* case in 1637, in which the Court declared the law on the question of ship-money, and of the *Dred Scot* case in 1857, in which the American Supreme Court declared the law on the question of slavery; each of these cases had its sequel in a civil war which was fought in part to determine afresh the very issues which the courts had decided.

Further, it ought never to be forgotten that law is not merely a convenient device for the settlement of disputes; it is not something that can be made an effective instrument at a crisis and left out of account at other times; it is useful as a means of settlement only when, and so far as, a society has accepted the rule of law as its way of life. It is only because the judicial organs of a state are part of the whole complicated machinery of a state's government that they are able to work with the relatively high degree of efficiency to which we are accustomed. In fact the example of the state, if it is examined more closely, is discouraging to the view that all disputes ought to or can be settled on the basis of existing law, for international disputes find their nearest analogy not in the disputes of individuals at all, but in a class of disputes which the practice of states itself tends to treat by political rather than judicial methods. By their very nature they are differences between large associated groups; and when such a group of persons within the state is discontented with its existing legal rights, a wise government does not merely refer them to the courts of law; it considers the arguments for and against a change of the law. When states are so minded and so organized that they too can deal with the more difficult disputes in this spirit, not only will peace be more secure than it is at present, but the judicial system itself, within its proper sphere, will be established on a firmer foundation.

Some of these difficulties of devising an all-inclusive scheme for the settlement of disputes would doubtless not apply if arbitrators or judges, instead of being required to give decisions based on existing law, were given a discretion to decide *ex aequo et bono* when the legal situation seems to them to be in conflict with the justice of the case. Proposals for a so-called 'equity tribunal' on these lines have often been made in recent years. It has already been mentioned that the Statute of the International Court provides for a decision of this kind 'if the parties agree'; and though this particular provision has not yet been used, the method is frequently used with advantage in the settlement of differences of secondary importance. After the proceedings before the Permanent Court in the *Free Zones* case,[1] France and Switzerland, being dissatisfied with the position established by the decision for the commerce between the Free Zones and Switzerland, but unable to agree on the changes to be introduced, empowered an arbitral tribunal to lay down a 'more liberal and legally more stable régime',

[1] *Supra*, p. 335.

and the regulations laid down by this tribunal themselves contain a provision that, in default of agreement, an arbitral tribunal, deciding *ex aequo et bono*, might in the future adapt them to new economic conditions.[1] It would, however, be a very different matter to extend this method of settlement by making it compulsory, even in the last resort, for all disputes.

A judge or an arbitrator applying legal principles is an expert, and his opinion that such and such are the rights of the parties has a special value; but an arbitrator's opinion of what is fair and just cannot be based on any objective standard and is worth intrinsically neither more nor less than that of any other equally fair-minded and intelligent person. The dissatisfaction of a state with the *status quo* raises a question which is not a judicial one, and cannot be turned into a judicial question by adopting judicial methods of procedure; it raises a question which is essentially *political*, susceptible of amicable settlement no doubt, but only by appropriate *political* methods, by negotiation, by compromise, by mediation, or conciliation; and when it relates to a matter which the states concerned regard as vital to their interests there is not the smallest chance that it will or can be settled by the *ipse dixit* of an arbitrator.

The true nature of the power which would be entrusted to an 'equity tribunal' should be understood; a power to decide *ex aequo et bono* is a power to abrogate or modify existing legal rights, and essentially that is

[1] For references see Habicht, 'Power of the International Judge o give a decision *ex aequo et bono*', pp. 78 and 84.

a power to *legislate*. However urgent it may be to create a procedure for the orderly modification of international legal rights in proper cases, it is inconceivable that the solution will be found in the simple plan of handing over to arbitral tribunals, responsible for their decisions only to their own consciences, a function which states are not yet prepared to concede to an international legislature. Legal rights ought not to be immutable, but a system in which one state could be required, on the mere demand of another, to put in issue its legal rights on any matter about which the two were in controversy would be as unreasonable as it is improbable.

§ 4. *Good Offices, Mediation, Conciliation*

In these modes of composing a quarrel, the intervention of a third party aims, not at *deciding* the quarrel *for* the disputing parties, but at inducing them to decide it for themselves. The difference between the two first terms is not important; strictly a state is said to offer 'good offices' when it tries to induce the parties to negotiate between themselves, and to 'mediate' when it takes a part in the negotiations itself, but clearly the one process merges into the other. Both, moreover, are political processes, which hardly fall within international law. The Hague Conventions for the Pacific Settlement of International Disputes declare it to be desirable that powers strangers to a dispute should offer their good offices and mediation, and such an offer is not to be regarded as an unfriendly act.

The same Conventions also introduced a new device for the promotion of peaceful settlements, in Commissions of Inquiry, whose function was simply to investigate the facts of a dispute and to make a report stating them; this report was not to have the character of an award, and the parties were free to decide what effect, if any, they would give it. The Commission was to be constituted for each occasion by agreement between the parties. This machinery was used with good effect in the Dogger Bank dispute between Great Britain and Russia in 1904.

The idea underlying these Commissions, that if resort to war can only be postponed and the facts clarified and published, war will probably be averted altogether, inspired the so-called 'Bryan treaties', the first of which was concluded between Great Britain and the United States in 1914. Under these the parties agreed to refer 'all disputes of every nature whatsoever' which cannot be otherwise settled to a standing 'Peace Commission' for investigation and report, and not to go to war until the report was received, which had to be within a year. The Commission consisted of one national and one non-national chosen by each party, and a fifth, not a national of either party, chosen by agreement. No disputes whatsoever were excluded from the operation of these treaties.

The method of the 'Bryan treaties' was extensively adopted in later developments of international organization, and as it is essentially different from the method of arbitration on the one hand, and not precisely the same as that of mediation on the other, it is convenient to refer to it as 'conciliation'. It has been defined as 'the process of settling a dispute by referring it to a commission of persons whose task it is to elucidate the facts and . . . to make a report containing proposals for a settlement, but not having the binding character of an award or judgement'.[1] Conciliation, therefore, differs from arbitration, because in it terms of settlement are merely proposed, and not dictated to the disputing states; it is therefore, unlike arbitration, a method appropriate to any dispute whatsoever. In the period between the two Great Wars machinery of conciliation was set up by many treaties between particular states, notably by those of Locarno in 1925. These so-called 'arbitration conventions' set up a 'Permanent Conciliation Commission' usually of five persons, consisting of one national of each of the signatory states and three nonnationals; disputes 'as to the respective rights' of the parties might by agreement be referred to the Commission, but if not settled there, they were to be referred to arbitration or to the Permanent Court; other disputes were to be referred to the Commission. Its task was to 'elucidate questions in dispute, to collect with that object all necessary information by means of inquiry or otherwise, and to endeavour to bring the parties to an agreement . . . at the close of its labours the Commission shall draw up a report'.

Treaties of conciliation have scarcely fulfilled the hopes placed in them; for, although nearly 200

[1] Oppenheim, *International Law*, 7th ed., vol. ii, p. 12.

commissions have been established, they have been little used, the number of cases dealt with by them being not much more than ten. There have, however, been a few encouraging examples of the use of conciliation in more recent years which have led to a revival of interest in this procedure for settling international disputes, and the development of its use is engaging the attention of international lawyers.[1]

§ 5. *The Covenant System of Handling Disputes*

The Covenant of the League contained a comprehensive scheme for the settlement of international disputes which is still of interest, especially for the contrast which it provides with that of the Charter of the United Nations. By Article 12 the members agreed that 'if there should arise between them any dispute likely to lead to a rupture' they would deal with it in one of three ways; they would submit it either to arbitration, or to the Permanent Court, or to inquiry by the Council. In the first alternative the award, and in the second the judicial decision, had to be given within a reasonable time; in the third the Council had to make its report within six months; and the members agreed that they would not 'resort to war' until three months after the award or the decision or the report as the case might be. The motive of this last provision was doubtless the feeling that if a war can be delayed long enough for excitement to cool and for the issues to be debated in an

[1] See H. Rolin, *European Yearbook*, vol. 3, p. 3; and *Annuaire de l'Institut de droit international*, 1959, vol. 1, p. 5.

impartial forum, it will probably be averted alto-gether, but subsequent events suggest that this was an over-optimistic view.

Article 13 dealt with the first two alternatives pro-vided by Article 12, and indicated the disputes which were considered 'generally suitable' for arbitration or judicial settlement. The disputes enumerated were the same as those in the optional clause of Article 36 of the Statute of the Court of International Justice, which has been quoted above.[1] The members agreed to carry out an award or judgment in good faith, and not to resort to war against a member which complied therewith. In the event of failure to carry out an award or judgment, the Council was to propose what steps should be taken to give effect thereto.

Article 15 dealt with the third alternative of Article 12, the submission of a dispute to the Council. The Council's first task was 'to endeavour to effect a settlement of the dispute', and if it succeeded it was then to publish a statement of the facts and the terms of settlement, the object of this provision being pre-sumably to reduce the chance that the Council, a political body, might be tempted to sacrifice the just claims of a weak power to political expediency. If, however, this attempt to get the parties to agree should fail, the Council's next duty was 'to make and publish a report containing a statement of the facts of the dispute and the recommendations which are deemed just and proper in regard thereto'. It is

[1] *Supra*, p. 355.

important to appreciate the exact effect of this report if we would understand the true nature of the scheme. The Council had no power to *dictate* a settlement to the parties; its function was not an arbitral one. The effect of its report differed according as it was reached unanimously (the votes of the parties to the dispute being excluded) or by a majority vote; if it was unanimous, 'the members of the League agree that they will not go to war with any party to the dispute which complies with the recommendations of the report'; if it was a majority report only, they 'reserve to themselves the right to take such action as they shall consider necessary for the maintenance of right and justice'. In other words, in neither case were the parties actually bound to accept the report, but a party which accepted a unanimous report was guaranteed against attack by the other, whereas a majority report did not carry this guarantee, and the parties were free to go to war, after the interval prescribed by Article 12, if they chose. The latter event was one of the so-called 'gaps in the Covenant', that is to say, one of a few cases in which the Covenant did not absolutely forbid states to resort to war; but the importance of these 'gaps' was often exaggerated. Though it was theoretically possible that an intending aggressor might first scrupulously observe all his obligations under the Covenant and then take advantage of one of the gaps to enter on a war from which he had not actually promised to refrain, that event was always most improbable, and none of the wars that occurred while the League was existing did in fact begin in that way; all of them either involved breaches of a state's obligations under the Covenant, or would have done so if the aggressor had been a member of the League.

Article 16 contained the 'sanctions' provisions, and the event in which these were to be put into force was clearly defined; it was that a member should 'resort to war in disregard of its covenants', namely those contained in the articles already quoted. There have been interminable discussions about the difficulty of defining 'aggression', but Article 16 did not use the word; it made a definition unnecessary by making the occasion for sanctions depend on the refusal of a prescribed procedure of peaceful settlement. The provisions relating to the form that the sanctions were to take when the occasion arose were not in all respects satisfactorily drafted; some of them were not free from ambiguity, and there was a tendency to rely too much on economic sanctions, the tremendous efficacy of which seemed to have been demonstrated by the war which had just ended, and to leave the possible need for military action somewhat obscure. But the points of principle which are of most interest today are (a) that the occasion for sanctions was not left indeterminate or discretionary, but was precisely defined; and (b) that it was left to each of the members to decide for itself whether the occasion had arisen, and consequently whether it was under obligation to join in the imposition of sanctions. The Council might recommend plans for co-ordinating the actions of the members in that event, but it could not make

380 INTERNATIONAL DISPUTES

decisions on their behalf nor issue directions which they would be bound to follow. There was thus, of course, a risk that the several members might not all decide alike, but as sanctions would never be contemplated except in a very clear case, it was practically certain that, if they acted honestly, they would; if they were not ready to honour their obligations, neither the Covenant nor any other system of sanctions could possibly work. In the event, sanctions were resorted to only once in the history of the League, namely against Italy in 1935–6, and then all the members except three small states which were entirely dependent on Italy's goodwill did reach identical decisions, and the fact that the sanctions failed had nothing whatever to do with the absence of a power in the League Council to make a decision on behalf of the League as a body. They failed because the leading powers in the League, for political reasons wholly unconnected with the merits of the case, were not willing to risk a total breach with Italy, and therefore refrained from any action which might seriously have affected her plans for the conquest of Ethiopia. The machinery prescribed by the Covenant for putting sanctions into operation on the whole worked well.

§ 6. *The Charter System of Handling Disputes*

Articles 24 and 25 of the Charter,[1] as already stated in an earlier chapter, provide:

'In order to ensure prompt and effective action by the

[1] *Supra*, p. 110.

United Nations, its members confer on the Security Council primary responsibility for the maintenance of international peace and security, and agree that in carrying out its duties under this responsibility the Security Council acts on their behalf. In discharging these duties the Security Council shall act in accordance with the Purposes and Principles of the United Nations. . . .'

'The members of the United Nations agree to accept and carry out the decisions of the Security Council in accordance with the present Charter.'

Later articles of the Charter contain certain 'specific powers' which are granted to the Security Council 'for the discharge of these duties'.

Unlike the Covenant the Charter does not lay down specific conditions for the exercise of the powers of the Security Council; but it does make an important distinction between powers relating to the Security Council's function of promoting pacific settlement under Chapter VI and those relating to enforcement action under Chapter VII. In fact, in relation to the former, the Council has in strictness no powers; its decisions are no more than recommendations to the parties. Thus it may call upon the parties to any dispute 'the continuance of which is likely to endanger the maintenance of international peace and security' to settle it by some peaceful method of their own choice. It may 'investigate any dispute, or any situation which might lead to international friction and give rise to a dispute' in order to determine whether its continuance is likely to endanger peace and security; and at any stage of such a dispute or situation it may 'recommend appropriate procedures or methods of settlement', as it did in the Corfu Channel incident when it recommended Albania and the United Kingdom to refer their dispute to the Court. If it should decide that the continuance of the dispute is, in fact, likely to endanger peace and security, it may go farther than this and 'recommend such terms of settlement as it may consider appropriate'. But it cannot dictate such terms.

When, however, the decisions of the Security Council concern action for the maintenance of peace, they may be more than recommendations; they may be directions which the members of the United Nations are bound to carry out. It is empowered to determine 'the existence of any threat to the peace, breach of the peace, or act of aggression', and to 'make recommendations *or decide* what measures shall be taken' to maintain or restore the peace; and before making such a recommendation or decision it may call upon the parties, in order to prevent an aggravation of the situation, to comply with any necessary provisional measures without prejudice to their rights or claims, and is to take account of any failure to comply with such provisional measures. But, unlike the Covenant, the Charter contains no tests for deciding whether an occasion for sanctions has arisen or not; it leaves it to the discretion of the Security Council to determine what constitutes a threat or a breach or an aggression. Nor, except for its general obligation to act in accordance with 'the Purposes and Principles of the United Nations', is there anything to ensure that the measures upon which the Council decides shall either respect the legal rights of the states affected or be just in themselves. When it has decided that action is needed, the Council may call for measures not involving the use of armed force, such as the interruption of economic relations and of means of communication, and the severance of diplomatic relations; but if it considers such measures inadequate, 'it may take such action by air, sea, and land forces' as may be necessary to maintain or restore the peace. For this purpose all members of the United Nations have bound themselves to make available to the Council on its call and in accordance with 'special agreements' armed forces and other forms of assistance and facilities, and these agreements are to state the numbers and types of forces, their degree of readiness and general location, and the nature of the facilities and assistance to be provided; and in order to enable 'urgent military measures' to be taken, the members are to 'hold immediately available national air force contingents for combined international enforcement action'. A Military Staff Committee, consisting of the chiefs of staff of the permanent members or their representatives, is to advise the Council on all questions relating to its military requirements, and is responsible under the Council for the strategic direction of the armed forces at its disposal. The negative attitude of the Soviet Union's representative, however, soon brought the work of the Military Staff Committee

to a standstill and no 'special agreements' have been
made between the Council and member states; in
other words, the Charter machinery for the taking
of enforcement action by the United Nations in
pursuance of a decision of the Security Council
simply does not exist. Consequently, in the Korean
War, when the absence of the Soviet delegate enabled
the Council to pass resolutions calling for action to
repel the aggression of North Korea,[1] it had to rely
on contingents voluntarily supplied by members in
response to its recommendation that members should
furnish the necessary assistance to repel the attack
upon South Korea; and the problem of unity of
command was dealt with by delegating the command
to the United States and inviting members to place
their contingents under that command. This expedient proved satisfactory enough as a means of
meeting the difficulty in the military sphere; but
much less so for dealing with political problems.[2]

In any event, the successful use of the Security
Council for initiating action in Korea was due to
the lucky chance of the absence of the Soviet delegate
from the Council table, and it is unlikely to be
repeated so long as the Great Powers remain divided.
As explained in a previous chapter,[3] each of the
permanent members, by the use of its veto, may
block the taking of any enforcement measures by the

[1] *Supra*, p. 115.
[2] The question of keeping the United Nations forces south of the
38th parallel of latitude made evident the awkwardness of a United
Nations chain of command placed under one member state.
[3] Chapter III.

Council against any state, including itself; and so, for example, the Soviet Union in the Hungarian incident and France and the United Kingdom in the Suez incident were in a position to block completely the taking of any resolutions by the Council for measures under Chapter VII of the Charter. Yet the only event which can seriously endanger the general peace of the world is an aggression or intervention undertaken or organized by a Great Power, and a system of collective security, like that of the Charter, which does not propose to deal with aggression or intervention by a Great Power is clearly something of a sham. It may be that no system of collective security can avail against a Great Power: no enforcement action, says the British official commentary on the Charter,[1] 'can be taken in such a case without a major war, and if such a situation were to arise the United Nations would have failed in its purpose and the members would have to act as seemed best in the circumstances.' This may be true. But if so, and if there never was any idea that the procedure of the Charter might, if necessary, be used against a Great Power, it is not easy to see the reason for the elaborate machinery described above. It does not make sense to provide that all members are to make armed forces available to the Security Council on its call, that they are to hold air forces immediately available, that the Military Staff Committee is to advise the Security Council on all questions relating to its

[1] Cmd. 6666 (1945).

military requirements, and so on, if the only purpose of these formidable plans is to deal with a small Power when it misbehaves. Small-power aggression can never be a serious problem to the peace of the world if the Great Powers are agreed among themselves to deal with it.

The explanation of the Charter provisions concerning the Security Council has to be sought in the circumstances in which they were drafted. Then it seemed that the dangers to be guarded against were those which Germany and Japan represented and the Charter therefore sought to forge an irresistible weapon to deal with just such dangers. At the same time the Soviet Union, with its constant fear of being outvoted by the Western states, the United States Government with its memories of the refusal of Congress to limit its sovereignty by joining the League, and the United Kingdom with its world-wide interests to protect, all had their reasons for insisting upon a veto. So it was that in the Charter there was fashioned a highly specialized instrument, useful only against a particular danger for which it is not in fact needed, and only on the assumption that the war-time unity of the Great Powers would be a permanent factor in their relations. Instead of a system that ensures 'prompt and effective action', the Charter provided one that could be jammed by the opposition of a single Great Power; instead of limiting further the sovereignty of States, it extended the effective sovereignty of the Great Powers, the only states whose sovereignty is still a formidable reality.

Happily, as already explained in Chapter III, the United Nations was not prepared in its search for collective security to be baulked by the defects of the Security Council system, and through the Uniting For Peace Resolution set about creating a secondary system centred upon the General Assembly. Under this Resolution, it will be recalled, when the Council is prevented from discharging its primary responsibility for maintaining peace owing to a Great Power's exercise of its veto, the matter may be transferred to the agenda of the Assembly, which can then deal with it by the procedure of *recommending* to the parties to the dispute measures for putting an end to the 'breach of the peace', 'threat to the peace', or 'act of aggression' which has arisen and, if necessary, recommending to the general body of the members collective enforcement measures for the purpose of maintaining or restoring peace. The Resolution also contained provisions designed to furnish the General Assembly with the necessary means for taking effective measures to keep the peace: (1) it established a Peace Observation Commission of fourteen members, which may be used either by the Assembly or the Council to observe and report on the situation in any area where there exists international tension dangerous to peace; (2) it recommended member states to maintain within their national armed forces elements capable of being made available promptly for United Nations service; and (3) it established a 'Collective Measures Committee' of fourteen members to study and report on the methods, including the use of armed forces, to be employed for maintaining and strengthening peace. The Assembly approved the establishment of a Balkan Sub-Commission of the Peace Observation Commission in 1951 to observe the situation on the Greco-Albanian and Greco-Bulgarian frontiers and a small mission was maintained in Greece for a considerable time; the Collective Measures Committee submitted yearly reports from 1951 to 1954 on the general principles and methods of collective security, and some member states specially earmarked contingents for United Nations duties. But in general the special machinery created by the Uniting for Peace Resolution has not so far been given much prominence and the United Nations has looked rather to the Secretary-General as the instrument for carrying out its measures for keeping the peace.

Beginning in 1955, both the Assembly and the Council have developed a practice of simply handing over to the Secretary-General the implementation of their decisions. The Council, for example, in 1956 instructed him to arrange with the parties to the Palestine armistice 'for adoption of any measures' which he should consider 'would reduce existing tensions along the demarcation lines.' A few months later the Assembly, acting under the Uniting for Peace Resolution, after France and the United Kingdom had vetoed the Security Council's proposals, authorized the Secretary-General 'to obtain compliance of the withdrawal of foreign forces'; and then

it instructed him to submit a plan for a United
Nations Force, to 'secure and supervise the cessation
of hostilities' and 'to take all necessary administrative
and executive action to organize this Force and dispatch it to Egypt'. Similarly, it was the Secretary-
General who was made responsible for the United
Nations arrangements for clearing the Suez Canal.
Again, in 1958, it was he, not the Peace Observation
Commission, who was requested by the Council to
establish an observer group in the Lebanon; and later
the Assembly, under the Uniting For Peace Resolution, gave him a general directive to make 'such
practical arrangements as would adequately help in
upholding the purposes and principles of the Charter
in relation to Lebanon and Jordan . . . and thereby
facilitate the early withdrawal of foreign troops'.
Finally, in the Congo crisis in 1960, first the Council
and later the Assembly delegated to the Secretary-
General virtually the whole execution of directives
given by them in the broadest terms for handling this
dangerous and complex situation. Thus the basic
mandate of the two bodies for his handling of the
Congo crisis was a resolution by the Council on
13 July 1960, which (a) called upon Belgium to withdraw her troops from the Congo and (b) authorized
the Secretary-General to provide the Government of
the Congo with such military assistance as might be
necessary, until with the technical assistance of the
United Nations the national forces of the Congo were
able to meet their responsibilities. That was all: the
formation of a United Nations Force, its introduction

into the Congo and its subsequent employment there were all left to the Secretary-General in consultation with the government—a government which promptly proceeded to disintegrate.

The United Nations Emergency Forces in Egypt and in the Congo represent constitutional experiments of the utmost significance. The first was established by the Assembly under the Uniting For Peace Resolution on the basis of a plan submitted by the Secretary-General; it was established as a 'subsidiary organ' of the Assembly which itself appointed the Chief of the United Nations Command. While the Secretary-General was responsible for taking the necessary administrative measures, the Chief of Command, in consultation with him, was directly responsible to the Assembly for the recruitment of the Force and for its operations; the general executive responsibility for securing compliance with its resolutions was, on the other hand, entrusted by the Assembly to the Secretary-General with whom, therefore, the political initiative always lay. The Secretary-General's political position was also strengthened by the creation of a small Advisory Committee of representatives of seven member states under his chairmanship, to which he could turn for guidance without, however, surrendering his personal responsibility and power of decision. The Force itself was composed of contingents selected from states other than the five permanent members of the Security Council and it was expressly recognized that Egypt—the 'host' country—was entitled to be consulted concerning the

Force's composition. The legal status of the United Nations contingents in Egypt—an urgent problem—was quickly agreed between the Secretary-General and the Egyptian Government in an important exchange of Notes, on the general basis that the Force, as a United Nations organ, and its personnel as United Nations officials, were in principle entitled to the privileges and immunities laid down in the Convention on the Privileges and Immunities of the United Nations. However, in order to protect the operational efficiency of the Force, criminal jurisdiction over its personnel in regard to offences committed in Egypt was reserved exclusively to the state to whose national forces the offender belonged, and special provisions were made in regard to the exercise of Egypt's civil jurisdiction with respect to members of the Force. The much larger Congo Emergency Force was established on similar principles, with the exception that its legal basis and its chain of command were different. Here, as already mentioned, the Security Council had simply requested the Secretary-General to provide the necessary military assistance to the Government of the Congo; and in consequence it was the Secretary-General himself who appointed the Chief of Command and recruited the Force. In short, both the political and military chain of command of the Force went through the Secretary-General, and the Force was not so much a 'subsidiary organ' as a military extension of the Secretariat. At first there was no Advisory Committee, and when after some five weeks an Advisory Committee of fifteen members was created, it was the Secretary-General again who established it.

The political initiative and executive responsibilities given to the Secretary-General in recent years is a reflection at once of the distrust of the Soviet Union and the Western Powers for each other and of the confidence of the general body of the member states in the high integrity and ability of the late Secretary-General, Mr. Hammarskjøld. But the new role given to the Secretary-General, as he himself pointed out,[1] brings certain risks to the independence and 'internationalism' of the Secretariat, since greater efforts may be made by governments to bring pressure to bear upon it. It may also complicate the relations of the Secretary-General with individual members who find their policies obstructed by the action of the United Nations; the very success of the Congo operation as a containing measure to prevent outside intervention led, for example, to strong criticism by the Soviet Union of Mr. Hammarskjold and of the whole institution of the Secretary-General as at present conceived. It must further be remembered that neither in Egypt nor in the Congo was it the mission of the Force to take enforcement action against one of the parties to the dispute;[2] in both

---

[1] *Lecture delivered at Oxford University on 30 May 1961* (Clarendon Press), pp. 19–28.

[2] In both cases the Secretary-General emphasized (1) that the Force could only operate in a territory with the consent of the government concerned and (2) the Force was not entitled to take the initiative in the use of armed force but could only use its arms in response to an armed attack.

cases it was to introduce the 'presence' of the United Nations into the dangerous area and thereby assist, in the one case, the restoration, and in the other, the maintenance, of international peace. The organization and employment of a military force to act as armed police to bring about a cease-fire, or to strengthen internal security, is a very different thing from undertaking full-scale combat operations against forces determined to resist, and whether the same procedure, perhaps in some developed form, can be used for mounting combat operations remains to be seen. Accordingly, while the Emergency Forces in Egypt and the Congo provide an encouraging demonstration of the feasibility and value of prompt United Nations action through the Secretary-General for the maintenance of peace, it may be too early yet to see in these Forces an adequate substitute for the international police force which the Charter envisaged and the world so clearly needs.

Two other points in the Charter system, both of which involve some mitigation of the paralysing power of the veto, require to be mentioned. The first is that Article 51 expressly reserves to member states their 'inherent right of individual or collective self-defence if an armed attack occurs' against another member, until the Security Council has taken the measures necessary to maintain peace. Hence, if an attack is made and a Great Power by its veto prevents the Security Council from taking any decision, member states are free to combine with the victim of the attack in the armed action against the aggressor, and their action cannot be stopped by the Council until it has itself taken effective action to put an end to the breach of the peace. This being so, when the Charter system of collective security showed signs of breaking down under the veto, members began to have recourse to mutual security pacts based on the right of collective self-defence under Article 51, the most notable being the North Atlantic Treaty; and Article 51 also furnished a secondary ground for justifying the recourse to armed force by many members of the United Nations in 1950 to repel the attack of North upon South Korea.[1]

The second point is that Articles 52–54 contemplate, and indeed encourage, the use of regional 'arrangements' or 'agencies' for dealing with matters relating to the maintenance of peace which are appropriate for regional action;[2] and members who are parties to such regional arrangements or agencies are enjoined to seek the pacific settlement of their local disputes through them before going to the Security Council. Moreover, where appropriate, the Council

[1] See *supra*, p. 117. It is true that Article 51 refers only to an armed attack against a 'member of the United Nations', and South Korea was not such; but the right of collective self-defence, as the Article itself recognizes, is an 'inherent' right which exists independently of the Charter and applies equally to the defence of a non-member; see L. C. Green, *World Affairs*, 1950.

[2] The Charter does not state exactly what is meant by the terms 'regional arrangement' and 'regional agency', and there has been some controversy as to whether defence arrangements such as the North Atlantic Treaty Organization are to be considered as falling within them. The *travaux préparatoires* of the Charter show that Articles 52–54 were originally inserted for the primary purpose of safeguarding the legality of the Pan-American system and of the Monroe doctrine.

is enjoined to utilize such regional arrangements for 'enforcement action' taken under its authority. Article 52, it is true, expressly reserves the right of the Council to investigate a local dispute, and Article 54 further requires the Council to be kept fully informed of activities undertaken or in contemplation under regional arrangements; but there is nothing in the Articles to make proceedings under a regional arrangement for *pacific* settlement of a local dispute subject to the prior approval of the Council, and therefore to this extent regional arrangements do offer a means of escape from the veto of the permanent members of the Council. Enforcement action under a regional arrangement is, on the other hand, subject to the prior authorization of the Security Council,[1] and it may therefore be blocked by the veto of a permanent member of the Council. Recently, however, the majority of the Security Council, in taking note of a decision by the Organization of American States condemning certain acts of the Dominican Government and calling for economic measures against it, expressed the view that the only 'enforcement action' that requires the *prior* authorization of the Council is action which would be illegal under the Charter without it, in other words, a threat or use of armed force.[2] In any event, it is clear that the parties to a regional arrangement are entitled to combine together in measures of collective self-defence

[1] Except the taking of measures against the renewal of aggressive policies on the part of ex-enemy states of the Second World War.
[2] *U.N. Bulletin*, October 1960, p. 68.

396 INTERNATIONAL DISPUTES

without the prior authorization of the Council, although the Soviet Union contended the contrary with reference to the North Atlantic Treaty Organization; the right of collective self-defence is governed by Article 51 and is entirely independent of the provisions regarding regional arrangements.

IX

INTERNATIONAL LAW AND RESORT TO FORCE

§ 1. *The Law of the Era before the League*

THE rules of international law governing the use of force by states have undergone profound changes during the past fifty years as the international community has sought, first in the League of Nations and then in the United Nations, to organize itself, politically, legally, and militarily, for the collective maintenance of peace and the pacific settlement of disputes. Before the League, international law was a decentralized system in which each state held itself entirely free both to decide and act for itself, and although the classical system knew of certain principles regulating the recourse to forcible measures short of war, their application was necessarily uncertain when each state claimed the right to be the judge of the merits of its own case. This is not to deny either the significance of these principles in shaping international public opinion on the merits of a case or the reality and importance of international public opinion in the era before the League; but in the absence of any central organization to apply it, the law governing the use of force was inevitably weak law.

Furthermore, despite earlier efforts by jurists and moralists to distinguish between *bellum justum* and *bellum injustum*,[1] international law had given up the attempt to regulate recourse to war, the most extreme form of the use of force, and made no distinction between a just and unjust war. 'International law', wrote Hall in 1880 in a much-quoted passage,[2] 'has no alternative but to accept war, independently of the justice of its origin, as a relation which the parties to it may set up, if they choose, and to busy itself only in regulating the effects of the relation'; and he added: 'Hence both parties to every war are regarded as being in an identical legal position, and consequently as being possessed of equal rights.' As long as this was the attitude of the law to war, the rules concerning recourse to lesser forms of force were somewhat illusory, since these could always be placed beyond criticism by the simple process of declaring war. How easily the law could be circumvented was shown by Great Britain and Germany in 1901 when, faced with a United States protest regarding measures of 'pacific blockade', they regularized their measures merely by acknowledging a state of war to exist.[3]

Measures of self-help under the classical system could be divided into four main legal categories: (*a*) retorsion, (*b*) reprisals, (*c*) intervention, and (*d*) self-defence. Although the law governing recourse to these measures has been radically affected by the development of new rules, first in the Covenant and

[1] *Supra*, p. 33.
[2] See *International Law* (8th ed.), 1924, p. 82.
[3] Cf. Moore, *International Law Digest*, vol. vii, p. 140.

then in the Charter, restricting the use of force, these categories of self-help still remain; and it is therefore proposed to begin by giving a brief account of the classical law and then to examine the position today.

Retorsion is a measure of self-help which, though unfriendly, is within the legal powers of the state employing it and is, therefore, necessarily a legal measure even if it involves the use of force in its application. For example, if State X adopts an economic policy damaging to State Y, it is a perfectly legitimate act of retorsion for the latter then to exclude State X's fishing vessels from its territorial waters where it has previously permitted them to fish.

Reprisals is an institution with a long history, and it involves the seizing of property or persons by way of retaliation for a wrong previously done to the state taking reprisals. In earlier times it was not uncommon for a state to issue 'letters of marque' to one of its own subjects, who had met with a denial of justice in another state, authorizing him to redress the wrong for himself by forcible action such as the seizure of the property of subjects of the delinquent state. This practice, called 'special reprisals', has long been obsolete and reprisals today are always taken by the state itself. Measures of reprisal commonly used in the era before the League included (*a*) embargo of the offending state's ships found in the ports and territorial waters of the state that claimed to have been wronged, (*b*) seizure of its ships or property on the high seas, and (*c*) pacific blockade. The last-mentioned measure was not infrequently used by naval Powers and the chief legal interest about it was the doubt whether a blockade of that kind could be legally enforced against the ships of third states. Practice on the matter varied, but the general legal opinion was that a pacific blockade was only enforceable against ships of the state which was the object of the reprisals. The right to take forcible reprisals of this kind was open to grave abuse by strong against weak states, and from early times it was recognized that, if they were to be valid, reprisals must satisfy certain conditions.

These conditions were re-examined in the award given in the *Naulilaa* arbitration[1] in 1928, which is generally considered to be the most authoritative statement of the customary law of reprisals. In 1915, while Portugal was still neutral in the First World War, an incident had taken place at Naulilaa, a Portuguese post on the frontier of Angola and the then German South-West Africa, in which three Germans were killed. On the evidence it was clearly established that the incident arose out of a pure misunderstanding. The Germans, however, as a measure of reprisals, had sent an expedition into Portuguese territory, attacked several frontier posts, and driven out the garrison from Naulilaa. In the regions which the Portuguese were thus compelled to evacuate, a native rising took place, and its suppression necessitated a considerable expedition by the Portuguese.

[1] *Annual Digest*, 1927–8, Case No. 360; the full award is printed in *Révue de droit international*, 1929, p. 255.

Germany's plea that it was a case of legitimate reprisals was rejected by the arbitrators, who said:

'Reprisals are acts of self-help by the injured State, acts in retaliation for acts contrary to international law on the part of the offending State, which have remained unredressed after a demand for amends. In consequence of such measures, the observance of this or that rule of international law is temporarily suspended, in the relations between the two States. They are limited by considerations of humanity and the rules of good faith, applicable in the relations between States. They are illegal unless they are based upon a previous act contrary to international law. They seek to impose on the offending State reparation for the offence, the return to legality and the avoidance of new offences.'

And they then laid down three conditions of the legitimacy of reprisals: (a) there must have been an illegal act on the part of the other state; (b) they must be preceded by a request for redress of the wrong, for the necessity of resorting to force cannot be established if the possibility of obtaining redress by other means is not even explored; and (c) the measures adopted must not be excessive, in the sense of being out of all proportion to the provocation received. In the case before them, however, Portugal had committed no illegal act; Germany had made no request for redress; and the disproportion between the German action and its provocation was evident.

The changes in the law concerning recourse to force have, of course, severely curtailed the kinds of reprisals which may lawfully be taken today; subject to that, however, the principles laid down in the *Naulilaa* case may be accepted as governing reprisals today.

Intervention is a word which is often used quite generally to denote almost any act of interference by one state in the affairs of another; but in a more special sense it means dictatorial interference in the domestic or foreign affairs of another state which impairs that state's independence. The law of intervention suffered from the same defect as the law of reprisals in that its legality could always be put beyond criticism by the simple expedient of calling it war; the question of its legality was also sometimes obscured under the cloak of a political doctrine such as the Monroe doctrine. Nevertheless, certain principles were fairly clear in customary law. Intervention, being a violation of another state's independence, was recognized to be in principle contrary to international law, so that any act of intervention had to be justified as a legitimate case of reprisal, protection of nationals abroad or self-defence or, alternatively, as authorized under a treaty with the state concerned.[1] Apart from the case of a special treaty right, therefore, intervention was not so much a right as a sanction against a wrong or threatened wrong.

In strict theory the legality of an intervention by many states acting together had to be judged by the

---

[1] e.g. the Treaty of Havana of 1903 gave the United States the right to intervene in Cuba for the preservation of its independence, the maintenance of a government adequate for the protection of life, property and liberty, &c.; it was abrogated in 1934.

same tests as that of an intervention by a single state, but politically and morally the distinction might sometimes be vital. On many occasions in the nineteenth century the Great Powers intervened, by action which technically and legally involved a usurpation of power, in order to impose the settlement of a question which threatened the peace of Europe. In the absence of an effective legislative procedure for altering international conditions, such extra-legal action was sometimes the only practicable alternative to war; but, lacking any constitutional authority, its basis was sheer power rather than law. Some support was, however, found among jurists for the view that humanitarian intervention by a number of Powers to prevent a state from committing atrocities against its own subjects or suppressing religious liberties, such as several times happened in the Turkish Empire in the nineteenth century, was recognized by international law.[1] Whether this really was so is doubtful in view of the strength in that period of the principle that a state's treatment of its own subjects was a matter exclusively within its own domestic jurisdiction; and Lauterpacht,[2] the great protagonist for the recognition of human rights, felt bound to concede that the doctrine of humanitarian intervention had 'never become a fully acknowledged part of positive international law'.

Self-defence[3] is a principle which applies to states no

---

[1] Winfield, *B.Y.I.L.*, 1924, p. 161.
[2] *B.Y.I.L.*, 1946, p. 46.
[3] See generally D. W. Bowett, *Self-Defence in International Law*, 1958.

404 INTERNATIONAL LAW AND FORCE

less than to individuals; and the legal content of the principle is clear, though its application in a specific case may be a matter of difficulty. In the nineteenth century, however, there was a tendency, by widening the principle to cover 'self-preservation', to give it a scope which is quite inadmissible. Even a writer so generally moderate in his views as Hall went so far as to say:[1] 'In the last resort almost the whole of the duties of states are subordinated to the right of self-preservation.' Such a doctrine would destroy the imperative character of any system of law in which it applied, for it makes all obligation to obey the law merely conditional; and there is hardly an act of international lawlessness which it might not be claimed to excuse. It was, for example, one of the pretexts advanced by Germany in 1914 to justify her attack on Belgian neutrality, although she herself was under no apparent threat of attack either from Belgium or any other state. Nor does the analogy of municipal law which influenced Hall[2] in any way support this extensive view of the principle of self-defence. In English law, for example, a plea of self-preservation will not justify an otherwise criminal use of violence against another person. Thus in *R.* v. *Dudley and Stephens*,[3] when two men and a boy were cast away at sea in an open boat and the men, after their food and water had been exhausted for many

---

[1] *International Law* (8th ed.), 1924, p. 322.

[2] Ibid., p. 65.

[3] (1884) 14 Q.B.D. 273. United States law is the same; *U.S.* v. *Holmes*, 1 Wallace Junior 1.

days, killed and ate the boy, they were convicted of murder, although the jury found that in all probability all three would have died unless one had been killed for the others to eat. The truth is that self-preservation in the case of a state as of an individual is not a legal right but an instinct; and even if it may often happen that the instinct prevails over the legal duty not to do violence to others, international law ought not to admit that it is lawful that it should do so.

Self-defence, properly understood, is a strictly limited right and the best statement of the conditions for its exercise is commonly considered to be found in the incident of the steamer *Caroline* in 1837. During an insurrection in Canada the *Caroline* was used to transport men and materials for the rebels from American territory into Canada across the Niagara river. The American Government had shown itself unable or unwilling to prevent this traffic, and in these circumstances a body of Canadian militia crossed the Niagara, and, after a scuffle in which some American citizens were killed, sent the *Caroline* adrift over the Falls. In the controversy that followed, the United States did not deny that circumstances were conceivable which would justify this action, and Great Britain for her part admitted the necessity of showing circumstances of extreme urgency. They differed only on the question whether the facts brought the case within the limits of the exceptional principle of self-defence. It is the formulation of the conditions for the exercise of self-defence in this case by the American Secretary of State, Daniel Webster, which has met with general acceptance.[1] There must be shown, he said, 'a necessity of self-defence, instant, overwhelming, leaving no choice of means and no moment for deliberation'; and, further, the action taken must involve 'nothing unreasonable or excessive, since the act justified by the necessity of self-defence must be limited by that necessity and kept clearly within it'. The second of these propositions is as important as the first, for there is a natural temptation, when force has been resorted to, to continue its use after the needs of defence have been fairly met. Thus whatever may have been the true view of the initial use of force by the Japanese in Manchuria in 1931,[2] it was impossible to regard their later operations as measures of defence.

The need to keep self-defence within strict limits has been demonstrated very often in recent history; for, aggressive war having been designated an international crime, nearly every aggressive act is sought to be portrayed as an act of self-defence. The right of self-defence was pleaded at Nuremberg and Tokyo on behalf of the German and Japanese major war criminals and rejected by the War Crimes Tribunals. The Nuremberg Tribunal expressly endorsed the statement of Secretary Webster in the *Caroline* as to

[1] See, however, Westlake's criticism of the words 'leaving no moment for deliberation', in *International Law*, part i, p. 300.

[2] On this the verdict of the Lytton Commission was that the operations were *not* measures of legitimate self-defence, but that the officers on the spot may conceivably have thought that they were. See the Report of the Commission, p. 71.

the proper limits of the right: 'It must be remembered that preventive action in foreign territory is justified only in case of "an instant and overwhelming necessity for self-defence leaving no choice of means, and no moment of deliberation".'

Another point needs underlining. It was sometimes said that in the nature of things every state must be competent to decide for itself whether a necessity for self-defence has arisen, with the implication that a state is sole judge of the need to have recourse to self-defence. Japan, for example, tried to read this meaning into the declaration made by the United States at the time of signing the Pact of Paris. The declaration read:

'Every nation is free at all times and regardless of treaty provisions to defend its territory from attack or invasion and it alone is competent to decide whether circumstances require recourse to war in self-defence. If it has a good case, the world will applaud and not condemn.

But if it must necessarily be left to every state to decide in the first instance whether or in what measure an occasion calls for defensive action, it does not follow that the decision may not afterwards be reviewed by the law in the light of all the circumstances. Here again the Nuremberg Tribunal, in dealing with the charge of German aggression against Norway, had something pertinent to say:

'It was further argued that Germany alone could decide, in accordance with the reservations made by many of the Signatory Powers at the time of the conclusion of the Briand–Kellogg Pact, whether preventive action was a necessity, and that in making her decision her judgment was conclusive. But whether action taken under the claim of self-defence was in fact aggressive or defensive must ultimately be subject to investigation and adjudication if international law is ever to be enforced.'

§ 2. *The Law of the League Period*

The Covenant radically changed the whole foundations of the law, (1) by creating express obligations to employ pacific means of settling disputes and not to resort to war without first exhausting those means, and (2) by establishing a central organization of states empowered to pass judgment on the observance of those obligations by individual states and to apply sanctions in the event of the obligations being violated. The relevant provisions of Articles 12–16 of the Covenant have already been set out in the previous Chapter, where it was seen that they made it illegal—at the risk of severe sanctions—for members of the League to go to war except in certain strictly defined circumstances. Moreover, although the renunciation of war under these Articles was not complete, they made it very improbable that an aggression-minded state would ever succeed in resorting to war without a breach of its obligations under the Covenant. In any event in 1928 the so-called 'gaps' in the Covenant were blocked by the conclusion of the Pact of Paris, to which we must now turn.

The Pact of Paris—the Briand–Kellogg Pact—is an instrument of outstanding importance: signed or adhered to by a great many members of the international community, it declares in the most categorical terms the absolute illegality of war in pursuit of national policies. Moreover, having been concluded outside the League, it did-not perish with the League, and being fully consistent with the provisions of the Charter, retains its full force today.[1] The Pact was the culmination of a strong movement in the early days of the League to outlaw any recourse to war otherwise than in self-defence, and it was preceded by a number of draft treaties and resolutions which declared aggressive war to be an international crime.[2] By its provisions the contracting Powers:

1. in the name of their peoples condemn recourse to war for the solution of international controversies and renounce it as an instrument of national policy in their relations with one another; and

2. agree that the settlement or solution of all disputes or conflicts, of whatever nature or origin, which may arise between them, shall never be sought except by pacific means.

In forbidding war as an 'instrument of national policy' the Pact did not forbid recourse to war in self-defence, and in the negotiations concerning the Pact several states made express declarations emphasizing

[1] See Lord McNair, House of Lords Debates, 12 September 1926, *Hansard*, vol. 199, col. 662.

[2] Draft Treaty of Mutual Assistance (1923), draft Geneva Protocol (1924), Resolution of the League Assembly (1927), and Resolution of the Pan-American Conference (1928).

that self-defence is a natural right not touched by the Pact.[1] But the Pact did intend to render wholly illegal all resort to war otherwise than in self-defence or as a sanction for the violation of the Pact.

It is true that the Covenant and the Pact of Paris, as international treaties, were in strict law binding only upon the parties to those instruments. But there can be no question that the general obligations contained in them, prohibiting recourse to war for the settlement of disputes and requiring disputes to be settled by pacific means, reflected and recorded a fundamental change in customary law in regard to the legality of war. These obligations had become part of general international law binding on states whether or not they were parties to the Covenant or the Pact. Whether a breach of these obligations— whether aggressive war—had become not merely a violation of international law but an international crime is a question on which commentators on the Nuremberg and Tokyo trials have been deeply divided; and some authorities have contended that Article 6 of the Charter of the two War Crimes Tribunals, in declaring the planning, initiation, or waging of a war of aggression to be crimes against peace, and attributing responsibility for it to individuals, infringed the maxim *nulla poena sine lege*.[2] In fact, as the Nuremberg Tribunal pointed out,[3] there is a good deal of evidence of the acceptance in

[1] See Hunter Miller, *The Peace Pact of Paris*, 1928, ch. 9.
[2] See generally Lord Maugham, *U.N.O. and War Crimes*, 1951.
[3] Judgment, pp. 38–42.

the League period of the concept that aggressive war is an international crime. But the point is anyhow now primarily of historical interest, for the principles of the Nuremberg Charter were expressly reaffirmed by unanimous resolution of the General Assembly in 1946, and are now undoubtedly accepted as part of general international law. This development of the law has been criticized in some quarters as carrying the danger that in any future war it will be abused and victors, who may themselves be the real aggressors, put their defeated opponents on trial on trumped-up charges of aggression. That there is such a danger cannot be denied, and it can only really be met by confining prosecution for crimes against peace to cases in which the prosecution can properly be said to be undertaken with the authorization of the international community as a whole.

The Covenant and the Pact, we have seen, did not touch the right of self-defence. Equally, they did not touch retorsion, reprisals, or intervention not involving the use of armed force. Less clear, however, was their effect on reprisals and intervention taking the form of a recourse to armed force short of war; for the express prohibitions of both instruments applied in terms only to 'resort to war'. The point was tested at an early stage in the Corfu incident in 1923, when Italy bombarded and occupied Corfu, claiming this action to be a legitimate reprisal for the murder of General Tellini by extremists on Greek territory while he was acting as chairman of the Greek-Albanian boundary commission. The Council of the

League appointed a committee of jurists to report whether measures of coercion not intended to be acts of war were consistent with Articles 12–15 of the Covenant, if taken without first seeking a solution by pacific means; and the jurists[1] gave the somewhat unhelpful reply that such measures might or might not be consistent with the Covenant according to the circumstances of the case. If this reply appeared to leave open the possibility of drastic armed reprisals being taken without infringing the Covenant, the general opinion of jurists was that such armed reprisals taken without prior recourse to pacific settlement were a violation of the Covenant; for, even if not regarded as a recourse to 'war', they were quite inconsistent with the observance in good faith of the express obligations in the Covenant and the Pact to have recourse to pacific means for settling disputes likely to lead to a rupture.[2] Accordingly, it is in the highest degree doubtful whether reprisals and intervention involving armed force were any longer admissible during the League period, except as sanctions for the violation of the Covenant and the Pact. The Corfu incident and the reply of the jurists at least served as a warning to the draftsmen of the Charter, with results which we shall now see.

[1] See Charles De Visscher, *Révue de droit international et de législation comparée*, 1924, pp. 213–30, 377–96.

[2] See Brierly, 'International Law and Resort to Armed Force', *Cambridge Law Journal*, 1932, p. 308.

§ 3. *The Law of the Charter*

The machinery established by the Charter and by the Uniting for Peace Resolution for maintaining peace has been explained in the previous Chapter. The Security Council—or, failing the Council, the General Assembly—may investigate any international dispute or situation likely to endanger peace and may recommend procedures for the settlement of the dispute or for the remedying of the dangerous situation; if in the opinion of the Council the dispute or situation already constitutes an actual breach of the peace, threat to the peace, or act of aggression, it may take the measures necessary to enforce the peace either by decisions binding on member states or by recommendations to members; and, failing the Council, the Assembly may do the same but by the process of recommendation only. The action neither of the Council nor the Assembly, it will be noted, depends on their having made a finding that there has been an illegal use of force by a particular State. For investigation it is enough that there should be a dispute or situation the continuance of which is likely to endanger peace; for enforcement action it is enough that there should be a breach of the peace or threat to the peace. Nevertheless, the provisions of the Charter, governing the use of force by individual states, are of the utmost importance for the maintenance of peace; and these provisions are strictly framed.

The fundamental law of the Charter is to be found in the twin principles stated in paragraphs 3 and 4 of

Article 2, which, however, have to be read in conjunction with the provisions of Articles 33 and 37 concerning the pacific settlement of disputes and with the reservation of the right of self-defence in Article 51.

Article 2 (3) binds members to settle their international disputes by peaceful means in such a manner that international peace and security and justice are not endangered; and this obligation is further developed in Articles 33 and 37, which require the parties to any dispute, the continuance of which is likely to endanger the maintenance of peace, to seek a solution by negotiation and other peaceful means of their own choice, and, if they fail to settle it by such means, to refer it to the Security Council. It is to be noticed that, while Articles 33 and 37 lay down more definite obligations and procedures with regard to the settlement of disputes likely to endanger peace, the only further provision concerning 'justice' is in Article 36, where it is said that the Security Council, in recommending procedures for the settlement of a dispute, should take into consideration that legal disputes should as a general rule be referred by the parties to the International Court in accordance with the provisions of the Statute. The truth is that the Charter, while it mentions 'justice' in its preamble and in Article 2 (3), does not occupy itself very much with insuring that 'justice' as distinct from 'peace' shall prevail among members of the United Nations

Article 2 (4), which is the corner-stone of the Charter system, reads as follows:

'All Members shall refrain in their international relations from the threat or use of force against the territorial
integrity or political independence of any State, or in
any other manner inconsistent with the purposes of the
United Nations.'

There seems to be general agreement that the 'force',
the use or threat of which is here forbidden, is *armed
force*, for in the Preamble to the Charter it is expressly stated that one of its aims is 'to ensure by the
acceptance of principles, and the institution of
methods, that *armed force* shall not be used, save in the
common interest'. Again, although it seems to be
generally accepted that internal disturbances in a
country may constitute a 'situation' which the
Security Council is entitled to investigate in the
interests of preserving peace, it is quite clear that
Article 2 (4), since it only covers resort to force in
international relations against *another* state, does not
touch a state's legal right to use armed force for the
suppression of internal disturbances. The broad effect
of Article 2 (4) is, therefore, that it entirely prohibits
the use or threat of armed force against another state
except in self-defence or in execution of collective
measures authorized by the Council or Assembly.[1]
Thus, today it is beyond argument that armed reprisals, such as Italy's bombardment of Corfu in
1923, would be a flagrant violation of international
law. Equally, it is clear that Article 2 (4) does not
preclude a state from taking unilaterally economic or

---

[1] This position was taken by a number of the members of the
Council in dealing with the Indonesian situation.

other reprisals not involving the use of armed force in retaliation for a breach of international law by another state.

Article 51, as we have already seen,[1] reserves to members their right of individual or collective self-defence; but this right is confined within certain limits and it is important to see exactly what those limits are. The main provision of the Article reads:

'Nothing in the present Charter shall impair the inherent right of individual or collective self-defence if an armed attack occurs against a Member of the United Nations, until the Security Council has taken the measures necessary to maintain international peace and security.'

The Article then goes on to provide that any measures of self-defence must be immediately reported to the Council, whose general responsibility and authority for taking action to maintain or restore the peace remains unaffected. Thus, any exercise of the right of self-defence is expressly made subject to the judgment and control of the Council; and if the veto is used to prevent the Council from intervening, the power of judgment and control can be transferred to the Assembly under the Uniting for Peace Resolution.

The precise scope of the right of self-defence under the law of the Charter is the subject of controversy.[2]

[1] Supra, p. 393.
[2] See D. W. Bowett, op. cit., ch. ix; Kelsen, Law of the United Nations, 1950, p. 791; Goodrich and Hambro, Charter of the United Nations, 1949, pp. 299–302; Stone, Aggression and World Order, 1958, pp. 98–101.

Some writers contend that the combined effect of Article 2 (4) and Article 51 is to cut down the right of self-defence to cases falling precisely within the words in Article 51 'if an armed attack occurs'; these writers, in short, take the view that today Article 51 is the exclusive source of the authority to have recourse to self-defence, so that any 'threat or use of force' not falling precisely within its terms—i.e. not amounting to self-defence with reference to an armed attack—is automatically a violation of Article 2 (4). The other view is that the opening words 'nothing in the present Charter shall impair the *inherent* right of individual or collective self-defence' show a clear intention not to impair the 'inherent', i.e. the existing, natural right of states to use force in self-defence; in other words, they show that the right of self-defence today does not have its source in the Charter but is an independent right rooted in general international law, and that the purpose of Article 51 was simply to remove possible doubts as to the impact of the Security Council's powers upon the right of states individually or collectively to have recourse to force in self-defence. This view derives some support from the *travaux préparatoires* of the Charter. Committee I at San Francisco, which dealt with Article 2 (4), said[1] outright that 'the use of arms in legitimate self-defence remains admitted and unimpaired'. Then the records show that Article 51 was introduced into the Charter in Committee III/4 primarily for the

[1] *United Nations Conference on International Organisation* (U.N.C.I.O.), vol. 6, p. 334.

418 INTERNATIONAL LAW AND FORCE

purpose of harmonizing regional organizations for
defence with the powers and responsibilities given to
the Security Council for maintaining peace; and they
do not indicate any conscious intention upon the part
of Committee III/4, in including the words 'if an
armed attack occurs', to put outside the law forcible
self-defence against unlawful acts of force not
amounting to an armed attack. One recent writer[1]
has insisted that the principle of 'effective interpretation' requires that the words 'if an armed
attack occurs', in order to give them full meaning,
should be treated as restricting the right of self-
defence to defence against armed attack. But the
words have to be read in their context, and Article 51
has to be interpreted as a whole; and when this is
done, the appropriateness of applying the principle
of effectiveness to the words in question so as to produce a maximum restriction on the right of self-
defence becomes very doubtful. The question at issue
is whether the words were intended to lay down an
express restriction on that right or are merely descriptive of a particular category of self-defence with
respect to which it was desired to underline that the
right of individual, and more especially of collective,
self-defence had not been taken away in the process
of conferring power on the Security Council to take
'preventive' and 'enforcement' measures for the
maintenance of peace. When the Article begins with
the statement that nothing in the treaty shall *impair*
an *inherent* ('imprescriptible' in the Russian, 'natural'

[1] I. Brownlie, *I.C.L.Q.*, 1959, p. 720.

in the French, texts) right, it is not easy to presume an intention in the following words drastically to impair that right; and there are too many uncertainties and contradictions in Article 51 to make it possible to solve the problem simply by giving maximum effect to the words 'if an armed attack occurs'.

First, the French text—*dans un cas où un Membre des Nations Unies est l'objet d'une agression armée*—is not expressed in the form of a condition and suggests that the English 'if' was used to express an hypothesis rather than a condition—which is, of course, one of the natural uses of 'if'. Secondly, if 'effective interpretation' is to be applied to the words 'if an armed attack occurs', so as to produce a restriction on the inherent right, is the same thing to be done to the very next words in the Article 'against a Member of the United Nations'? If these words are given their full effect, the right of collective self-defence cannot be invoked to justify recourse to armed force in defence of a non-member state which is the victim of a flagrant aggression; but we know that this interpretation of the words was completely rejected by the United Nations with respect to the invasion of South Korea. Another difficulty lies in the word 'occurs'. Those who treat the words 'if an armed attack occurs' as restricting the right of self-defence also insist that it limits the right to cases where the 'armed attack' has actually begun, thus excluding the legitimacy of any recourse to force in the face of even the most imminent invasion or attack. Here again, the French text is a little different and more equivocal:

est l'objet d'une agression armée. But in any event, if anticipatory recourse to force in face of an actually impending attack is never to be permitted, the limitation of self-defence to action 'until the Security Council has taken the measures necessary to *maintain* international peace' is not very aptly worded, for if the peace must first have been broken, it can only be 'restored', not 'maintained'; nor is the unsuitability of the word 'maintain' made less by the fact that in the second sentence of Article 51 we find the Council expressly empowered to intervene to *maintain or restore* peace. Further queries can be raised, for example, as to what exactly is covered by the words 'armed attack', and as to whether measures of pure self-defence can ever constitute 'a use or threat of force against the territorial integrity or political independence' of a state or an act 'inconsistent with the purposes of the United Nations' which are the acts prohibited by Article 2 (4).

Accordingly, the drafting of the Charter leaves the scope of the right to resort to force in self-defence in some uncertainty—an uncertainty which is not removed by the inconclusive nature of the state practice and United Nations practice up to date. What can be said with confidence is that under the Charter, as under general international law, a minimum condition of resort to armed force in self-defence is 'an instant and overwhelming necessity for self-defence, leaving no choice of means, and no moment for deliberation', the criterion applied by the Nuremberg Tribunal and originally formulated by the United

States Secretary of State in the *Caroline* incident. What is also clear—and was rightly emphasized in the *Caroline*—is that acts of self-defence must be strictly limited to the needs of defence and may not be converted into reprisals or punitive sanctions. More difficult is the question of the kinds of action to which it is permissible to react by forcible measures of self-protection, and here it is necessary to take into account certain pronouncements of the International Court in the *Corfu Channel*[1] case.

In May 1946 Albanian shore batteries fired without warning on two British cruisers as they were making passage through Albanian territorial waters in the North Corfu Strait by a channel swept through a former German minefield. Albania in diplomatic Notes maintained that in the Strait foreign warships had no right of passage through her territorial waters without her authorization; the United Kingdom, on the contrary, asserted that they had a right of innocent passage and gave warning that, if fire was again opened on British warships passing through the Strait, the fire would be returned. In October of the same year two British cruisers and two destroyers were sent northwards through the Strait from Corfu for the express purpose of seeing whether Albania would 'behave' and allow the ships to pass without interference. The crews were at action stations with instructions to fire back if attacked; but their guns were in their normal positions with the main armament trained fore and aft and there was

[1] *I.C.J. Reports*, 1949, p. 4.

no question of force being used except in reply to an attack. The two destroyers were mined within the swept portion of the Strait with heavy loss of life, and the United Kingdom, though not yet in possession of any evidence, naturally suspected that this was the work of Albania. Fearing that any approach to the Security Council for the sweeping of the area to ascertain the cause of the explosions would be blocked by a Soviet veto, the United Kingdom decided itself to look for the evidence. A large force of minesweepers was sent into Albanian waters, covered by powerful ships outside territorial waters, with the result that a number of newly laid mines of German type were found in the area. The United Kingdom then did refer the case to the Council which, after three months of investigation and debate, recommended that the dispute should be submitted to the Court. In the proceedings the Court upheld the United Kingdom's view that under international law warships have a right of passage through the Corfu Strait, and found Albania responsible in law for the mining of the ships, on the ground that she must have been aware of the laying of the new minefield. But the Court also had to pronounce on counter-claims by Albania that her sovereignty had been violated by reason of the acts of the British Navy on the two separate occasions of (1) the abortive passage in October and (2) the subsequent sweeping of the Strait; and it is the Court's pronouncements with respect to these counter-claims which throw an important light on some aspects of the law governing recourse to force.

The question at issue in regard to the October passage was essentially the innocence of the passage both in regard to its object and the manner in which it was carried out. The passage had been made not only for navigation but to test Albania's attitude, and as to this the Court said:

'As mentioned above, the Albanian Government, on May 15th, 1946, tried to impose by means of gunfire its view with regard to the passage. As the exchange of diplomatic notes did not lead to any clarification, the Government of the United Kingdom wanted to ascertain by other means whether the Albanian Government would maintain its illegal attitude and again impose its view by firing at passing ships. The legality of this measure taken by the Government of the United Kingdom cannot be disputed, provided that it was carried out in a manner consistent with the requirements of international law. The 'mission' was designed to affirm a right which had been unjustly denied. The Government of the United Kingdom was not bound to abstain from exercising its right of passage, which the Albanian Government had illegally denied.'

Then the Court dealt with the objection that the ships were at action stations ready to retaliate:

'In view of the firing from the Albanian battery on May 15th, this measure of precaution cannot, in itself, be regarded as unreasonable. But four warships—two cruisers and two destroyers—passed in this manner, with crews at action stations, ready to retaliate quickly if fired upon. They passed one after another through this narrow channel, close to the Albanian coast, at a time of political tension in this region. The intention must have been, not only to test Albania's attitude, but at the same time to demonstrate such force that she would abstain from firing again on passing ships. Having regard, however, to all the circumstances of the case, as described above, the Court is unable to characterize these measures taken by the United Kingdom authorities as a violation of Albania's sovereignty.'

A number of writers have sought, for understandable reasons, to minimize the implications of these two passages by confining them to the particular context of innocent passage. But it is not easy to do so, since the first passage appears so clearly to assume the existence of a more general principle that a state may 'affirm' a right which has been 'unjustly denied', and is not bound to abstain from exercising it, even although this may involve the risk of having to use force to ward off interference with its exercise.

The issue in the second pronouncement was the innocence of the passage; but, since this issue turned upon the question of the legitimacy of the preparations and the instructions for the use of force in self-defence during the passage, the Court's pronouncements clearly have a bearing on the right of self-defence. In this pronouncement the Court states that precautions with a view to immediate resort to force in self-defence, if attacked whilst affirming a right of passage, are legitimate. It did not say in terms that actual recourse to force in self-defence would have been legitimate in the event of an attack occurring; as, however, the ships were under express instructions to fire back, it clearly must have held that view, or it could scarcely have found the passage to be innocent. Moreover, this view would certainly seem correct. In another respect, however, this pronouncement does seem perhaps to go too far by appearing to allow the legitimacy of a demonstration of force to deter Albania from future attacks on passing ships. Force to assure the safety of ships actually in passage is one thing. Force to frighten Albania into future respect for the right of passage is another thing, and goes near to being a form of 'police action'.

The question at issue in regard to the subsequent mine-sweeping operation was whether there was any ground on which this question could be regarded as a justifiable intervention, for intervention it undoubtedly was. The United Kingdom first argued that there was grave danger that the mines, the essential evidence of the cause of the injury done to its ships, would be removed by those who laid them; and that she was entitled, as a strictly limited measure of self-help, to investigate the minefield and preserve the evidence, provided always that she immediately afterwards brought the case before the Court or another organ of the United Nations, as she had done. This argument the Court summarily rejected:

'The Court can only regard the alleged right of intervention as the manifestation of a policy of force, such as has in the past given rise to most serious abuses and such as cannot, whatever be the present defects in international organization, find a place in international law. Intervention is perhaps still less admissible in the particular form it would take here; for, from the nature of things, it would be reserved for the most powerful states, and might easily lead to perverting the administration of international justice itself.'

Then it rejected no less summarily a further United Kingdom argument that a minefield in an international strait is an international 'nuisance' which any interested state is entitled to remove, if the coastal state will not do so; and, in doing so, it said:

'Between independent States respect for territorial sovereignty is an essential foundation of international relations. The Court recognizes that the Albanian Government's complete failure to carry out its duties after the explosions, and the dilatory nature of its diplomatic Notes, are extenuating circumstances for the action of the United Kingdom. But to ensure respect for international law, of which it is the organ, the Court must declare that the action of the British Navy constituted a violation of Albanian sovereignty.'

The Court thus drew a sharp distinction between forcible affirmation of legal rights against an expected unlawful attempt to prevent their exercise and forcible self-help to obtain redress for rights already violated; the first it accepted as legitimate, the second it condemned as illegal. But although the legitimacy of affirming the exercise of a legal right was upheld, the scope of this ruling must not be exaggerated. It is very far from meaning that a state may resort to force whenever another state threatens to violate its rights; for in its second pronouncement the Court said with the utmost emphasis that respect for territorial sovereignty is an essential rule. It is not the *enjoyment* of every right possessed by a state under international law that may be affirmed by force; it is the *exercise* of a right, and it is only exceptionally that a state is entitled, either by treaty or by custom, to exercise a right in or through another state's territory. An exercise of rights of passage through territorial waters, on the high seas and in free air space and of rights of fishing on the high seas would seem to be within the principle admitted by the Court, as would also exercise of a treaty right of passage over land, such as that through the corridor to West Berlin. But the dispatch of troops to another state's territory to prevent an unlawful expropriation of the property of nationals and other acts of a similar kind are outside the principle and are forbidden by Article 2 (4) of the Charter. Whether the landing of detachments of troops to save the lives of nationals under imminent threat of death or serious injury owing to the breakdown of law and order may be justifiable is a delicate question. Cases of this form of intervention have been not infrequent in the past and, when not attended by suspicion of being a pretext for political pressure, have generally been regarded as justified by the sheer necessity of instant action to save the lives of innocent nationals, whom the local government is unable or unwilling to protect. Clearly, every effort must be made to get the local government to intervene effectively and, failing that, to obtain its permission for independent action; equally clearly every effort must be made to get the United

Nations to act. But, if the United Nations is not in a position to move in time and the need for instant action is manifest, it would be difficult to deny the legitimacy of action in defence of nationals which every responsible government would feel bound to take, if it had the means to do so; this is, of course, on the basis that the action was strictly limited to securing the safe removal of the threatened nationals. The question arose recently in striking circumstances in the Congo when, after the United Nations had already intervened, Belgium dispatched troops to protect Belgian nationals said to be in imminent danger of being murdered wholesale. Some delegates in the United Nations, while calling for the withdrawal of the Belgian troops, appeared not to discountenance the idea that in extreme cases troops might be dispatched to save life; others roundly condemned the Belgian action, but as these delegates entertained a profound suspicion of Belgium's motives in regard to the Congo, no clear conclusions can be drawn as to their attitude on the general legal question.

One further point needs to be underlined in the *Corfu Channel* case, since it is generally overlooked: the Court upheld the United Kingdom's assertion of its rights of passage in October 1946, despite the fact that this could scarcely be regarded as consistent with its obligations under Article 2 (3) to settle its disputes by peaceful means, in such a manner that international peace and justice are not endangered. The exchange of diplomatic protests after the incident in May had resulted in a position where the views of the two governments as to their legal rights were in complete conflict and each was proposing to back its view by force; moreover, although the Court ultimately decided in favour of the United Kingdom's view, it was impossible before that decision to say that the right of warships to innocent passage through the Corfu Strait was free from doubt. No suggestion was made by either side that the legal dispute should be settled by arbitration or other peaceful means. But if the United Kingdom, in threatening the use of force and asserting its view of the law, may have failed to act in accordance with the spirit of Article 2 (3), Albania was in no position to rely on that fact; for her own act in firing completely without warning on the two cruisers in May was a most flagrant and prior violation of the principle in Article 2 (3). What, in effect, the Court held was that if a state has a right which it is entitled to exercise and another state wrongfully and forcibly persists in interfering with its exercise, the first state is not bound to submit to the lawless use of force by the second but may *lawfully* assert its right by the threat and use of force. This seems clearly correct when the second state—the wrong-headed state—is insisting on using force and refusing to have recourse to any peaceful means of resolving the dispute; otherwise Article 2 (4) becomes a shield for those who break the law by force.

Some commentators seem to fear that the Court's decision may unduly encourage breaches of the peace;

but this would only be so if no attention were paid to Article 2 (3) and Articles 33 and 37. Under these Articles, as we have seen, the parties to a dispute the continuance of which is likely to endanger peace are bound to seek a solution by pacific means and, if they fail to settle it, to refer it to the Security Council, while the Council itself has the right at any time to call upon them to settle it by pacific means. Moreover, if one party is intransigent, the other may unilaterally bring the dispute before the Council or the Assembly under Article 35. Accordingly, the conditions for a forcible affirmation of legal rights under the *Corfu Channel* doctrine would not seem to exist unless the other party was not only wrongfully denying by force the exercise of those rights but also unwilling to use pacific means to settle the dispute. The Court did not refer to this aspect of the question in its judgment; but it can hardly be credited that the Court would have considered legitimate the United Kingdom's 'demonstration of force' and instructions to force a passage if interfered with, had Albania previously referred the dispute to the United Nations or proposed the settlement of the legal issue by arbitration or other pacific means.

The political organs of the United Nations, the Council and Assembly, have had as their almost constant occupation the handling of breaches of the peace and threats to the peace in one part of the world or another: Korea, the Formosa Strait, Laos, Indonesia, Kashmir, Jordan and the Lebanon, the Arab–Israeli borders, Suez, the Greek frontiers with

Albania and Bulgaria, Algeria, Bizerta, the Congo, and Cuba, to mention only some of the more conspicuous examples. In handling these dangerous situations the United Nations has bent its energies for the most part to bringing the hostilities to an end and containing the danger within narrow limits, without pronouncing on the legality or illegality of the actions of the states concerned. Nevertheless, it has shown itself in the highest degree critical of any forcible action initiated against another state, whatever the pretext, and has set its face against attempts either to take a large view of the right of self-defence, such as Egypt's claim to be entitled to close the Suez Canal against Israeli ships in self-defence, or to claim other measures of self-help such as the British and French claim in the Suez incident to take 'police action'. It has also roundly condemned the armed intervention of the Soviet Union in Hungary in 1956 at the alleged request of the Government of Hungary for the purpose of suppressing an internal rising of the people. On the other hand, while uneasy at the sending of United States and British troops to the Lebanon and Jordan at the request of the respective governments, it seems to have accepted that there is a distinction between intervention to suppress a popular rising and one to assist in repelling attempts at subversion directed from a neighbouring state. In general, despite the aberrations of individual states and despite the political cross-currents that affect votes, the United Nations as a whole has shown itself strongly attached to the law of the Charter regarding the use of force. The 'cold war' has imposed severe limits on the possibilities of United Nations action to enforce peace, but the Organization, as we have seen, has developed certain techniques for bringing about a cease-fire and even for providing a limited form of international policing of critically dangerous areas. The more effective the executive arm of the United Nations is made, the stricter, we may be sure, will become the attitude of members to the use of force and their insistence that, except in case of urgent self-defence, lawful use of force is a monopoly of the United Nations itself.

The Council and Assembly, as already indicated, have shown comparatively little interest in the obligations of members under Article 2 (3) to settle their disputes by peaceful means; and the United Nations period has seen virtually no development in the techniques for settling disputes by peaceful means, and little application of existing techniques. No doubt this may in part be explained by the 'cold war', and by the fact that major revolutions are taking place in the structure of political society. Nevertheless, the United Nations' lack of interest in seeing that justice prevails in the settlement of disputes has been profoundly disturbing to many. As Mr. Dulles said[1] in the Assembly debate on the Suez crisis: 'Peace is a coin which has two sides—one is the avoidance of the use of force and the other is the creation of conditions of justice'; and he added: 'In the long run you cannot expect one without the other.'

[1] *United Nations Bulletin*, December 1956, p. 93.

INDEX OF CASES CITED

INDEX OF SUBJECTS